$30.⁰⁰

JOURNAL FOR THE STUDY OF THE OLD TESTAMENT
SUPPLEMENT SERIES
310

Sheffield Academic Press

Sexual Politics in the Biblical Narrative

Reading the Hebrew Bible as a Woman

Esther Fuchs

Journal for the Study of the Old Testament
Supplement Series 310

This book is dedicated to Dr S. Kleiman
with my greatest love

Copyright © 2000, 2003 Sheffield Academic Press (*A Continuum imprint*)
Hardback edition first published 2000

Published by Sheffield Academic Press Ltd
The Tower Building, 11 York Road, London SE1 7NX
370 Lexington Avenue, New York NY 10017-6550

www.continuumbooks.com

British Library Cataloguing-in-Publication Data
A catalogue record for this book is available from the British Library

Typeset by Sheffield Academic Press
Printed on acid-free paper in Great Britain by Biddles Ltd
www.biddles.co.uk

ISBN 1-84127-138-1 (hardback)
      0-8264-6954-X (paperback)

CONTENTS

PREFACE

When critics talk about biblical patriarchalism they usually describe the ways in which the biblical narrative reflects the ancient patriarchal societies that produced it. In this book, 'patriarchalism' refers to a political ideology that inspires the present shape of various biblical narratives. Recognizing the biblical narrative as a prescriptive text, this work focuses on the ways in which it legislates and authorizes the political supremacy of men over women. The recent outpouring of scholarly work on the art or the poetics of the biblical narrative remains, despite its objective posturing, an androcentric venture. As they admire the virtuosity of the biblical narrator, and the artistic ingenuity of the biblical narrative, critics choose to ignore the patriarchal ideology that inspires so much of what they glorify. In questioning the sexual politics of the biblical narrative, I also question the contemporary approaches to it which reinscribe—by failing to notice and comment on it—the Bible's patriarchal ideology.

This is not to say that I seek to deny the artistic complexity of the biblical narrative. On the contrary, my argument here is that it is primarily for their rhetorical effectiveness that so many of the Bible's constructions of femininity seem natural, or non-ideological. Poetic ingenuity and ideological forcefulness complement rather than exclude each other. That the biblical narrative is a literary masterpiece does not mean that it is not prescriptive or that it is nonpolitical. The biblical narrative does not merely valorize the power-based relations between men and women, it also legislates and authorizes the political subordination of women. To read a narrative about male and female relations as art is to read it scripturally, or to accept its claim to authority; in other words, to read it anachronistically.

In 1982, when I first began to publish articles on biblical sexual politics, I had few models to draw on. Feminist literary criticism was defined by the pioneering work of Phyllis Trible's *God and the Rhetoric of Sexuality* (Philadelphia: Fortress Press, 1978). I published my first critique of the patriarchal representation of women in a journal whose focus was neither literary nor feminist. In, 'Status and Role of Female Heroines in the Biblical Narrative,' published in the *Mankind Quarterly* (23. 2 [1982], pp. 149-60), I offered the first critique of the presentation of heroic women in the Hebrew Bible. My only theoretical models at that time were Mary Daly's *Beyond God the Father* (Boston: Beacon Press, 1973) and Rosemary Radford Ruether's anthology *Religion and Sexism* (New York: Simon & Schuster, 1974), which included a single article on the Hebrew Bible by Phyllis Bird. None of these sources included a discussion of the power relations between men and women. None of these sources discussed the relationship between literary strategies and the ideology of male supremacy, which I later defined as patriarchal ideology. And none of these sources discussed the ways in which the biblical narrative constructs women. Images of women were discussed in terms of their relationship to the historical context of ancient Israel, as if they reflected a certain ancient reality.

The books that inspired me to search for the ideologically motivated constructions of women were Simone de Beauvoir's *The Second Sex* (New York: Vintage, 1974 [1952]) and Kate Millet's *Sexual Politics* (New York: Ballantine Books, 1969). Much has changed since the early 1980s. Women, gender and sexuality in the Bible have become respectable areas of inquiry and research. In the late 1980s, Mieke Bal published *Lethal Love: Feminist Literary Readings of Biblical Love Stories* (Bloomington: Indiana University Press, 1987), in which she introduces narratological approaches to so-called biblical 'love stories'. In 1993, Danna Nolan Fewell and David M. Gunn published a political inquiry into the intersection of discourse, power and the construction of gender entitled *Gender, Power, and Promise* (Nashville: Abingdon Press, 1993). In the same year, Cheryl Exum published her political critique of the Hebrew Bible in *Fragmented Women: Feminist (Sub)versions of Biblical Narratives* (Valley Forge, PA: Trinity Press International, 1993) and Alicia Suskin Ostriker published *Feminist Revision and the Bible* (Oxford: Basil Blackwell, 1993).

The wealth of feminist companions and commentaries on the Bible and the various anthologies that have appeared in the 1990s notwithstanding, literary criticism of biblical narratives, most recently in its postmodern incarnation, refuses to take the challenge of ideological criticism seriously. It seems to me that the challenge I posed to male-dominated poeticism as defined by Robert Alter's and Meir Sternberg's approaches still stands. In recent years, this androcentric poeticism has been replaced by the so-called postmodern approach, which continues to delight in the playfulness of words and the multidimensionality and relativity of language and discourse as such. It is therefore more urgent than ever to restate the feminist position in no uncertain terms. This book questions the ways in which the biblical narrative universalizes and legislates its hierarchical endorsement of the power relations between male and female characters. It calls attention to the interrelationship of patriarchal ideology that sanctions the subordination of women and literary constructions, such as type-scenes, characterizations, dialogue and narrative endings. All these publications seek to explore and expose the collusion of power, gender and discourse in the biblical narrative.

Chapter 1

INTRODUCTION

The purpose of this book is to expose the link between the politics of male domination and the representation of women in the Hebrew Bible. My goal is not to read the text as a religious or historical text, but rather as a cultural-literary text. As a literary text authored by men, the Bible is androcentric, or male-centered. Most tales revolve around male characters. The large segments of the narrative portion of the Bible from Genesis to 2 Kings focus on the stories of the patriarchs—Abraham, Jacob; the national leaders—Moses, Joshua; the judges; the early prophets—Samuel, Elijah, Elisha; the kings—Saul, David. No amount of trotting out exceptional female figures, such as Deborah the judge and Miriam the prophet, should blind us to the overwhelming presentation of women as male-dependent and male-related ciphers, who appear as secondary characters in a male drama. No amount of searching for pre-biblical or extrabiblical sources and traditions can mitigate the fact that in its final presentation the biblical text reduces women to auxiliary roles, suppresses their voices and minimizes their national and religious significance. The argument of this book is that the Hebrew Bible not only presents women as marginal, it also advocates their marginality. It is not merely a text authored by men—it also fosters a politics of male domination.

Most stories displaying women as ancillary, insignificant and morally flawed have been taken in stride. Some are even historicized, thus exonerating the biblical authors of the responsibility that is placed on an ancient society that exists no more. Some argue that the inferior status of women in Israelite society is post-monarchic and some argue that women wielded power in ancient Israel.[1] If indeed women played a

---

1. Carol Meyers, *Discovering Eve: Ancient Israelite Women in Context* (New York: Oxford University Press, 1988); Savina J. Teubal, *Sarah the Priestess: The First Matriarch of Genesis* (Athens, GA: Swallow Press, 1984).

crucial role in early Israelite history, if there were female-centered institutions and communities as some would have it, the question we face is
all the more serious: why was this role distorted, suppressed, obscured
and erased? In this book I do not argue that there is no correlation between the Bible's literary representation of women and their historical
oppression in ancient Israel. Rather, I argue that patriarchy as the fundamental social system of ancient Israel is justified, universalized and
naturalized in the biblical text. My contention is that the Bible does
not merely project a male consciousness, but that it promotes a male-
supremacist social and cognitive system. According to this system, man
is a more 'authentic' representative of God because God is male, and
God is male because the Bible reflects a masculine construction of the
divine. The imaging of God as male redefined roles previously assigned
to female Goddesses in the ancient Near East.[2] It is possible that the
argument against human females is an extension of a broader onslaught
of patriarchal monotheism on Goddess worship—the anti-Goddess polemic that is especially conspicuous in the latter prophets. It is possible
that the polemic against the Goddess is one manifestation of the symbolic counter-order established by ancient Near Eastern patriarchy. By
definition, a shift is a movement from one representational system to
another. Representational vestiges of repressed female power remain in
the text, but the process of patriarchal rewriting is—I would argue—undeniable.[3] Though the Bible certainly did not invent patriarchy in its

2.   Gerda Lerner, 'The Goddesses', *The Creation of Patriarchy* (New York:
Oxford University Press, 1986), pp. 141-60. For a nuanced study of the absorption
of various aspects of ancient Near Eastern Goddesses by a single male God, see
Tikva Frymer-Kensky, *In the Wake of the Goddess: Women, Culture and the Biblical Transformation of Pagan Myth* (New York: Free Press, 1992). See also Carole
R. Fontaine, 'A Heifer from thy Stable: On Goddesses and the Status of Women
in the Ancient Near East', in *The Pleasure of her Text: Feminist Readings of
Biblical and Historical Texts* (Valley Forge, PA: Trinity Press International, 1990),
pp. 69-96. For a different interpretation of the symbolic meaning of the phallic God,
see Howard Eilberg-Schwartz, *God's Phallus and Other Problems for Men and
Monotheism* (Boston: Beacon Press, 1994). For an analysis of the rise of patriarchy
in the Hellenistic world, see Eva Cantaella, *Pandora's Daughters: The Role and
Status of Women in Greek and Roman Antiquity* (Baltimore: The Johns Hopkins
University Press, 1987).
3.   The 'both and' approach detecting in the text patriarchal repression and
gynocentric validation is in my opinion methodologically weak. See, e.g., Ann
Marmesh, 'Anti-Covenant', in Mieke Bal (ed.), *Anti-Covenant: Counter-Reading*

religious or social sense, it has contributed to validating it, especially because of its wide reception as a reflection of divine truth, or word.[4] Be that as it may, the biblical representation of women is an interpretive act that is anchored in a particular ideology of male domination.

The term 'Sexual Politics' refers to the discursive validation of the power asymmetry, the gender-based hierarchy that is at the heart of patriarchy.[5] I read the biblical narrative as a political speech act, one that justifies the political subordination of women. All narratives, all texts are in a sense speech acts; they prescribe or proscribe certain behaviors, actions and beliefs, they favor a certain position, they offer a certain interpretation.[6] The Bible promotes a patriarchal ideology in its legal texts, in long lists of male genealogies, in prophetic texts whose genre is poetry rather than prose narrative.[7] Traditionally, until the emergence of a feminist critical consciousness in the late 1960s, stories about male and female behavior have been taken at face value. With the emergence of literary criticism in biblical studies, the Bible began to be re-evaluated as a literary text of both aesthetic and universal human value. The premise of universality is allied to the hypothesis of objec-

Women's Lives in the Hebrew Bible (Sheffield: Sheffield Academic Press, 1989), pp. 43-58. See also, Ilana Pardes, *Countertraditions in the Bible: A Feminist Approach* (Cambridge, MA: Harvard University Press, 1992).

    4. Carole R. Fontaine, 'The Abusive Bible: On the Use of Feminist Method in Pastoral Contexts', in Athalya Brenner and Carole R. Fontaine (eds.), *A Feminist Companion to Reading the Bible* (Sheffield: Sheffield Academic Press, 1997), pp. 84-113.

    5. Esther Fuchs, 'The Literary Characterization of Mothers and Sexual Politics in the Hebrew Bible', and 'Who is Hiding the Truth?', in Adela Yarbro Collins (ed.), *Feminist Perspectives on Biblical Scholarship* (Chico, CA: Scholars Press, 1985), pp. 117-44.

    6. John R. Searle, *Speech Acts: An Essay in the Philosophy of Language* (London: Cambridge University Press, 1969); Mary Louise Pratt, *Toward A Speech Act Theory of Literary Discourse* (Bloomington: Indiana University Press, 1977); Fredric Jameson, *The Political Unconscious: Narrative as a Socially Symbolic Act* (Ithaca, NY: Cornell University Press, 1981); Terry Eagleton, *Literary Theory: An Introduction* (Minneapolis: University of Minnesota Press, 1983).

    7. Athalya Brenner, *A Feminist Companion to the Latter Prophets* (Sheffield: Sheffield Academic Press, 1995); see especially Yvonne Sherwood, 'Boxing Gomer: Controlling the Deviant Woman in Hosea 1–3', pp. 101-25. Carolyn Pressler, 'Sexual Violence and Deuteronomic Law', in Athalya Brenner (ed.), *A Feminist Companion to Exodus to Deuteronomy* (Sheffield: Sheffield Academic Press, 1994), pp. 102-12.

tive and neutral reading. Both are vestiges of an Enlightenment legacy that shifted the evaluative criterion from God to man. The reason much of the Bible has been seen as an unmediated, disinterested reflection of the human condition as such lies in the continuity of biblical patriarchal ideology and European Enlightenment thought positing at its center man as the measure and purpose of creation.[8] Because both men and women have been constructed by such belief systems, it is not possible for us fully to critique biblical patriarchalism. This kind of critique will forever be incomplete.[9]

In general, the Bible creates empathy and admiration for its central male character, God, or Yhwh. Women are often portrayed as supporting God's intentions, whether explicitly described or implied in the text. When they are shown to be supportive of this plan, they usually work to achieve a patriarchal goal (e.g. giving birth to and securing the position of sons). All too often, stories about male and female behavior have been taken at face value, as accounts of historical 'facts' or as naive yet charming and aesthetically satisfying works.[10] My point is that there is nothing innocuous or quaint about biblical narratives. These narratives do not merely describe a male-dominated social order, but justify it as morally requisite and sanctioned by God. They do not merely tell us how women came to be inferior, they also tell us that this inferiority is necessary. In other words, though they often seem to be descriptive, they are more often than not prescriptive. As such they deserve careful analysis. As mechanisms justifying male dominance they use various

8.   Christine DiStefano, *Configurations of Masculinity: A Feminist Perspective on Modern Political Theory* (Ithaca, NY: Cornell University Press, 1991).

9.   'Ideology in action is what a group takes to be natural and self-evident, that of which the group as a group, must deny any historical sedimentation.' Gayatri Chakravorty Spivak, *In Other Worlds: Essays in Cultural Politics* (New York: Methuen, 1987), p. 118. On ideological approaches to the Bible, see 'Ideological Criticism', Elizabeth A. Castelli *et al.* (eds.), *The Postmodern Bible* (New Haven: Yale University Press, 1995), pp. 272-308. For suggestive analyses of 'ideology' and 'power' see Irene Diamond and Lee Quinby (eds.), *Feminism and Foucault: Reflections on Resistance* (Boston: Northeastern University Press, 1988).

10.   On the historical, literary, theological and anthropological 'codes' or disciplinary approaches to the biblical text, see Mieke Bal, *Murder and Difference: Gender, Genre, and Scholarship on Sisera's Death* (trans. Matthew Gumpert; Bloomington: Indiana University Press, 1988), pp. 13-94. Bal makes the important point that all disciplinary approaches are restrictive to the extent that they build on methodological conventions and specific discourses and premises.

literary ploys in specific and calculated ways. Repeated motifs and scenes, the construction of point of view and the characterization of women should be considered not merely as literary means of enlightenment, but as a rhetoric of persuasion, as political strategies.

The male biblical author, or narrator, constructs not only a narrative, but an argument for a particular configuration of power relationships.[11] By attributing certain words, gestures or actions to female characters and by evaluating the characters as positive or negative the narrator constructs what womanhood is and what it should be. More often than not biblical female characters reflect male fears and desires rather than historical women. The male narrator wields rhetorical control, he has the power of discourse.[12] He also has the power to omit or close off alternatives, options and narrative possibilities that may interfere with or challenge this politics. He has the ability to 'prove' women's moral inferiority or to valorize women's reproductive abilities as suits his purpose.

By referring to a 'narrator' I do not intend to suggest that we are dealing with a particular individual. The 'narrator' here refers to a construct, a collective male-centered consciousness spanning many periods, styles and approaches. By describing the narrator as male I do not mean to suggest that 'he' is empirically male, but rather that he represents a male-centered perspective. Even if we are to accept recent suggestions according to which certain sources have been authored by women, the basic perspective of the stories remains androcentric.[13]

11. I use the terms 'narrator' and 'author' interchangeably to denote the agency responsible for the final version of the narrative as we have it. I understand the biblical narrative and the biblical narrator to be expressions of a broader ideological position. See Michel Foucault, 'What is an Author?', in Josué V. Harari (ed.), *Textual Strategies: Perspectives in Post-Structuralist Criticism* (Ithaca, NY: Cornell University Press, 1979), pp. 141-60.

12. The narrator is a figure in the text who appears to be omniscient and transparent. See Alice Bach, 'Signs of the Flesh: Observations on Characterization in the Bible', in A. Bach (ed.), *Women in the Hebrew Bible* (New York, 1999), pp. 351-65.

13. Compare J. Cheryl Exum, *Fragmented Women: Feminist (Sub)versions of Biblical Narratives* (Valley Forge, PA: Trinity Press International, 1993), pp. 9-15. For hypotheses dealing with the possibility of female-authored sources, see Bal, *Murder and Difference*, pp. 111-34; Harold Bloom and David Rosenberg, *The Book of J* (New York: Grove Weidenfeld, 1990); Pardes, *Countertraditions in the Bible*; Athalya Brenner and Fokkelien van Dijk-Hemmes, *On Gendering Texts: Female and Male Voices in the Hebrew Bible* (Leiden: E.J. Brill, 1993).

A recognition of the political nature of the biblical text reveals that even the most basic narrative ploys, such as characterization, point of view, dialogue and type-scene are motivated by an ideological perspective. For lack of a better term I define it as a patriarchal ideology, the interlocking set of beliefs and premises based on the idea of Man's centrality.[14] Patriarchal ideology manipulates literary ploys as political strategies. Patriarchal ideology is based on the belief in the propriety of male leadership and centrality. Linked to the other major biblical ideologies of monotheism and ethnocentrism, patriarchal ideology promotes the idea that men rather than women should be God's representatives and the nation's leaders (hence the centrality of men as priests, scribes, judges, kings and prophets). Patriarchal ideology is the theory of biblical sexual politics, the literary strategies that validate women's secondary status are its practice.

Traditionally, women accepted the biblical construction of their nature and status; they read the text as men. In recent decades literary theory and feminist theory have refined concepts and terms that help us question and challenge the authority of the text. My subtitle defines 'woman' in opposition to the biblical construction. The woman I have in mind is a cautious and suspicious reader. She does not accept her male-centered and male-authored representations. She refuses her implicit definition as the Other—as a human who is different and inferior to the normative male. She refuses her construction as an object of male epistemology. She rejects her political subservience and dependence on male authority for survival and legitimacy. The woman in my subtitle affirms her right to refuse the authority of the Bible, the manipulations of the biblical narrator and the long history of male-centered authorizations and interpretations of the text. To read as a woman means to practice a counter-reading that is made possible by a long familiarity with the status of the outsider.[15] Women's reading experience is a divided one: for we have been alienated from an experience appropriate to our condition as women. Women are expected to identify with a masculine experience and perspective, presented as human. The 'woman'

---

14. 'Patriarchy' refers usually to the social and symbolic system. See Gerda Lerner, 'Introduction', *The Creation of Patriarchy*, pp. 3-14. For a more limited definition of patriarchy, see Carol Meyers, 'The Problem of Patriarchy', *Discovering Eve*, pp. 24-46.

15. Alice Bach, *Women, Seduction and Betrayal in Biblical Narrative* (London: Cambridge University Press, 1997), pp. 1-33.

then in my subtitle is a construct, based on a generalization: it is a hypothesis.[16] The hypothesis of the woman reader is a metaphor for the position of women as a social class. The woman reads on behalf of all members of her class, including herself.[17] Reading as a woman means reading as an 'Other', as an outsider, as the reader refusing her position in the margins. Reading as a woman means reading with distrust and disbelief: 'a fundamental questioning of the masculine definitions and the social mythology they serve, which puts forward both an explanation of why the world works as it does, and prescribes proper behavior for living here successfully—or at least for living'.[18]

To read as a woman entails the assumption that all interpretations are anchored in the reader, rather than in the text. It means to engage a hermeneutics or interpretive method based on resistance. A hermeneutics of resistance, or 'reading against the grain' affirms a woman's ability to challenge the Bible's sexual politics. This reading process requires shifting the litmus test of interpretive validity from the authority of the text to the authority of an interpretive community.[19]

A hermeneutics of resistance is the first step in a process of liberation. As we resist the political messages and as we question the function of the Bible's narrative strategies we loosen the grip of the myth of male supremacy over our consciousness and imagination. No woman is free of this grip, because the biblical narrative has in many ways been inscribed in Western culture and its consumers. To some extent we have become the male-authored texts, and by re-reading the biblical text, one of the most powerful sources of male hegemony, we in fact also re-read ourselves. [20]

Naturally, I am aware that the first person plural 'we' is a rather risky label. It is based on a broad-based abstraction, equating all women. The

16. Jonathan Culler, 'Reading as a Woman', *On Deconstruction: Theory and Criticism After Structuralism* (Ithaca, NY: Cornell University Press, 1982), pp. 43-64.

17. Robert Scholes, 'Reading Like a Man', in Alice Jardine and Paul Smith (eds.), *Men in Feminism* (New York and London: Methuen, 1987), pp. 204-18.

18. Elizabeth Janeway, 'Women and the Uses of Power', in Hester Eisenstein and Alice Jardine (eds.), *The Future of Difference* (New Brunswick: Rutgers University Press, 1985), pp. 327-44 (330).

19. Stanley Fish, *Is there a Text in this Class? The Authority of Interpretive Communities* (Cambridge, MA: Harvard University Press, 1980).

20. Barbara Johnson, *The Critical Difference: Essays in the Contemporary Rhetoric of Reading* (Baltimore: The Johns Hopkins University Press).

label 'we' has been questioned, just as the categories of sex, gender, woman and man have come under feminist analytical scrutiny.[21] Increasingly, feminist biblical scholars argue for a recognition of diversity and heterogeneity of interpretive communities and theoretical approaches.[22] I would like to caution that too much emphasis on 'difference' and inclusiveness is paralyzing.[23] Though theoretically pleasing—mostly because it refuses valuation, exclusion and hierarchic stratification—methodologically the 'both and' approach leads to a dead end. Feminist biblical theory has come a long way in the last two decades, but the tension between 'critics' and 'reconstructionists' remains.[24] This is perhaps a debate that should remain unresolved, as it may generate new approaches and theories. But to fall prey to the vague promises of an inclusive approach, embracing all possibilities and committing to none is potentially self-destructive. The rejection of theoretical and methodological hegemonies should not prevent us from articulating a coherent approach, or one that seems coherent to us. As we search for answers to the question, 'Why is it difficult to do feminist biblical criticism today?', we may perhaps entertain materialist answers.[25] One materialist explanation is that feminist biblical criticism has not yet generated enough independent journals, and has established no independent scholarly associations or presses that may give free expression to feminist thinking. Accommodating the present status quo and controlling

21. See Judith Butler, *Gender Trouble: Feminism and the Subversion of Identity* (New York: Routledge, 1990).

22. See, e.g., in Elisabeth Schüssler Fiorenza (ed.), *Searching the Scriptures: A Feminist Introduction* (New York: Crossroad, 1993). Heather A. McKay, 'On the Future of Feminist Biblical Criticism', in Athalya Brenner and Carole Fontaine (eds.), *Reading the Bible: Approaches, Methods and Strategies* (Sheffield: Sheffield Academic Press, 1997), pp. 61-83; 'Feminist and Womanist Criticism', in The Bible and Culture Collective, *The Postmodern Bible* (New Haven: Yale University Press, 1995), pp. 225-71.

23. By 'difference' I refer to the categories that separate women (race, class, sexual orientation) and the analytical categories of postmodernism that question the very term 'woman' as essentialist. See Elaine Showalter, 'Feminism and Literature', in Peter Collier and Helga Geyer-Ryan (eds.), *Literary Theory Today* (Ithaca, NY: Cornell University Press, 1990), pp. 179-202.

24. Katheryn Pfisterer Darr, *Far More Precious than Jewels: Perspectives on Biblical Women* (Louisville, KY: John Knox Press, 1991); Pamela J. Milne, 'Toward Feminist Companionship: The Future of Feminist Biblical Studies and Feminism', in Brenner and Fontaine (eds.), *Reading the Bible*, pp. 39-60.

25. McKay, 'On the Future of Feminist Biblical Criticism', p. 61.

our voices may not necessarily be the right direction for a feminist future in biblical studies. By pointing the finger at ourselves, as responsible for the impasse in feminist biblical studies, we collude with the powers that be—and male-centered scholarship and the status quo. We should not seek accommodation with institutional frameworks and conventional discourses, but rather expand the field of play.

Hardly any feminist scholar would disagree that, as one of the paradigmatic immasculating texts of Western culture, the biblical narrative continues to be in need of a comprehensive critical hermeneutics.[26] Though there have been attempts to articulate a hermeneutic theory that 'affirms women's point of view by revealing, criticizing and examining its impossibility', more needs to be done.[27] While the study of women and biblical texts and traditions has come a long way in the last two decades, we are still lacking a theoretical articulation of biblical sexual politics—the ways in which the biblical narrative universalizes and legislates its male-centered epistemology.[28] Despite the tendency to stereo-

26. 'Immasculation' is a term coined by Patrocinio P. Schweickart to designate the process by which male-authored and male-centered texts produce in the female reader an identification that obliterates her sense of herself as a woman. The process of immasculating teaches the female reader to see the world and herself in masculine terms and it is latent in the text, though it can only be actualized in the process of reading, by the female reader herself. See her essay 'Reading Ourselves: Toward a Feminist Theory of Reading', in Elizabeth A. Flynn and Patrocinio P. Schweickart (eds.), *Gender and Reading: Essays on Readers, Texts and Contexts* (Baltimore: The Johns Hopkins University Press, 1986), pp. 31-62.

27. Catherine A. MacKinnon, 'Feminism, Marxism, Method, and the State: Toward a Feminist Jurisprudence', in Nanneil O. Keohane *et al.* (eds.), *Feminist Theory: A Critique of Ideology* (Chicago: University of Chicago Press), pp. 1-30.

28. See Kate Millet, *Sexual Politics* (New York: Ballantine Books, 1969). See also Simone de Beauvoir, *The Second Sex* (trans. H.M. Parshley; repr. New York: Vintage, 1974 [1952]); Mary Ellman, *Thinking about Women* (New York: Harcourt Brace Jovanovich, 1968); Eva Figes, *Patriarchal Attitudes: Women in Society* (New York: Persea Books, 1970). For an elaboration of sexual politics in literature see Carolyn G. Heilbrun and Margaret R. Higonnet (eds.), *The Representation of Women in Fiction* (Baltimore: The Johns Hopkins University Press, 1983). See also Lillian S. Robinson, *Sex, Class and Culture* (New York: Methuen, 1978). For responses to the concept and theory of sexual politics see, Toril Moi, *Sexual/Textual Politics: Feminist Literary Theory* (New York: Methuen, 1985). For redefinitions and challenges to the concept of 'patriarchy' see Michele Barrett, *Women's Oppression Today: Problems in Marxist Feminist Analysis* (London: Verso, 1980).

type feminist theory as an assault on the Bible, much of the interpretive work on biblical women has been rehabilitative if not outright apologetic. I would go as far as saying that, in some ways, the most dominant theories in the field indirectly foreclose the articulation and elaboration of a critical hermeneutics of the Hebrew Bible. After two decades of feminist scholarship, especially in biblical history and theology, we are still lacking a coherent feminist critical hermeneutics of the biblical narrative, we are still in need of a political hermeneutics that might help us disrupt the process of immasculation. We are still lacking what I might call a hermeneutic theory of resistance by which we expose to consciousness the political implications of apparently innocuous literary constructions.[29] While some traditionalist feminists read biblical texts for a liberating message, some literary critics argue that the biblical narrative is too complex, or heterogeneous for a sustained feminist critique. The recognition of multiple disciplinary codes, of multiple hermeneutic models and the recognition that reading is an endless process of approximations, rather than an articulate articulation of a single Truth lead to a general reluctance to question the political implications of the Bible's patriarchal ideology.[30]

In one of the first theoretical articulations of biblical literary feminism Phyllis Trible wrote '[The] hermeneutic challenge is to translate the Bible without sexism'.[31] The idea that sexism—the discriminatory

For a critique of the concept of woman and a discussion of sex versus gender, see Butler, *Gender Trouble*.

29. For feminist-literary models of resisting reading, see Judith Fetterley, *The Resisting Reader: A Feminist Approach to American Fiction* (Bloomington: Indiana University Press, 1977); Teresa de Lauretis, *Alice Doesn't: Feminism, Semiotics, Cinema* (Bloomington: Indiana University Press, 1984). See also Teresa de Lauretis, *Feminist Studies/Critical Studies* (Bloomington: Indiana University Press, 1984). Critical analyses whose explicit objective is to interrogate biblical patriarchal discourse are relatively few. See, e.g., Exum, *Fragmented Women*; Danna Nolan Fewell and David M. Gunn, *Gender, Power, and Promise: The Subject of the Bible's First Story* (Nashville: Abingdon Press, 1993); Athalya Brenner, *The Intercourse of Knowledge: On Gendering Desire and 'Sexuality' in the Hebrew Bible* (Leiden: E.J. Brill, 1997); Bach, *Women, Seduction and Betrayal*.

30. Mieke Bal, 'The Emergence of the Lethal Woman, or the Use of Hermeneutic Models', *Lethal Love: Feminist Literary Readings of Biblical Love Stories* (Bloomington: Indiana University Press, 1987), pp. 10-36; *Murder and Difference*, pp. 13-94. On the impossibility of reading, see Jane Gallop, *Reading Lacan* (Ithaca, NY: Cornell University Press, 1985).

31. Phyllis Trible, 'Depatriarchalizing in Biblical Interpretation', *JAAR* 41.1

attitude to women—can be excised from the biblical narrative entails a cut and paste method, which selects what appear to be nonsexist passages as representative of the 'real' Bible.[32] This approach endorses a reading that picks and chooses what appeals or does not appeal to the reader who proceeds to label the text under discussion in evaluatively dichotomous terms. This kind of operation results in what I might call the argument of heterogeneity, namely the idea that the Bible is both 'good' and 'bad', sexist and nonsexist, providing an experience that is both 'painful and exhilarating'.[33] The argument of heterogeneity forecloses a critical analysis—a critique of ideology—of the immasculating narrative. The reader is forewarned that the text is so plural, it cannot possibly be subjected to a systematic questioning. The recognition that the biblical text is composed of diverse sources, and that it displays several genres should not forestall a feminist theory of critical hermeneutics. The listing of biblical women according to various organizational principles, from the chronological to the typological creates an impression of fullness and critical balance.[34] This inclusive picture, however, often obscures the pernicious implications of biblical construction of both 'good' and 'bad' women.

Another hermeneutic approach to the biblical narrative historicizes narratives about exceptional women arguing for a non-patriarchal, egalitarian social order in ancient Israel. This approach is often speculative and interpretive though it presents itself as historical. The problem of this approach for literary critics is the tendency to give priority to historical context over the biblical narrative in its final shape. Conceived mainly as the product of 'real' social circumstances, the biblical nar-

(March, 1973), pp. 30-48 (31). This approach is further elaborated in various essays included in Letty M. Russell (ed.), *Feminist Interpretation of the Bible* (Philadelphia: Westminster Press, 1985). See especially the introduction by Letty M. Russell, pp. 11-18.

32. See Phyllis Trible, *God and the Rhetoric of Sexuality* (Philadelphia: Fortress Press, 1978); *Texts of Terror: Literary-Feminist Readings of Biblical Narratives* (Philadelphia: Fortress Press, 1984).

33. Carol A. Newsom and Sharon H. Ringe, 'Introduction', in Carol A. Newsom and Sharon H. Ringe (eds.), *The Women's Bible Commentary* (Louiville, KY: Westminster/John Knox Press, 1992), pp. xiii-xix (xv).

34. See, e.g., Edith Deen, *All of the Women of the Bible* (New York: Harper & Row, 1955); also Susan Niditch's survey in her article 'Women in the Old Testament' in Judith Baskin (ed.), *Jewish Women in Historical Perspective* (Detroit, MI: 1991), pp. 41-88.

rative is analyzed as a given rather than as a constructed or fabricated text. It approaches the text as a reflection of a certain reality, a historicized 'truth', rather than as a product of ideology. The argument of historical placement explains the discriminatory attitudes toward women by reconstructing (or inventing) events or ancient institutions. The argument of historical placement can easily be used as an apologetic theory for canonic sexist texts.[35] The argument of historical placement implies that it is impossible to challenge the narrative's patriarchal ideology because we are dealing with an ancient text which must be 'understood' within its own historical context. The apology by historical placement tends to bracket off questions of ideology as irrelevant for scholarly inquiry, by implying that the Bible merely 'reflects' or describes an ancient society. A strange collusion thus arises between the argument of historical placement and the 'scriptural' that takes the biblical text as the manifestation of truth or divine discourse. A historiographic-reconstructionist approach has evolved in the context of the Greek Bible and early Christianity that is based on the recognition that the biblical narrative does not reflect even partially a women's history, but rather interprets it from an androcentric point of view.[36] According to this approach a feminist-critical hermeneutics must move from androcentric texts to their gynocentric historical-social context.[37] A recommendation to shift from text to context not only re-encodes the traditional definitions of these disciplines, but also privileges historical criticism over literary criticism. Literary criticism thus becomes an auxiliary subcategory of historical research. Embedded in the program to shift from androcentric text to gynocentric context is also the risk that we re-entrust a founda-

35. Wayne C. Booth, 'Freedom of Interpretation: Bakhtin and the Challenge of Feminist Criticism', in W.J.T. Mitchell (eds.), *The Politics of Interpretation* (Chicago: University of Chicago Press, 1982), pp. 51-82.

36. Elisabeth Schüssler Fiorenza, *In Memory of Her: A Feminist Theological Reconstruction of Christian Origins* (New York: Crossroad, 1983). See also her *Bread Not Stone: The Challenge of Feminist Biblical Interpretation* (Boston: Beacon Press, 1984) and *But She Said: Feminist Practices of Biblical Interpretation* (Boston: Beacon Press, 1992). On the combination of a 'hermeneutics of suspicion' and 'a hermeneutics of revision' see Elisabeth Schüssler Fiorenza, 'Transforming the Legacy of The Woman's Bible', in Schüssler Fiorenza (ed.), *Searching the Scriptures*, pp. 1-24.

37. On the problems entailed in a 'simple' gynocentric reconstruction of history, see Joan Wallach Scott, *Gender and the Politics of History* (New York: Columbia University Press, 1988).

tional text to immasculating critics, who present themselves as objective scientists of the past.

A critical hermeneutics of the biblical text places women at the center of the frame of inquiry. In my opinion, however, it is just as important to understand the lives of ancient women as it is to understand ourselves as reading subjects. In essence, when we struggle with mechanisms of immasculation, we are peeling off layers of indoctrination and false consciousness that we are carrying as parts of our own self-definitions. The distinction between 'historical women' and the attitudes toward them presupposes that we can reconstruct their lives without taking account of the patriarchal oppressions that shaped them. A critique of ideology is always and forever incomplete, and the assumption that we should be capable of discovering an authentic feminine voice, through a 'hermeneutics of revision' should itself be subjected to a hermeneutics of suspicion. Patriarchal attitudes toward women, whether ancient or modern, are integral to our histories and lives. They do not only explain how men treated women, but also to what extent and why women accepted this treatment. As long as feminist historians and critics agree that all we have is interpretation, there is neither opposition nor competition between a historiographic-reconstructionist approach and the literary-critical approach. As has been recognized in one of the earliest articulations of feminist criticism, critique and reconstruction are interpretive strategies that can coexist in dialogue. There is no need to dichotomize or hierarchalize the gynocentric reconstructions of history and the literary-critical analysis of biblical narrative.[38] At the same time, we must appreciate the pervasiveness and constantly self-reproducing nature of ideology in order to appreciate the essentialist illusion of an authentic female voice or past. We also should be able to advance an effective model of a doubled feminist interpretation that should let these interpretive strategies coexist without teasing out the contradictions and theoretical inconsistencies they imply.

Literary-critical approaches to the biblical text are varied and there is no point in listing the many methods that have been used by feminist critics so far.[39] The critical approaches to the biblical text have been

38. I am referring here to Carolyn Heilbrun and Catherine Stimpson, 'Theories of Feminist Criticism: A Dialogue', in Josephine Donovan (ed.), *Feminist Literary Criticism: Explorations in Theory* (Lexington: University Press of Kentucky, 1975), pp. 61-73.

39. It is impossible to list the many collections that have recently been pub-

informed by the understanding that the Bible neither reflects a historical situation, nor tells an innocent story. By calling attention to the complex and effective interrelations between the ideology of male dominance and repeated narrative paradigms, I seek to question the tendency to ignore the ideological nature of the Hebrew Bible.[40] Structuralist readings of the 'Bible as Literature' obscure the ways in which power and language collude in the biblical text. A feminist-critical hermeneutics always has a double focus: the biblical text itself and 'objective', 'literary' readings of the biblical narrative that re-encode biblical patriarchal epistemology.[41]

Implicit in this work is my belief in the urgency of a feminist critique of as obvious a foundational cultural script as the biblical narrative. The contemporary appropriations by literary scholars of the biblical narrative make it imperative for us not to dismiss the Bible as an irrelevant and outdated freak of culture. A dismissal of this kind would be both intellectually and politically unsound. For the Bible continues to define our own perceptions of gender and sexual politics. By dismissing the biblical text we end up colluding with the appropriation of the Bible by conservative theologians. It is not only that the past is essential for our attempt to build a different future. It is more importantly that where literature—and especially canonic literature—is concerned, the past is the present and—in the absence of a comprehensive feminist revision— must become the future. Far from being an outdated collection of

lished on this subject. See J. Cheryl Exum and D.J.A. Clines (eds.), *The New Literary Criticism and the Hebrew Bible* (Valley Forge, PA: Trinity Press International, 1993). See also Elizabeth Struthers Malbon and Janice Capel Anderson, 'Literary-Critical Methods', in Schüssler Fiorenza (ed.), *Searching the Scriptures*, I, pp. 241-54. See also The Bible and Culture Collective, *The Postmodern Bible* (New Haven: Yale University Press, 1995), especially the section on 'Feminist and Womanist Criticism', pp. 225-71.

40. One of the most effective critiques of biblical historical criticism as a discipline is offered by Mieke Bal, *Death and Dissymmetry: The Politics of Coherence in the Book of Judges* (Chicago: University of Chicago Press, 1988), especially pp. 12-39.

41. Esther Fuchs, 'Contemporary Biblical Literary Criticism: The Objective Phallacy', in Vincent L. Tollers and John Maier (eds.), *Mappings of the Biblical Terrain: The Bible as Text* (Lewisburg: Bucknell University Press, 1990), pp. 134-42; Alice Bach, 'Contending with the Narrator', *Women, Seduction, and Betrayal*, pp. 13-24.

ancient writings, the Bible is not only a literary document worthy of close attention, but also a political text *par excellence.*

> Our canonized texts convey the working myths of the culture. We are to blame if we read them as gospel instead of as myth... Feminists need to re-evaluate the notorious canon—to discover not only what it excludes, but also how it constructs what it includes.[42]

Feminist critics have always been aware of the complexity of the biblical text. The Bible is a compilation of writings spanning over a thousand years. It is an eclectic collection of fragments of unknown origin. Some may argue that the Bible cannot be reduced to a single conceptualization. One of the earliest articulations of feminist biblical theory offers a list of caveats to the feminist critic of the Hebrew Bible.[43] Since its inception, feminist biblical criticism has also been aware of its own positions. Feminist critics have warned us to be conscious of the agenda behind our questions to the material. In other words, because we as readers bring our own set of priorities and concerns to the text we may be biased in our critical interpretation of the Bible. This approach ignores the fact that the biblical text is itself an interpretation of historical circumstances as well as of other oral or written texts. The over-cautious insistence on our agenda obscures the fact that the biblical narrative has an agenda of its own. Coupled with the notion that the Bible is merely a collection of fragments with no overarching agenda of its own, too much feminist theoretical self-consciousness may result in a pious repetition of traditional male-centered approaches to the biblical narrative. While it is sensible to emphasize the complexity of the documents that make up the Bible, it is also valid to read it as a unitary text. Indeed, outside the academy the Bible has been read as a unitary whole, and this is how it continues to exert its ideological influence. The Bible is not read in religious or literary circles as a compilation of fragments originating from various historical and textual strata. An emphasis on a holistic or integrative reading does not entail a globalizing or careless reading. On the contrary, the more careful our reading, the more easily

42. Adrienne Munich, 'Notorious Signs, Feminist Criticism and Literary Tradition', in Gayle Greene and Coppelia Kahn (eds.), *Making a Difference: Feminist Literary Criticism* (London: Methuen, 1985), pp. 238-60.

43. Katherine Doob Sakenfeld, 'Old Testament Perspectives: Methodological Issues', *JSOT* 22 (1982), pp. 13-20. This cautious approach characterizes Susan Niditch's essay (see above).

we are likely to see the text's patriarchal investments. In addition, the idea of the biblical narrator has become accepted in biblical criticism and the notion that the Bible presents a continuous story of national origins and an explanation of national demise no longer requires proof or argumentation.

Some feminist critics have referred to a critical approach to the Bible as 'negative' and defined the gynocentric focus on women and women's lives in ancient Israel as 'positive'.[44] The differentiation between these two typologies along evaluative lines obscures the fact that they are in essence complementary. I find the dichotomous categories of 'positive' versus 'negative' criticism restrictive and confusing. It seems to me that this distinction is based on a misguided equation between two very different concepts: 'critical' and 'negative'. A critical activity need not be negative. A critical reading of the Bible does not entail its rejection as an important cultural source, though it may very well reject its claim to divine or absolute truth. It is not clear to me why the gynocentric study of women and their status is presented as valid and positive, and the criticism of women's presentations is perceived as negative. That the biblical narrative is patriarchal does not mean that it lacks value. On the contrary, by analyzing such a text we stand to learn quite a bit about ourselves as constructed subjects. It is just because the biblical text is both androcentric and patriarchal that we must pay closer attention to narratives we have so often taken for granted. It is just because the Bible continues to be canonic in both religious and secular communities that we must investigate carefully what it excludes and how it constructs what it includes.

A recognition of the 'patriarchalizing' tendencies of later traditional readings of the Bible does not entail an exoneration of the biblical text itself. This recognition ought to lead rather to a greater awareness of both the patriarchal bias of the original text and its subsequent interpretations. Re-reading certain biblical passages in an attempt to demonstrate that they are not sexist, or not as sexist as they first appear to be is not as effective a method as a critical analysis of later 'patriarchalizing' traditions. To purge the Bible of its sexism is not necessarily a feminist hermeneutics. This approach is often used by apologists of various reli-

---

44. Mary Ann Tolbert, 'Defining the Problem: The Bible and Feminist Hermeneutics', *Semeia* 28 (1983), pp. 113-26. The 'negative' approach has also been labeled 'rejectionist'. These labels fail to do justice to the critical project.

gious strands who are more concerned with the authority of the canon than with the status of women past or present.[45]

It is possible that some readers confuse the meaning and purpose of hermeneutics, or textual theories of interpretation, with its traditional definition as explication, understanding and application from past to present.[46] The traditional understanding of the term 'hermeneutics' ought then to be revised. For if we restrict this activity to application from past to present we already map out an agenda of obedient reading. The understanding of reading as explication and appropriation of the past entails by definition a rejection of the present in favor of the past. If the past is presented as a venerated object of knowledge, as something that needs to be understood and therefore accepted, it is surely difficult if not impossible for the modern reader to come up with a critical analysis of its biases and agendas. A traditional understanding of 'hermeneutics' undermines our attempt to resist the immasculation of the biblical narrative. There is then a paradox in the very collocation 'feminist hermeneutics' if by 'hermeneutics' we mean application from past to present. On the other hand, to point to only one hermeneutic method as authoritative is to imitate the male-centered phallacy of objective and ultimate truth.[47] A reinterpretation of interpretation may be necessary before we engage seriously with a feminist-critical interpretation of the Bible.

The Bible's claim to divine truth or absolute knowledge has often been misinterpreted as a manifestation of divine truth and absolute knowledge. If we take the text as 'Scripture', that is as a script for conceptualizing the world and the text, we 'authorize' the text, we claim authority for the text. It is up to us to accept or refuse the narrator's self-presentation as the mouthpiece of divine Truth. But my reference to ideology leads me to yet another problem that requires explanation: the problem of intentionality. When discussing the political investments of the biblical narrative, or in describing how the biblical narrator conveys a certain patriarchal message, am I implying that the latter does so purposely? The assumption of this question is that ideology is a conscious set of values and interrelated agendas. And yet, ideology is very

45. See, e.g., Virginia Ramney Mollenkott, *Women, Men and the Bible* (Nashville: Abingdon Press, 1977) and Adin Steinsaltz, *Women in the Bible* (Tel Aviv: The Ministry of Defense, 1983) (Hebrew).

46. Trible, *God and the Rhetoric of Sexuality*, p. 7.

47. On the use of multiple hermeneutic models, see Bal, *Lethal Love*, pp. 10-36.

often the political unconscious of literary works, or any other truth-claiming discourse. The power of any truth-claiming discourse is not in the intrinsic value of statements or the veracity of facts but rather in the perception of the reader who ascribes to this discourse the power of knowledge.[48] The impression that the biblical narrative imparts to the reader universal truths about the nature of Man is anchored in the reader's prior indirect absorption of biblical doctrine regarding the power relations between men and women. The question of intentionality assumes a 'psychologizing conception of hermeneutics' that presumes that the 'real' meaning of a text depends on the reconstruction of the original intention of the author.[49] My references to the biblical narrator infer an ideological position, not a conscious intention of a particular individual.

The attempt to exonerate the Bible of the charge of sexism is not necessarily unique to traditionalist feminist critics. This attempt to rehabilitate the Bible takes on different methodological guises and ranges from simplistic paraphrases of biblical stories to sophisticated arguments regarding female textual sources.[50] Some traditionalists theologize and idealize women's reproductive function as well as their status as outsider. Others use the argument of heterogeneity, namely that the Bible includes good, bad and ambivalent attitudes to women and that it lacks an overall agenda.[51] The terms 'bad' and 'good' are applied to various female characters without asking for whom, from whose point of view and who profits from this evaluation. The lack of a political perspective often leads to a confusion of 'good women' and good attitudes. The listing of women according to these criteria offers the impression of objectivity and inclusiveness. Still other critics elaborate on Woman's symbolic function as a 'mediatrix' between the world

48. Michel Foucault, *Power/Knowledge: Selected Interviews and Other Writings 1972–1977* (ed. Colin Gordon; New York: Pantheon, 1980). My references to Foucault are not meant to obscure the masculinist bias in his own work.

49. Paul Ricoeur, *Interpretation Theory: Discourse and the Surplus of Meaning* (Fort Worth: Texas Christian University Press, 1976), p. 22.

50. John H. Otwell, *And Sarah Laughed: The Status of Woman in the Old Testament* (Philadelphia: Westminster Press, 1977); Leonard Swidler, *Biblical Affirmations of Women* (Philadelphia: Westminster Press, 1979); Janice Nunnally-Cox, *Foremothers: Women of the Bible* (New York: Seabury, 1981); Bloom and Rosenberg, *The Book of J.*

51. E.g. Swidler, *Biblical Affirmations of Women.*

and the hero.[52] By mystifying the feminine role this approach precludes the critique of the absence of the female hero. By glorifying the mythical feminine we risk losing sight of the power-based hierarchy between men and women. Yet other critics argue for authentic women's voices or women's texts in the Bible based on a stylistic analysis of recurrent images, metaphors, motifs and certain linguistic expressions.[53]

My critique is premised on the proposition that the biblical narrative is not merely a historical interpretation of past events, but a prescriptive interpretation of culture. It is neither neutral nor objective, though its narrator is usually omniscient and authoritative. The concept of a neutral historiography is in fact alien to the biblical 'historian'. Neither is the biblical narrative merely an explanation of human and national origins. The prescriptive nature of the biblical narrative does not mean that it is a primitive text lacking in artistic sophistication. There is no necessary contradiction between the Bible's art of persuasion and its prescriptiveness. A hermeneutics of resistance is based on the recognition that the Bible's rhetorical art and its patriarchal ideology are inseparable and complementary. Critique is not a reductive procedure, though every analysis is to some extent selective. It is a procedure that is based on the understanding that every interpretation is ideological and that all fiction is interpretive.[54] Ancient literature and ancient readers were interested in the power the text exerted on their societies rather than in its aesthetics. In this sense, feminist criticism is paradoxically in theoretical and methodological terms a return to ancient rhetorical principles.[55] The biblical narrative is a political text not despite its poetic sophistication but because of it. The political dimension of any literary text is its unconscious, and the feminist reader is not different from the psychoanalytic investigator in probing the linguistic and structural symptoms of its ideology.[56]

52. James G. Williams, *Women Recounted: Narrative Thinking and the God of Israel* (Sheffield: Almond Press, 1982).

53. See, e.g., Brenner and van Dijk-Hemmes, *On Gendering Texts*.

54. Naomi Schor, 'Fiction as Interpretation, Interpretation as Fiction', in Susan R. Suleiman and Inge Crosman (eds.), *The Reader in the Text: Essays on Audience and Interpretation* (Princeton, NJ: Princeton University Press, 1980), pp. 165-82.

55. Jane P. Tompkins, 'The Reader in History: The Changing Shape of Literary Response', *Reader-Response Criticism: From Formalism to Poststructuralism* (Baltimore: The Johns Hopkins University Press, 1980), pp. 201-32.

56. Jameson, *The Political Unconscious*; Shoshana Felman, *Writing and Madness: Literature/Philosophy/Psychoanalysis* (Ithaca, NY: Cornell University Press,

In the above paragraphs I discussed such interrelated terms as 'sexist', 'patriarchal' and 'androcentric'. In what follows I would like to suggest some definitions that may help us negotiate the maze of interrelated terms that nevertheless infer different problems. 'Androcentrism' is the epistemology of masculine normativity, the presumption that the male is the center and supreme manifestation of what is right and good in the order of things. 'Patriarchalism' is the politics of male domination and the ideological validation of androcentrism. 'Misogyny' is a psychological phenomenon: it refers to the hatred and fear of women. Misogyny and patriarchalism are clearly interrelated, but it is important to draw a distinction between these terms. While the portrayal of women as 'good' or 'positive' in a particular narrative may perhaps indicate that this narrative is not misogynous, it does not necessarily mean that the narrative is not patriarchal. The portrayal of women as deceptive or dangerous is the hallmark of misogynous fiction. A patriarchal narrative by contrast aims at affirming the political subordination of women and so it may portray women as 'good'. Obviously, women who are obedient and eager to accept male authority are 'good' from a patriarchal point of view and provide the author with desirable models that he is eager to reproduce and highlight. There is no contradiction between the affirmative presentation of women as the reproducers of male heirs, for example, and the interests of patriarchy. By distinguishing misogyny and patriarchal ideology, feminist critics should be able to see through the fallacy of the 'good woman' as reflective of 'positive' or affirming trends in the biblical narrative.

What I hope to accomplish in this book is a reconsideration of the implications of the arguments of plurivocality in feminist interpretive communities, in the biblical text and in contemporary theory. The differences between and among female readers ought to strengthen rather than weaken our feminist interrogation of biblical texts. The recognition of the inherent multiplicity of the biblical text should not obscure the ideological collusion of violence and monotheism.[57] The recognition of various valencies of patriarchy, and the complexity of the concept of ideology itself should not blind us to the fundamental message of bibli-

1985). Psychoanalytic theories emphasize the elusiveness of meaning and the impossibility of a knowing subject.

57. Regina M. Schwartz, *The Curse of Cain: The Violent Legacy of Monotheism* (Chicago: University of Chicago Press, 1997).

cal patriarchal ideology. Heterogeneity as a theory must not preclude the development and refinement of a method of resisting reading.

In the following chapters I call for a recognition of the various aspects and emphases of patriarchal ideology—at the expense of women. The assertion of the father's power plays itself out in certain narrative contexts. Different scenarios are conjured up to legitimate the husband's power, the son's power and the brother's power. In each context the mother, wife, daughter and sister are devalued in relation to their male counterparts, but in each context this is done differently. The various 'gynotypes' or 'figures' reflect the degree of phallic stereotyping, or the logic of sameness in phallocentric thought.[58] The structural categories of male-related women often overlap. Characters are presented as both wives and mothers, as both sisters and daughters. Yet, in their capacity as mothers women are usually valorized. There is a growing effort to create a causal link between their procreative ability and their moral status. In their capacity as wives, women are increasingly devalued or ambiguated. In both contexts they are rarely shown to be victims of male aggression. This is a representation usually reserved for daughters and sisters. The woman's vulnerability in both these categories justifies the intervention of the father and the brother. It is significant, however, that the biblical narrator rarely presents the wife as a mother or the daughter as a sister. The logic of sameness and fragmentation makes it necessary for the biblical narrator to deal with only one aspect of the female character.

What helps us identify the ideological investments of the biblical narrative is the type-scene, a literary scene that repeats with variations in various contexts.[59] Nativity narratives and conjugal narratives include type-scenes, such as the annunciation and temptation type-scenes, the adultery and contest type-scenes, the rape type-scenes. The type-scene helps clarify the function of the woman in the text vis-à-vis her male counterpart. The repetition of type-scenes inculcates a certain message. This message is inculcated through the orchestration of motifs in a given type-scene, and by the sheer cumulative power of repetition. A synchronic and diachronic reading of the text helps highlight this mech-

58. Luce Irigaray, *Speculum of the Other Woman* (trans. Gillian C. Gill; Ithaca, NY: Cornell University Press, 1985).

59. 'Plot' refers to a sequence of events, while 'scene' refers to a stationary or 'synchronic' narrative structure. A type-scene repeats several times in various contexts.

anism. By pointing to repetition as well as to omission and silences or gaps I suggest that certain 'innocuous' narrative techniques are deployed as strategies of persuasion. These techniques are examined for the ways in which they construct and validate the ideal of male normativity. The first step of the literary hermeneutics of resistance is distanciation, that is, the description of female characters as constructs rather than self-evident beings. The second step consists of exposition, that is, assessing the political meaning, the ideological function of the message conveyed by the literary configuration. The third step is critique: an interrogation of the fundamental premises of patriarchal ideology as expressed in the literary techniques considered in the analysis. Male and female characters are juxtaposed in order to bring out the hierarchical power differences between them. In addition various gynotypes are juxtaposed to bring out the difference between the wife and the mother, the sister and the daughter.

What emerges is an ideology that affirms in women their ability and willingness to support the patriarchal arrangement. The prerogative of the husband to marry several wives is justified by the wife's interest in male progeny. The authority of the father is not linked to his moral status, whereas the mother's procreative ability is. The status of the bride as deserving of respect and attention dwindles. The sister needs her brother to protect her and the daughter is blamed for taking the initiative, for venturing outside. The sister and the daughter are victim figures as long as they do not give birth to male sons. Their liminal existence is a source of social instability and war, and their self-destructive behavior justifies greater male control. Women are objects of male desire and the causes of men's downfall. Female sexuality needs to be controlled, female procreativity is to be used, female political power needs to be contained and female spiritual/religious potential suppressed. When all is said and done, the biblical narrative justifies the domination of women and children—by male heads of households, and male national and religious leaders. The fictional world constructed along these androcentric perceptions and patriarchal precepts has become a powerful discourse that continues to shape our collective imagination and cultural scripts, our lives and our histories.

Most of the characters selected for discussion here have normally been designated by various critics as 'positive' characters, and as such expressive of a presumed anti-patriarchal counterculture. As I will argue in Chapter 2, however, positive female actors are every bit as effective a patriarchal strategy as negative characters. The question is not how often we find positive female characters, but for what purpose are these characters portrayed as positive, and what does their valorization mean in the context of biblical sexual politics. The distinction between positive and politically useful is especially central to my discussion of the mother-figure in Chapter 3, the most valorized gynotype in biblical narrative. Chapter 4 on the biblical bride is a sort of interlude between my discussion of the mother-figure and the wife-figure. By highlighting the differences in the portrayals of mothers and wives, it foreshadows the basic questions I will be asking in Chapter 5, namely: What do the various conjugal narratives teach about male–female power relations? Chapters 6 and 7, about the biblical daughter and the biblical sister, respectively, are based on intensive rather than extensive reading offered in Chapters 3–5.

Needless to say, there is a considerable degree of overlap among the various gynotypes. Biblical mothers are often characterized as wives, just as biblical sisters are often unmarried daughters. By distinguishing among them I do not intend to imply that the same characters never figure in several roles at the same time. The point is rather to highlight the fact that each role is usually presented in separate narrative contexts. The biblical narrator splits off the conjugal and maternal roles; when the father appears as a factor, the brother is suppressed and vice versa. An intertextual reading brings out the narrative fragmentation that underlies the biblical representation of women.

Chapter 2

CONTEMPORARY BIBLICAL LITERARY CRITICISM: THE OBJECTIVE PHALLACY

The recent proliferation of literary approaches to the biblical narrative confirms that in regard to biblical women, *plus ça change plus c'est la même chose*. The dominant critical trends in the field manifest a disconcerting degree of what Catherine MacKinnon, in another context, calls 'aperspectivity': an objective, neutral posture of male-centered scholarship.[1] There is a stunning resemblance between the objective posturing of contemporary Bible critics and the aperspectivity which is one of the master tropes of biblical discourse. Just as the biblical narrator presents the power relations between men and women as divinely ordained, so do androcentric critics write about biblical men and women with an air of unperturbed disinterestedness. Just as patriarchal ideology is taken for granted by the biblical narrator, so does it remain unchallenged in the works of most contemporary rhetorical and literary critics. By assuming a 'nonpartisan' stance, biblical critics end up legitimizing the marginalization of biblical women and the relentless focus on male-oriented concerns. The aperspectival stance of most biblical literary critics re-encodes biblical sexual politics that seeks to universalize and absolutize the dominance of women by men. Though most literary critics agree that the biblical narrative is androcentric, they rarely allow this fact to interfere with their analytical procedures. Coupled with a scriptural vision that ignores the ideological nature of biblical literature

---

1.   'Feminism not only challenges masculine partiality, but questions the universality imperative itself. Aperspectivity is revealed as a strategy of male hegemony.' Catherine A. MacKinnon, 'Feminism, Marxism, Method, and the State: An Agenda for Theory', in Nannerl O. Keohane, Michelle Z. Rosaldo and Barbara C. Gelpi (eds.), *Feminist Theory: A Critique of Ideology* (Chicago: University of Chicago Press, 1981), pp. 1-30 (23).

in general, contemporary biblical criticism re-endorses biblical sexual politics.

In a classical analysis of the biblical narrative, Erich Auerbach insists on the latter's prescriptive nature, a feature that often eludes contemporary critics. Unlike Greek epic, Auerbach notes, the biblical narrative lays

> claim to absolute authority... If the text of the biblical narrative, then, is so greatly in need of interpretation on the basis of its own content, its claim to absolute authority forces it still further in the same direction. Far from seeking, like Homer, merely to make us forget our own reality for a few hours, it seeks to overcome our reality: we are to fit our own life into its world, feel ourselves to be elements in its structure of universal history... Everything else that happens in the world can only be conceived as an element in this sequence.[2]

In their attempts to show how artful, how intricate, how ironic, how carefully crafted the biblical narrative is, contemporary critics ignore the prescriptive aspect that is in many ways its most obvious characteristic.

Substituting for the search for truth an indefatigable search for beauty (often understood to mean textual complexity), the modern critic does not, in essence, abandon the scriptural approach that accepts rather than questions biblical ideology. Moshe Greenberg, for example, draws an analogy between the traditional exegete and the modern critic. Assuming that the modern reader is male, he urges this reader to subjugate his concerns to the designs of the biblical text:

> As the religious person approaches the text open to God's call, so must the interpreter come 'all ears' to hear what the text is saying. He [*sic*] must subjugate his habits of thought and expression to the words before him and become actively passive—full of initiatives to heighten his receptivity.[3]

Since 'receptivity' and the reader's self-subjugation to the biblical text are the order of the day in what is known today as rhetorical or literary criticism of the Bible, it is not surprising that most if not all contemporary analyses of the biblical narrative have failed to question the latter's

---

2. Erich Auerbach, *Mimesis: The Representation of Reality in Western Literature* (trans. Willard Trask; Garden City, NY: Doubleday, 1953), pp. 12-13.

3. Moshe Greenberg, 'The Vision of Jerusalem in Ezekiel 8–11: A Holistic Interpretation', in James L. Crenshaw and Samuel Sandmel (eds.), *The Divine Helmsman: Studies on God's Control of Human Events, Presented to Lou H. Silverman* (New York: Ktav, 1980), pp. 145-46.

patriarchal prescriptions. For one thing, that would mean criticizing an ancient text, which 'good' historians cannot afford to do. For another, this would mean allowing the reader's habits of thought to interfere with the poetic designs of the text, which a good poetician is not supposed to do. The only thing the 'good' reader of the biblical text is enjoined to do, then, is to marvel at the text's complexity and wisdom. The 'good' reader, who in recent theoretical articulations of biblical literary criticism is invariably male, must not bring 'his' own concerns into the process of deciphering and enjoying the biblical text. As a good obedient son, the contemporary literary critic is not supposed to question the Bible's claim to authority and its interpretation of human history and destiny. A peculiar collusion thus emerges between the procedures of traditional religious readings of the Bible and contemporary rhetorical or literary readings.

For all of the controversy sparked by the modern procedures of biblical literary criticism, the fact remains that the deviations from traditional rules of reading the biblical text have not been so great after all. For the fundamental disposition of the modern reader is to paraphrase and exfoliate the original text. Whether primarily aesthetic or hermeneutic, modern literary criticism of the Bible remains by and large paraphrastic. The absence of a critical perspective in contemporary criticism of the Bible delegitimizes a priori any attempt to question the Bible's patriarchal ideology, which sanctions the dominance of men over women. Bracketed as irrelevant, the prescriptive character of the biblical narrative is sidestepped by the poeticians who do not cease to find new ways to glorify its poetic ingenuity. What traditionalists like James Kugel denounce as the 'unmediated encounter between Modern Man and Ancient Text'[4] is in fact mediated by the assumption that the reader is a man and that the encounter consists in the son's acceptance of the father's word.

The rare critic who does acknowledge that the biblical narrative is fundamentally ideological tends to ignore the patriarchal aspect of this ideology. Meir Sternberg, for example, focusing exclusively on the Bible's theistic ideology interprets most of its poetic principles as strategies in 'justifying the ways of God to Man'.[5] Sternberg's aper-

---

4.   James Kugel, 'On the Bible as Literature', *Prooftexts* 2 (1982), p. 332.
5.   Meir Sternberg, *The Poetics of Biblical Narrative: Ideological Literature and the Drama of Reading* (Bloomington: Indiana University Press, 1985), p. 482; see esp. pp. 84-128. Hereafter, *PBN*, cited parenthetically in the text.

spectival approach, much as the omniscient stance of the biblical narrator lays an implicit claim to absolute truth, postulates an ideal androcentric reader. The ideal reader's sensitivity to gaps, repetition, shifty perspectives, and other literary subtleties can only be matched by *his* obliviousness to the androcentric premises that bind him to the text. It should not surprise us, for example, that his theory of 'gapping', which invites the androcentric reader to fill the gaps, does not recognize as a gap the suppression of a female perspectivity. In his discussion of the story of David and Bathsheba in 2 Samuel 11, the only gaps that seem to be legitimate have to do with what one or another male character does, thinks, wants, and with what the male narrator tells the male reader.[6] The marginalization of Bathsheba is for Sternberg a nonquestion. 'Between the Truth' sought by the androcentric critic and the 'Whole Truth' often hidden by the patriarchal narrator, the female character is dismissed, and the female reader made invisible.

Just as Bathsehba gets lost in Sternberg's system of gaps, so is Rebekah lost in 'the movement from divergence to convergence' (*PBN*, p. 136), which is primarily concerned with the perspectives of the male characters involved in the narrative. In a similar fashion Dinah's rape is subsumed under the broader concern with the 'delicate balance' between the points of view of Dinah's brothers and father and the points of view of her male rapist and his father (*PBN*, p. 445).

Needless to say, Dinah in Genesis 34 and Bathsheba in 2 Samuel 11 are already peripheral characters. By construing the antagonistic relationship of male characters as the fundamental frame of his analysis, Sternberg validates and contributes to the marginalization of the female characters.

Though he presents his questions as neutral, objective responses to the informational gaps of the text, Sternberg's questions are often based on androcentric presuppositions. In his discussion of the rape of Dinah, for example, he argues without explaining his own axiological priorities that rape is less heinous a crime than murder. 'The trouble is,' he states, 'that mass slaughter will not balance against rape according to conventional normative scales' (*PBN*, p. 445). Just what these 'conventional scales' are, when, how, by whom and to whom they have become normative, is not made clear. Glossed over is the fundamental question of the narratee. The implicit assumption is that the same 'conventional

---

6.   'Between the Truth and the Whole Truth' is Sternberg's title for Chapter 7, pp. 230-63, in which he discusses ambiguity and temporary versus permanent gaps.

scales' are normative, both in biblical and in modern times, to male and female alike. We are expected to believe that the narrator performs a feat of manipulative artistry in order to balance out Shechem's murder and the revenge of Dinah's brothers. The objectification of Dinah, the informational gaps about her perspective, her motivations, and her response to her own rape, are problems that remain untouched. Despite the hair-splitting analysis to which almost every single verse in Genesis 34 is subjected, the entire first verse describing Dinah as a subject who 'goes out' on her own 'to see the daughters of the land' (*PBN*, p. 446) is presented without commentary. Because she does not fulfil a function in the male-centered scheme of things, the female character is discarded. Sternberg refers to Dinah only when and if she illuminates in some fashion her brothers' conduct. The androcentric obsession with the male parties forecloses otherwise interesting informational gaps that could have pointed up the investments of the Bible's patriarchal ideology. Thus, for example, one might ask, Why rape? Is it mere coincidence that Dinah, the first and only Israelite daughter, is presented as a rape victim who is subsequently disqualified from becoming a licit heiress to her father and a tribal leader in the same way as brothers? One can also ask, of course, why is Dinah, the rape victim, silenced by the narrator? Why are we not told what she feels about Shechem or, for that matter, about her brothers? These questions are no longer possible within the male-centered bipolar scheme erected by Sternberg. If gaps are by definition those empty spaces that the phallocentric critic is expected to penetrate and fill with the help of his logos, then it is also up to him, one assumes, to decide what qualifies as a gap and what does not.

In a similar vein, Sternberg all but eliminates Bathsheba from what he calls 'the David and Bathsheba story' (*PBN*, p. 188). While he dedicates considerable space to the question 'does Uriah know about his wife's infidelity and pregnancy?', Sternberg does not explain why he judges Bathsheba's actions as 'infidelity'. Surely this is not a term suggested by the text. The fact is that the text is peculiarly silent about Bathsheba's motivations and responses to David's actions. This, however, does not seem to represent a problem or a gap for Sternberg. While he seems to think that what Joab and the servant think are urgent problems of specific as well as heuristic value, he ignores the obvious gap concerning the presentation of Bathsheba. What the female character thinks or knows belongs to the category of nonquestions, and trying to

understand the ideology behind the reticent presentation of female characters amounts to what Sternberg calls 'illegitimate gap-filling'. The
theoretical law set down by the critic invalidates any attempt to question the marginalization of Bathsheba. 'Illegitimate gap-filling is one
launched and sustained by the reader's subjective concerns...rather than
by the text's own norms and directives' (*PBN*, p. 188). But are not
Sternberg's numerous questions about what Uriah knows inspired by an
androcentric subjectivity? Are not the many questions about what the
husband knows motivated by a set of male-centered anxieties and pre-
occupations? After all, there is nothing in the text indicating that what
the husband knows about his wife is more important than what the wife
knows about her husband. Nowhere in his analysis does Sternberg explain why Uriah's awareness is more important than Bathsheba's. Sternberg judges Bathsheba's actions as 'infidelity' (*PBN*, p. 201), but is this
definition justified by the text? The concept of infidelity entails a voluntary crime. But the extent to which Bathsheba was coerced into adultery by the king is a question left open. It is in fact one of the most
interesting gaps in the narrative: Did Bathsheba object? Could she
object? What did *she* know? Sternberg's failure to consider these questions as gaps leaves serious gaps in his own theory of the biblical narrative.

By ignoring the ideological problem posed by stories of rape and
adultery, by ignoring the patriarchal implications of the way in which
the woman in the text is silenced, the modern andocentric critic rein-
scribes biblical sexual politics. The poeticist reinscription of patriarchal
ideology is made possible by combining on the one hand an aperspectival stance and on the other a submissive stance vis-à-vis the text. The
ideological identification of father-text and the obedient son results in
the latter's adjusting his voice to that of the biblical narrator, which
according to Sternberg projects itself as the 'voice of the one and indi-
visible truth' (*PBN*, p. 128). The choral harmony of the authoritative
narrators and the 'objective' critics re-encodes the silence about
women's oppression.

The aperspectival poeticist approach to the biblical narrative excludes
questions about gender, which consequently renders the Bible's patriarchal ideology invisible. The fundamental premise of contemporary biblical poeticism is that it is possible to articulate rules about the way in
which the biblical narrative 'behaves' regardless of its male voice.
Dialogue, characterization, point of view, gaps, repetition and omission

are discussed in a neutral 'objective' fashion as if the ideology of male supremacy had nothing to do with the construction of these elements. The godlike gaze of the critic seems unperturbed by the interactions of patriarchal ideology and poetics—poetics seems to be 'outside' the vexing presence of *this* kind of ideology. Promulgating the poetic rules by which the biblical narrative allegedly operates, the modern andro-centric critic imitates the biblical omniscient narrator whose prescriptive interpretations of reality preclude women from the sphere of consciousness and will.

One of the most important premises of current poeticist approaches is that the biblical narrative is not didactic. Thus, for example, the repetition of certain motifs and what Robert Alter brilliantly identifies as type-scenes have been interpreted as poetic strategies aimed mainly at heightening the aesthetic pleasure of the audience:

> The only plausible hypothesis, then, is that these intriguing instances of recurrent sequences of motif reflect a literary convention which, like other narrative conventions, enabled the teller of the tale to orient his listeners, to give them intricate clues as to where the tale was going, how it differed delightfully or ingeniously or profoundly from other similar tales.[7]

The ingenuity, delight and profundity marking the permutations of various annunciation type-scenes are to be enjoyed by the modern audience at least to the same degree that they have been appreciated by the ancient audience. A careful reading of Alter's analysis reveals the collusions of aesthetic bliss and the ancient *and* contemporary concern with the male protagonist. Though, as its name suggests, the annunciation type-scene is at least equally interested in the fate of a prospective mother as it is with the son, Alter interprets it as a foreshadowing mechanism alluding to the fate of the son as a male adult. Similarly, in his discussion of the betrothal type-scene, which by its very name suggests a measure of heterosexual reciprocity, Alter focuses on the function of the type-scene as foreshadowing the future of the groom.[8] With the groom as protagonist, the bride cannot help but be consigned to the periphery, signaling a mere stage in the multiphased evolution of the male protagonist. Alter speaks of the 'archetypal expressiveness' of

---

7.   Robert Alter, 'How Convention Helps Us Read: The Case of the Bible's Annunciation Type-Scene', *Prooftexts* 3 (1983), pp. 115-30.

8.   Robert Alter, *The Art of Biblical Narrative* (New York: Basic Books, 1981), pp. 47-62. Hereafter, *ABN*, cited parenthetically in the text.

the betrothal type-scene as he explains that the foreign land to which the groom travels 'is chiefly a geographical correlative for the sheer female otherness of the prospective wife' and, as he points out, the 'well in the oasis' is 'obviously a symbol of fertility, and in all likelihood, also a female symbol' (*ABN*, p. 52). Does this mean that femaleness is by definition other? That female otherness is a universal archetype or a biblical convention? These questions are neither raised nor answered. What is clear is that Alter perceives the adventures of the groom as central to the betrothal type-scene, for it is in the latter that the future exploits of the groom are foreshadowed. While the entire convention of the type-scene is interpreted as an ingenious literary means by which the narrator presents the groom's story, the bridge becomes willy-nilly a point of reference in the male-centered frame. The bride shrinks in the course of the analysis from a full-fledged character to a stage on the groom's road to adulthood, to a symbol of fertility, and in the case of Rachel to an object of the groom's desire, to a womb.

> If the well of the betrothal scene is in general associated with woman and fertility, it is particularly appropriate that this one should be blocked by an obstacle, for Jacob will obtain the woman he wants only through great labor, against resistance (*ABN*, p. 55).

Rachel's desire for Jacob and for sons, Rachel's labor against resistance, are not discussed in this context. The preoccupation with the groom eclipses the bride's significance.

To enjoy as an archetypal motif what Alter calls the 'sheer female otherness' of the mother or the bride presupposes an androcentric vision continuous with biblical definitions of femininity. To construe as aesthetic ingenuity type-scenes that progressively write female characters out of existence reveals a poeticist viewpoint that remains oblivious
to the political and didactic aspects of the biblical type-scene. To say that the problem does not exist uses aestheticism and aperspectivity as excuses for modern patriarchalism in knowledge-producing communities.

That modern poeticism ends up validating biblical definitions of womanhood becomes evident in works whose declared object of inquiry is women. In *Women Recounted* James Williams mystifies the problematic marginalizations of women as symptomatic of a poetic construction he calls 'the arche-mother'.

> The arche-mother performs symbolic functions as the progenitress [*sic*],
> the object of love and inspiration, and agent of change for the hero,
> enabling him to move successfully into the world or actually determining
> his destiny. In these functions, especially as mediatrix between world
> and hero, her acts and character are reminiscent of the mythical
> feminine.[9]

The poetic construct of the arche-mother is used as an explanation/
justification for the subordinate roles played by female characters.
Williams associates the arche-mother with the 'mythical feminine' with
the same ease that Alter refers to women's archetypal otherness in the
betrothal type-scene. Just what this 'mythical feminine' is remains
unexplained; it is assumed that we all know what this mysterious concept is. Williams writes as if Simone de Beauvoir, Kate Millet and
Mary Ellman never existed, and as if the mythical feminine has not
been exposed as one of the most oppressive stereotypes of the androcentric canon.[10] Williams describes the arche-mother as the male hero's
'object of love' or 'agent of change' without bothering to problematize
these terms. The auxiliary role of many female characters is thus
naturalized and neutralized as the obvious result of a transhistorical
truth embodied by the arche-mother. What Sternberg does by dismissal,
Williams does by mystification. Though their methods differ, the result
remains the same, for both reinscribe woman as Other. The symbolic
interpretation of biblical womanhood diffuses the ideological problems
and risks repeating the less sophisticated apologetic work of, for example, John H. Otwell and Leonard Swidler.[11]

To a considerable degree, biblical patriarchalism continues to inspire
the most dominant literary approaches to the Hebrew Bible. While the

9.   Williams, *Women Recounted*, p. 113.

10.   See de Beauvoir, *The Second Sex* (New York: Knopf, 1974); Ellman, *Think-ing about Women* (New York: Harcourt Brace Jovanovich, 1968); Millet, *Sexual Politics*.

11.   It is instructive to compare Williams's treatment of biblical women with Otwell's *And Sarah Laughed*. Otwell, too, tends to emphasize the 'positive' in woman's alleged role as mediatrix between God and the people of Israel. See also Swidler, *Biblical Affirmations of Woman*. Swidler's taxonomies appear to give us an inclusive picture of biblical women by considering 'negative', 'positive' and 'ambivalent' images of women. For a critique of Swidler, see Bernadette J. Brooten, 'Early Christian Women and Their Cultural Context: Issues of Method in Historical Reconstruction', in Collins (ed.), *Feminist Perspectives on Biblical Schol-arship*, pp. 73-77.

biblical narrator marginalizes women, the contemporary critic takes this marginalization for granted or mystifies it. Just as the biblical narrator lays claim to absolute truth so does the modern androcentric critic endorse this claim through his aperspectival posturing. Man is a self-evident point of reference in both biblical literature and in modern scholarly discourse about this literature. Worse, contemporary criticism suppresses women as characters and readers even more than the original text tends to do.[12]

If the Bible has been understood as a prescriptive compilation of documents, modern biblical scholarship presents itself as a descriptive and neutral venture. The apparent transparency of contemporary literary approaches to the biblical narrative risks reinscribing what I call elsewhere biblical sexual politics.[13] The continued obliviousness of contemporary scholars to the implications of biblical sexual politics risks as well turning what we understand today as literary biblical scholarship into a secular form of obedient reinscription of attitudes that have long become untenable.

12. On the traditional androcentric interpretation of biblical texts, see Trible, *God and the Rhetoric of Sexuality*. How subsequent readings of the Hebrew Bible have further marginalized biblical women is exemplified in Mieke Bal's *Lethal Love*.

13. Esther Fuchs, 'The Literary Characterization of Mothers', pp. 117-36. See also my forthcoming book, *Sexual Politics in the Biblical Narrative: Toward a Feminist Hermeneutic of the Hebrew Bible* (Bloomington: Indiana University Press, forthcoming).

Chapter 3

THE BIBLICAL MOTHER:
THE ANNUNCIATION AND TEMPTATION TYPE-SCENES

Mother-Figures and Nativity Narratives

The most detailed biblical narratives about motherhood describe how, against all odds, prospective mothers succeed in giving birth to one or more sons.[1] Narratives about the relationships of mothers and sons, beyond the themes of maternity (the desire/ability to give birth to sons) and maternality (the desire/ability to protect sons) are few and brief.[2] Narratives about mother–daughter relations or about the birth of daughters are nonexistent. As we shall see, the telos of nativity narratives is the birth of a male heir, and the happy re-establishment of patrilineal continuity. Mother-figures—prospective, actual or surrogate mothers—are frequently valorized as male-controlled wives or widows successfully warding off the threat of patrilineal disruption. While the biblical narrative has much to tell us about motherhood as a patriarchal institution whose aim is to ensure patrilineal continuity, it has little to tell us about motherhood as experience or political privilege.[3]

1. Motherhood refers here to the Israelite institution that interpreted a man's wife/mother and offspring as his legal possessions. See Roland de Vaux, *Ancient Israel*, I (New York: McGraw–Hill, 1965), pp. 19-52. See also Phyllis Bird, 'Images of Women in the Old Testament', in Rosemary Radford Ruether (ed.), *Religion and Sexism: Images of Women in the Jewish and Christian Traditions* (New York: Simon & Schuster, 1974), pp. 41-88.

2. For further details on this point, see Bird, 'Images of Women', pp. 61-64. See also my article, 'The Literary Characterization of Mothers', pp. 131-36.

3. For a discussion of the conceptual distinction between motherhood as institution and experience, see Adrienne Rich, *Of Women Born: Motherhood as Experience and Institution* (New York: Bantam Books, 1976). For a sociological analysis of the institution of motherhood, see Dorothy Dinnerstein, *The Mermaid and the Minotaur: Sexual Arrangements and Human Malaise* (New York: Harper Colophon,

The patrilineal interest in the services of the institution of mother-hood explains why mother-figures are the most common and affirmed gynotypes in the biblical narrative. The superiority of this gynotype in relation to other gynotypes, like the wife, sister and daughter can be gauged in mimetic, structural and axiological terms.[4] Mimetically, mother-figures are more likely than other gynotypes to be characterized as resourceful, courageous, active and autonomous. Though they are capable of petty rivalry with other mothers and co-wives (Sarah and Hagar, Rachel and Leah, Hannah and Peninnah), toward their sons they are solicitous, protective and jealously loyal. Diegetically, mother-figures are permitted to control the activity of a particular narrative, and thus become its protagonists. As mothers, female characters are likely to be the initiators of a series of significant events. Axiologically, mothers emerge from various narratives as heroic, victorious or—for lack of a better term—positive. The axiological validation of mother-figures is most often signaled by the kind of attributes ascribed to them, the extent of narrative attention granted to them, their successful accomplishment of their goal (i.e. the birth of a male child) and various manifestations of Yhwh's interest in their plight. Unlike other gyno-types, mother-figures are the most likely female characters to elicit a favorable response from Yhwh of 'His' representatives. Procreative contexts are the only ones in which women address Yhwh and hold a dialogue with him. Yhwh either responds to the actions of mother-figures, or sends emissaries to them. As mothers, women are also most often shown to act in accordance with a broader divine plan.

A closer look at the mimetic aspect of the mother-figure reveals, however, that their impressive characteristics often serve as explana-

1976). For a sociological and psychoanalytic approach, see Nancy Chodorow, *The Reproduction of Mothering: Psychoanalysis and the Sociology of Gender* (Berkeley: University of California Press, 1978). For a historical and anthropological analysis of the institution of motherhood, see Robert Briffault, *The Mothers* (2 vols.; New York: Johnson, 1927), I. For an analysis and bibliographical survey of recent studies of motherhood, see Nancy Chodorow and Susan Contratto, 'The Fantasy of the Perfect Mother', in Barrie Thorne and Marilyn Yalom (eds.), *Rethinking the Family: Some Feminist Questions* (New York: Longman, 1982), pp. 54-75.

4.   'Mimetic' refers to the extent to which the character corresponds to a 'real' human mother. 'Diegetic' refers to the literary, compositional strategies involved in the creation of characters, as well as plots, dialogue, etc. 'Axiological' refers to the explicit (e.g. a narrator's comment) or implicit (e.g. Yhwh's attitude to the character) evaluation of the character.

tions for their success in securing the interests of their husbands, sons and fathers-in-law. The courage and wisdom of Tamar, Judah's daughter-in-law, results in the successful re-establishment of Judah's patrilineage (Gen. 38). Shiphrah's and Puah's resourcefulness leads to the redemption of the Israelite sons who were condemned to death by the Egyptian Pharaoh, while Moses is saved from death thanks to the ruse of Yochebed and Miriam. Men are also the direct or indirect beneficiaries of mothers' rivalry and pettiness. The rivalry between Rachel and Leah produces twelve sons for Jacob.

As prospective mothers, female characters are likely to control center stage. The prospective mother initiates actions, holds speeches and dominates other characters. Yet, her thoughts and words will be 'reported' only inasmuch as they are related to the implied telos of the story—the birth of a male heir. Upon the birth of a male heir, mother-figures slip out of the literary scene and are rarely mentioned in subsequent narratives. The birth of the son leads to the inevitable mimetic and diegetic death of the mother. She will either die at childbirth, like Rachel, or, as happens most of the time, through the suppression of information.

In her article on the biblical mother, Cheryl Exum interprets the positive portrayal of mother-figures as indicative of an anti-patriarchal trend:

> Within the admittedly patriarchal context of the biblical literature, we find strong countercurrents of affirmation of women: stories that show women's courage, strength, faith, ingenuity, talents, dignity, and worth. Such stories undermine patriarchal assumptions and temper patriarchal biases, often challenging the very patriarchal structures that dominate the narrative landscape.[5]

5.   J. Cheryl Exum, ' "Mother in Israel": A Familiar Figure Reconsidered', in Russell (ed.), *Feminist Interpretation of the Bible*, p. 74. Exum's definition of 'mother-figures' is both concrete and metaphorical: she refers both to women who give birth, and to women who enable the survival of children (e.g. Shiphra and Puah) and who protect the nation (e.g. Deborah). Exum revises her position in a later article where she discusses patriarchal strategies against mother figures. The first article was reproduced as ' "You Shall Let Every Daughter Live": A Study of Exodus 1.8–2.10', in Athalya Brenner (ed.), *A Feminist Companion to Exodus to Deuteronomy* (Sheffield: Sheffield Academic Press), pp. 37-61. See also 'The (M)other's Place', in *Fragmented Women*, pp. 94-147. Mieke Bal uses the term in metaphorical terms as well in her psychoanalytic approach to the murderous women in the book of Judges. See *Death and Dissymmetry*, pp. 197-230.

As we have seen, however, positive portrayals of mothers do not run counter to the political interests of patriarchy. As the 'enablers' and sustainers of patrilineal continuity, mothers are necessary.[6] By intruding into the plot in highly critical moments so as to enable its continued domination by male protagonists, the mother-figures are acting in accordance with the requirements of the patriarchal plot. Exum's interpretation is based on the identification of patriarchy, the politics of male domination, with misogyny, the psychology of negating women. To be sure, condemnatory representations of women appear in both misogynous and patriarchal literature, but in the latter only certain roles and aspects are likely to be condemned. Roles (such as motherhood) will be valorized because of their potential to enhance male dominance. A general belittlement of women is the logical extension of a misogynous frame of mind. Patriarchy, by contrast, has little to gain from a total negation of women. It has much more to gain from valorizing the contribution of mothers to the patriarchal system. The interests of patriarchy are better served by routing the resourcefulness of mothers in the 'proper' direction. The proper direction is the sustenance and perpetuation of patrilineal continuity. Therefore, it is not women's procreative powers that are celebrated in most nativity narratives, but rather their initiative in obviating obstacles to patrilineal continuity. This explains the preponderance of narratives about barren wives, who manage to give birth despite the odds. This also explains the repeated validation of childless women who succeed against the odds in giving birth to a male heir. Such mother-figures are indeed implicitly or explicitly praised not despite but because of the Bible's patriarchal policy.

All nativity narratives tell about the successful reinstitution of a temporarily disrupted patrilineage. The birth of a male heir is therefore the telos of all biblical nativity scenes, but it is not their focus. Most of the narratives detail the problems and the successful resolutions leading up

6.   On the role of the 'enabler', see J. Cheryl Exum, ' "You Shall Let Every Daughter Live": A Study of Exodus 1:8–2:10', in Mary Ann Tolbert (ed.), *The Bible and Feminist Hermeneutics* (Chico, CA: Scholars Press, 1983), pp. 63-82. Exum reverses her position in a later article, in which she analyzes the female characters in this narrative as male constructs serving a patriarchal ideology. See 'Second Thoughts about Secondary Characters: Women in Exodus 1.8–2.10', in Athalya Brenner (ed.), *A Feminist Companion to Exodus to Deuteronomy* (Sheffield: Sheffield Academic Press, 1994), pp. 75-87.

to this telos. It is significant that no biblical nativity scene makes reference to a man's impotence or sterility as the cause of childlessness. The denial of male infertility complies with yet another patriarchal strategy: the denial of the father's interest in a male heir. This interest is usually displaced onto the mother-figure. Significantly, although the father's name, patrilineage and inheritance are at stake, the biblical narrative projects onto the mother-figure the concern for patrilineal continuity; the mother-figure rather than the father-figure is most interested in giving birth to a male heir, though her name will inevitably be omitted from the patrilineal genealogy she tries so hard to sustain. Significantly, it is not the father who is shown to be desperate for sons, but rather the mother. All nativity narratives displace the patriarchal investment in patrilineal continuity to a female character, who has much less to gain from the birth of a male heir than the male character.

The major obstacles to the birth of a male heir are the wife's barrenness and the premature death (or the unavailability) of a husband. Appropriately, these are the thematic foci of the two major categories of nativity narratives. What has come to be known as the annunciation type-scene describes the happy transition of a prospective mother from barrenness to fertility (Sarah, Rachel, Samson's mother).[7] The widow's redemption narrative (Tamar, Ruth's daughter-in-law) tells how a childless woman manages to rebuild the temporarily disrupted patrilineage of her husband or father-in-law.

Both type-scenes, however, indicate that the mother-figures act in accordance with the divine plan. Both type-scenes indicate a growing interest in the prospective mother, her character and conduct. One motif that repeats in both annunciation and seduction type-scenes is the denial of a woman's 'natural' ability to give birth. By repeatedly presenting women as barren, by emphasizing that birth is an extraordinary event, and by insisting that maternity is determined by an agency external to the mother-figure, the annunciation type-scene offers again and again a patriarchal interpretation of motherhood.

But if the didactic nature of the biblical text explains the repeated presentation of certain motifs, narrative situations and characterizations, how does it account for the specific variations, or different presentations, of the same narrative material? As I suggested elsewhere, a com-

---

7.   For a general explanation of the biblical type-scene, see Alter, *The Art of the Biblical Narrative*, pp. 47-62. For a comparative analysis of the annunciation scenes, see Alter, 'How Convention Helps Us Read', pp. 115-30.

parative analysis of the various annunciation type-scenes reveals a progressive emphasis and growing affirmation of the mother-figure.[8] From a passive and peripheral character in the earlier scenes, the mother-figure grows into an ever more central and active character, while her male counterpart, in most cases her husband, tends to drift into the background. It is tempting to interpret this progression as an expression of an antipatriarchal trend. But such an interpretation would be too simplistic in its identification of positive evaluations of certain male-oriented female roles with the political interests of women. As we shall see, the growing emphasis on the prospective mother's moral stature implies that barrenness may be overcome by the barren woman's efforts to become a 'better' person. The implication that 'good' women are in the end rewarded with sons associates barrenness with moral deficiency. This justifies and validates the patriarchal indictment of childless women. In addition, by repeatedly focusing on barrenness as the major obstacle to securing offspring, the annunciation type-scene singles women out as the exclusive culprits of childlessness. Thus, men are associated with permanent fertility, while in women fertility is a contingency if not a rarity. This interpretation of female sexuality justifies the institution of polygyny in addition to the institution of fatherhood which gives the father exclusive authority over both his wife(ves) and children.

The Annunciation Type-Scene

The first biblical annunciation type-scene is preceded by Yhwh's direct address to the potential father, Abram, regarding the future conception of his barren wife, Sarai:

> And God said to Abraham, 'As for Sarai your wife, you shall not call her name Sarai, but Sarah shall be her name. I will bless her, and moreover I will give you a son by her [mimena]; I will bless her, and she shall be [the mother] of nations; kings of peoples shall come from her' (Gen. 17.15-16).

Although Sarah's new name, status and future are discussed here, she is excluded from the dialogue. Referred to through the third person singular, she is not recognized as a subject in her own right, neither is she blessed directly by Yhwh. Her prospective respectable status as the

8. 'The Literary Characterization of Mothers', pp. 117-27.

mother of nations and kings of people is presented as the happy result
of her successful reproductive performance. Her new, elevated status as
the recipient of divine blessing is contingent on her procreativity, and
her conjugal relationship with Abraham. But her procreative potential is
visibly separated from the moral-religious significance of Yhwh's relationship with Abraham. In other words, Sarah is excluded from the
covenantal framework despite her role as progenitrix. The latter confers
on Sarah a higher status than she has heretofore enjoyed, but it nevertheless does not permit her to cross into the privileged locus of her
husband's covenantal relationship with Yhwh.

The transformation of the barren Sarai into a fertile Sarah is a logical
and necessary procedure required by Yhwh's commitment to Abraham.
It is carefully indicated that Sarah's fertility is a product of God's
promise to Abraham: 'And I will make my covenant between me and
you, and will multiply you exceedingly' (Gen. 17.2). 'Behold the covenant *is with you*, and you shall be the father of a multitude of nations'
(Gen. 17.4). The repeated emphasis on the second person singular stresses not only the special bond between Yhwh and Abraham, but also the
exclusion of Sarah. Furthermore, the text emphasizes that it is Abraham
who is the true recipient of the promised son: 'and I shall also give you
a son from her'. Verse 19 repeats this emphasis: 'and also Sarah your
wife is bearing for you a son'. The son is to be born *to* and *for* (ל)
Abraham *by* Sarah. 'By' Sarah is implicitly defined as a reproductive
means, while Abraham's authority is ratified through his power to re-
name her and name his son.[9]

In the annunciation scene itself, Abraham continues to occupy center
stage. The scene opens with an introductory verse which leaves no
doubt as to whom is Yhwh's true addressee: 'And the Lord appeared to
him by the oaks of Mamre, as he sat in the tent door in the heat of the
day' (Gen. 18.1). When the three messengers arrive at the tent, Abraham, the generous and hospitable host, invites the guests to rest up and
refresh themselves, while instructing Sarah, who is inside the tent, to
prepare cakes for the men. Sarah's function in this context is not different from that of Abraham's servant who is enjoined to prepare a calf for
the meal. Unlike Abraham, who is implicitly praised for his generosity

---

9. On the significance of maternal naming, see Ilana Pardes, 'Beyond Genesis
3: The Politics of Maternal Naming', pp. 39-59. On the significance of the act of
naming in the Bible, see Nahum M. Sarna, *Understanding Genesis: The Heritage of
Biblical Israel* (New York: Schocken Books), pp. 129-31.

and eagerness to please his guests, Sarah, who is not privy to what is happening outside the tent, receives no credit for her work, since she functions as her husband's adjunct. Throughout the meal, Sarah shows no interest in the guests. The text repeats the fact that Sarah remains inside the tent in Abraham's response to the messengers' query concerning her whereabouts (Gen. 18.9). This repetition is not coincidental; it emphasizes Sarah's absence from this fateful scene and, by contrast, Abraham's central role in it. Instead of become actively involved in the conversation, Sarah eavesdrops on her husband and guests 'at the tent door behind him [Abraham]' (18.10). Once again, although Sarah is the subject of Yhwh's message, she is referred to in the third person while her husband functions as the actual addressee: 'Yhwh said, "I shall surely return to you when the season comes round and Sarah your wife shall have a son" ' (18.10).[10] Even when Sarah is reprimanded for laughing to herself in disbelief, she is addressed through her husband. Only when she denies having laughed, does Yhwh speak directly to her, 'saying "No, but you did laugh" ' (18.15). Yhwh's only direct reference to Sarah takes the form of an implicit reprimand.

The juxtaposition of the husband and wife in this scene enhances the attributes of the former and the drawbacks of the latter. Abraham's activity outside the tent is contrasted with Sarah's passivity. Seventeen verbs articulate Abraham's dedication to this guests. The verbs 'run' (רוץ) and 'hasten' (מהר) are repeated twice. Sarah, on the other hand, is reported to be the subject of four verbs, none of which demonstrates a high level of exertion or initiative: she hears (שמע), laughs (צחק), denies (כחש), and fears (ירא). The text also prefers implying that Sarah prepared a meal for her guests to describing her preparations with any detail. Sarah emerges from the scene as confined, passive, cowardly, deceptive and, above all, untrusting of Yhwh's omnipotence.[11]

Sarah's participation in the annunciation scene amounts to a troublesome interference. She is not only inferior to Abraham in the literary

10. כעת חיה, is translated by RSV 'in the spring'. Here I use the Jewish Publication Society version (Philadelphia, 1955). Speiser translates the Hebrew as 'when life would be due', that is, at the end of the pregnancy period. See E.A. Speiser, *Genesis: A New Translation with Introduction and Commentary* (AB; New York: Doubleday, 3rd edn, 1983), pp. 128-31.

11. Although Abraham too laughs at the prospect of having a child in his old age (Gen. 17.17), Yhwh does not rebuke him for his faithlessness, but instead reassures him that 'His' promise will be realized.

sense, serving as a foil to bring out his admirable attributes, she is also made inferior to him morally. If the text is trying to establish a correlation between Yhwh's benevolence and the uprightness of his subjects, it is clear that the manifestation of this benevolence, namely the annunciation scene, is related causally to the man's demeanor and concessively to the woman's. The implication is that Yhwh violates nature's rules and gives the barren woman a child because of her husband's magnanimity and despite her pettiness. But the fulfillment of the divine promise does not follow the annunciation in the narrative sequence; instead, it is postponed to ch. 21, which opens with a characteristic formula: 'And the Lord remembered Sarah' (Gen. 21.1). The interpolated narrative material refers to Abraham's intercession on behalf of the citizens of Sodom and Gomorrah, the destruction of the iniquitous cities by Yhwh (Gen. 19) and the episode in Gerar in which Abraham presents his wife as his sister (Gen. 20). Sarah is absent from ch. 19 which dramatizes Abraham's compassion and altruism. Abraham's ardent appeal to Yhwh on behalf of the 'foreign' Sodomites highlights by contrast Sarah's heartless expulsion of her Egyptian maid, Hagar (Gen. 16). In ch. 20, Sarah appears as a passive object of male sexual interest as she is taken by Abimelech, king of Gerar, and narrowly saved from committing adultery by the direct intervention of Yhwh.

Although Sarah is given full credit for giving birth to Isaac in ch. 21, the text continues to stress that she is mostly the instrument, and that the miracle is performed for Abraham. Verse 2 does not simply state that Sarah bore a son but that 'she bore [to] Abraham a son'. Verse 3 repeats this idea twice: 'Abraham called the name of *his* son who was born *to him*, whom Sarah bore [*to him*], Isaac.' Abraham proceeds to name and circumcise his son (v. 4), two acts that symbolically convey paternal authority and divine intervention. Sarah is excluded again on the laughability of her belated conception (v. 6), which faintly reminds us of her embarrassing verbal interchange with Yhwh.

As noted, the first annunciation scene starts with Yhwh's promise to Abram. In the second annunciation type-scene, Isaac initiates the first move; he pleads with Yhwh on behalf of his barren wife and Yhwh grants his prayer (Gen. 25.21). Once again the wife's conception is attributed to the close relationship of her husband with Yhwh; it is not contingent upon the qualities or actions of the wife. Nevertheless, it is Yhwh's response to Rebekah that the text reports and not 'His' response to Isaac. The divine message about Isaac and Rebekah's prospective sons is not offered through a messenger before Rebekah conceives. Rather, it is mediated through an oracle addressed to the already pregnant Rebekah. What Rebekah learns from Yhwh is not *that* she will give birth, but the futures of the twins in her womb. In response to Rebekah's desperate complaint about the commotion in her womb, Yhwh explains that she is sensing the future conflict between her sons, the younger of whom will prevail over the older (Gen. 33.22-23). This is the only annunciation scene making any reference at all to a mother's gestation period, or to a pregnant woman's initiative. The contrast between the anacoluthon attributed to Rebekah ('If so, why do I?') and the solemn, coherent and detailed quartet attributed to Yhwh makes it clear that the difficult pregnancy is used as a prelude and a pretext for a divine message about Rebekah's twins, putting to rest any speculation about the religious symbolism of the pregnancy itself.[12]

Nevertheless, the reference to Rebekah's pregnancy may foreshadow and explain the attention given to her intervention on behalf of her son, Jacob (Gen. 27.5-17). The logical connection between these episodes is that Rebekah won a right to determine her sons' future because she put up with a long period of discomfort that preceded their birth. As already noted however, an explicit awareness of the mother's gestation period is a rarity in the annunciation scene and in nativity episodes in general and so is the description of a mother's intervention in her son's life.

It is undeniable, however, that Rebekah is much more active a character than her counterpart in the first annunciation scene. It is true that she conceives thanks to Isaac's plea, but she does not wait for Isaac's intercession when troubled by what is described as her sons' 'clashing [ויתרצצו] inside her' (Gen. 25.22). Yhwh seems also better disposed to Rebekah, offering a rather detailed response to her inquiry (vv. 23-24). Unlike Sarah, Rebekah is also shown to participate in the naming of her sons. Whereas in the case of Isaac, Yhwh endows Abraham with the exclusive right to name his son, here the children are named by both parents: 'The first came forth red, all his body like a hairy mantle; so *they* called his name Esau. After, his brother came forth...so his name was called Jacob' (Gen. 25.25-26; emphasis added).[13] Unlike Sarah,

12. The RSV renders Rebekah's broken speech as 'If it is thus, why do I live?' Speiser suggests: 'If this is how it is to be, why do I go on living?' Most translations sacrifice the rhetorical effectiveness of the syntactic disruption to coherence.

13. The Hebrew in v. 26 reads 'and he called his name Jacob', but it does not specify a subject; it is therefore acceptable to render it in the passive form.

Rebekah appears at center stage, alongside Isaac. She receives greater recognition from Yhwh as potential mother, and there is not so much as an allusion to a moral discrepancy between husband and wife, at this point.

If in the second annunciation scene pregnancy is represented as a sort of curse (in compliance with Gen. 3.16), in the third one barrenness is so conceived. The third scene resembles the first in its emphasis on the barren woman's plight. Echoing the rivalry between Sarah and Hagar, the story of Rachel and Leah also evokes the rivalry between a fertile and a barren wife. Unlike Rebekah, who suffers from her pregnancy, Rachel is tortured by her barrenness. In her despair, Rachel turns to Jacob with an impetuous demand, whose despair is slightly evocative of Rebekah's explosion. Unlike Rebekah, however, Rachel does not turn to Yhwh, but rather to Jacob: 'Give me sons, or I shall die' (Gen. 30.1). Robert Alter argues that Jacob's angry response 'points simultaneously to the theological impropriety of Rachel's importunate plea and to its violation of the conventional requirements of the annunciation type-scene'.[14] But this interpretation offers an all too literalistic reading of Rachel's plea. As an illocutionary act, Rachel is demanding sons from Jacob, but the perlocutionary aspect of this act can easily be taken as an attempt to elicit in Jacob sympathy or reassurance.[15] Rachel's impetuous demand is an exasperated plea for Jacob to become involved in her plight. From this perspective, Rachel's plea is by no means a violation of 'the conventional requirements of the annunciation type-scene', as Alter would have it. For the preceding scene shows us Isaac's intercession on behalf of Rebekah. Whereas Isaac prays for Rebekah without being asked to do so, Jacob's angry response indicates a new vision of a woman's procreative responsibilities. Jacob's rhetorical question: 'Am I in the place of God who has withheld from you the fruit of the womb?' (Gen. 30.2) implies both that he has no control over and no responsibility for Rachel's barrenness.

It is here that the patriarchal redefinition of procreation comes full circle: the father has the prerogative of owning his sons, without however bearing responsibility for their absence. Implicitly blamed for a

14. I am borrowing and adapting the concepts of illocutionary and perlocutionary speech acts from J.L. Austin, *How to Do Things with Words* (Cambridge, MA: Harvard University Press, 1962). See also, Searle, *Speech Acts*.

15. For a psychoanalytic interpretation of Rachel's plight, see Ilana Pardes, 'Rachel's Dream: The Female Subplot', in *Countertraditions in the Bible*, pp. 79-97.

couple's childlessness, the mother will never exercise authority over the children she does bear. While the prospective father can never lose, the prospective mother, whether fertile or not, will have to remain politically inferior to her male counterpart. With Abraham we learn that sons belong to their fathers. With Jacob, we begin to learn that the absence of sons is the exclusive responsibility of the prospective mother. Yhwh is said to have withheld the 'fruit of the womb' from Rachel, and the 'fact' that Jacob fathered Leah's sons lends authority to this figural interpretation of the divine conduct.

The ensuing list of sons born to Jacob by Bilhah and Zilpah, and Leah (vv. 4-13) may explain the conditions that made it possible for Jacob to be vituperative toward his preferred wife. I shall discuss the political implications of the co-wife paradigm in the chapter on the wife-figure. For now, suffice it to say that the exclusive attribution of barrenness to the wife-figure serves as an implicit justification for polygyny, which in turn ratifies Jacob's impatient response to his most beloved wife. If the co-wife permits the husband to scold his other wife, her fertility permits the narrator to stretch the description of her despair and helplessness. Since Rachel's despair is now an inconvenience easily separated from Jacob's concerns about progeny—in other words, the prospective mother's barrenness does not entail any harm to the prospective father's patriliny—the delay in Yhwh's response to Rachel's misery can by no means signal anything in terms of 'His' special relationship to Jacob. After another unsuccessful attempt by Rachel to become fertile (she purchases mandrakes, assumed to be an aphrodisiac, from Leah in return for a night with Jacob [vv. 14-15]), and after Leah manages to bear 'to [ל] Jacob' (vv. 17, 19) two additional sons (vv. 17-20), Yhwh finally responds to Rachel's indirect pleas for sons of her own: 'Then God remembered Rachel, and God hearkened to her and opened her womb' (Gen. 30.22). This formula of divine intervention, differs from those we encountered in the previous annunciation scenes.

The first formula presents Yhwh's intervention as a fulfillment of a promise: 'Yhwh visited Sarah as He had said, and Yhwh did to Sarah as He had promised' (Gen. 21.1). The second formula presents divine intervention as a direct response to the husband's plea: '...Yhwh granted his prayer' (Gen. 25.21). The third formula, however, stresses the fact that Yhwh intervenes in response to Rachel's plight, by repeating that Yhwh 'remembered her' (ויזכר), 'and hearkened to her' (וישמע) (Gen. 30.22). In addition, Rachel and Leah are shown to give names to their sons, names that Jacob accepts with the exception of his last son, Benjamin. Rachel's attempt to inscribe her suffering in her son's name, Ben-oni ('the son of my sorrow'), is overridden by Jacob's preference for Benjamin ('the son of my right arm'), a name resonant with potency and optimism (Gen. 35.18).

The fourth annunciation scene leaves little doubt as to the real addressee of the divine message. Although Judges 13 never reveals Samson's mother's name, and though she is referred to as Manoah's wife, she does not depend on him for significance. As J. Cheryl Exum demonstrates, in many ways the nameless woman outshines her bumbling husband.[16]

In pointed contrast to Sarah, confined in a tent and positioned behind Abraham's back (Gen. 18.10), Manoah's wife meets Yhwh's messenger in an open field, and it is her husband who must 'follow her' in order to meet the messenger (Judg. 13.11). While Sarah is excluded from the more detailed agreements between Yhwh and Abraham, here it is Manoah who learns less than his wife about the future and fate of his sons. Though his request to meet personally with the messenger is granted, Manoah 'never receives as much information concerning the child or his wife'.[17]

Whereas the woman perceives immediately that the messenger is 'a man of God' and compares his appearance to the 'countenance of an angel of God, very terrible' (Judg. 13.6), Manoah treats the divine messenger as a human being, inviting him to a meal (v. 15). When the angel declines Manoah's invitation, hinting at his divine identity by suggesting that Manoah should use the meal as a burnt offering for Yhwh, Manoah misses the hint and proceeds to inquire about the stranger's name, so that 'when your words come true, we may honor you' (v. 17). This request contrasts with the woman's conscientious and respectful silence (Judg. 13.6). We do not know at this point whether she knows that the guest is specifically Yhwh's messenger, but it is

---

16. See J. Cheryl Exum, 'Promise and Fulfillment', *Journal of Biblical Litera-ture* 99 (1980), pp. 43-59. See also her analysis of Manoah's wife as the good mother prototype in contradistinction to the seductive women in Samson's life in 'Samson's Women', in *Fragmented Women*, pp. 61-93.

17. See Robert Polzin, *Moses and the Deuteronomist: A Study of the Deutero-nomic History* (New York: Seabury, 1980), p. 183. Polzin argues that Manoah's wife is both 'ignorant' and 'presumptuous' in her reasoning.

clear that in contrast to her husband she knows that he is a divine messenger. Manoah's wife does not insist on learning the messenger's name, which is in line with the angel's cryptic and reluctant reference to his 'wondrous' (פלא) name in response to Manoah's insistent question (v. 18). Only when he witnesses the miraculous ascent to heaven in the flame of the burnt offering does Manoah realize that the 'man' is Yhwh's messenger: 'Then Manoah knew that he was the angel of Yhwh' (v. 21). This realization, however, causes Manoah to panic: 'We shall surely die, for we have seen God [אלהים]' (v. 22). By contrast, Manoah's wife, remains calm and reasons that Yhwh would not have sent an angel to them had 'He' planned to bring about their deaths (v. 23). The woman's explicit reference to Yhwh demonstrates, contra Robert Polzin, that she does not remain ignorant of the angel's true identity.[18] The prospective mother's response is implicitly vindicated by the verse that immediately follows it: 'And the woman bore a son and called his name Samson' (v. 24). The subject of the verse is once again the mother, who is not shown to consult with her husband as she names her son. The woman is implicitly vindicated by the fact that Yhwh indeed does not punish them for 'seeing God', but rather gives them a son as his angel promised, and 'blesses' him (v. 24).

The thematic and structural parallels between Judges 13 and Genesis 18 highlight the progressive transposition of the mother-figure as the focus of the annunciation scene. Whereas Abraham's hospitality is graciously accepted by the three messengers, Manoah's hospitality is rejected. The first scene uses Abraham's hospitality to enhance his uprightness, the latter exposes Manoah's hospitality as maladroitness. In the first scene, Yhwh's messengers address the prospective father first, and refer to Sarah indirectly and peripherally. In the fourth scene, Yhwh's messenger appears twice to the woman first (Judg. 13.3, 9), though his second appearance is occasioned by Manoah's request. Sarah emerges from the first scene as a skeptical and confined housewife, vastly overshadowed by Abraham's magnanimity. Her skeptical remarks and her deceptive self-justifications do not contribute much to the development of the plot. As already noted, her participation in the scene amounts to an unwelcome interference with the progression of the plot toward a satisfactory resolution. In structural terms, we can say that Sarah is associated with the digressive incidents which delay the

18. See Polzin above.

plot progression. In the fourth annunciation scene, it is the prospective father who is the subject of digressive incidents, while his wife controls the progressive events that propel the plot toward the satisfactory solution of the fundamental diegetic dilemma. Manoah's interventions are largely digressive. It is Manoah who slows down the progression of the plot through questions that seem to annoy the angel and that elicit answers known by him, his wife and the reader. The angel's explicit references to his previous communications with Manoah's wife, 'all that he said to the woman' and 'all that he commanded her' (vv. 13-14) also imply that Manoah's importunities did not contribute substantively to what he already established with his wife.[19]

Like Rachel, Hannah, the protagonist of the next annunciation scene, is a barren co-wife, who in addition to her childlessness must contend with her fertile rival, Peninnah (1 Sam. 1.6-7). But unlike Rachel, Hannah does not turn to her husband, Elkanah, for help. Unconsoled by his love (v. 5), and tormented by Peninnah's provocations (v. 6), Hannah turns directly to Yhwh. She does not even call on Eli, the priest, who is seated at the entrance of Yhwh's house (v. 9). Pouring out her bitter heart in prayer (v. 10), Hannah makes a vow to dedicate her son to Yhwh, in return for the latter's help.[20] While in the second annunciation scene, the narrator reports briefly that Rebekah 'went to inquire of Yhwh' (Gen. 25.22), in this scene the narrator finds it necessary to 'report' Hannah's vow through direct speech (1 Sam. 1.11). Like Manoah's wife, Hannah is the subject of the major plot events. Unlike Manoah's wife, who is presented as the recipient of the good tidings about her imminent conception, Hannah is shown to initiate the series of events leading to the birth of her son. And whereas Manoah's wife is told about her son's special vocation, Hannah proposes of her own initiative that her son be dedicated to Yhwh's service.[21]

---

19. This is not to say that Manoah's importunities are nonfunctional. While they do not add to the progression of the plot, their apparent redundancy can be profitably interpreted on another level. For some of the functions of the narrative's repetitions, see Exum, 'Promise and Fulfillment', pp. 50-55.

20. For two conflicting assessments of Hannah's vow and prayer of thanks, see Carol Meyers, 'Hannah and her Sacrifice: Reclaiming Female Agency', in Athalya Brenner (ed.), *A Feminist Companion to Samuel and Kings* (Sheffield: Sheffield Academic Press, 1994), pp. 93-104; and Fewell and Gunn, *Gender, Power, and Promise*, pp. 136-40.

21. I am following here the Anchor Bible. See P. Kyle McCarter, *I Samuel*

Clumsy as he may be, Manoah insists on meeting the divine messenger and learning directly from him about his prospective son. In this later scene, the prospective father and the divine messenger never meet. Elkanah is not aware of Eli's promise, and Eli does not seem to be aware of Elkanah's existence. Neither man is aware of the extent of Hannah's despair and resolve. While Elkanah tries to console her by reassuring her of his great love for her ('for I am better to you than ten sons' [v. 8]), Eli the priest mistakes her ardent prayer for drunkenness. The threefold question Elkanah addresses to his wife expresses not only his concern for her, but also his incomprehension of her suffering: 'Hannah, why do you weep? And why do you not eat? And why is your heart sad?' (v. 8.) Elkanah's thrice-repeated 'why' parallels Eli's rhetorical question 'How long will you be drunken?' (1 Sam. 1.14) Both men are at a loss as to Hannah's behavior. And both men's dialogues touch on Hannah's problem, but only circuitously. Elkanah's statement that he is better to her than ten sons refers only indirectly to Hannah's source of misery. Much in the same way, Eli refers rather vaguely to Hannah's 'request' and promises its fulfillment without ever referring explicitly to the content of the request or the promise: 'And Eli answered: "Go in peace, and may the God of Israel grant you the request you asked of Him"' (v. 17). Despite Eli's ambiguity, Hannah appears to know in advance that her request will be answered: 'Then the woman went her way and ate, and she no longer wore her [sad] expression' (v. 18). Hannah's implicit premonition is confirmed in the next two verses which indicate that 'God remembered her' (v. 19), and that she 'gave birth to a son' (v. 20).

If Hannah stands out as an exceptionally pious woman who trusts that Yhwh will redeem her from barrenness, the 'great woman' of Shunem (2 Kgs 4.8), the protagonist of the next annunciation scene, seems to supersede her in the degree of her piety. For the Shunammite opens up her home to Yhwh's prophet, Elisha, and feeds him generously long before he promises that she will bear a son. The text gives us vivid details about her generosity and hospitality: 'and she seized him to eat bread, and it came to pass that whenever he passed [though] he would stop by to have bread there' (v. 8). The text also makes it clear that it

---

(New York: Doubleday, 1980), p. 55. The RSV translates: 'And her countenance was no longer sad.' The original text reads something like: 'And she no longer had her face.'

was the woman rather than her husband who was insisting on offering the prophet food and lodging:

> And she said to her husband: 'I do know that a holy man of God often passes by our house. Let us make a small attic and put up for him there a bed and a table and a chair and a lamp, so that when he comes to us he could stay there' (vv. 9-10).

The Shunammite's actions are further highlighted by the episodes that precede and follow this annunciation scene. For whereas the nameless widow entreats Elisha for help (vv. 1-7), the Shunammite does not ask for anything. And while both the widow and the prophets' sons (vv. 38-44) are fed by Elisha, the Shunammite provides Elisha with food. Even when Elisha offers to reciprocate her generosity, she does not mention her barrenness, and does not ask for anything. Her proud response is: 'I am dwelling among my people' (v. 13). It is only through his servant, Gehazi, that Elisha (and the reader) learns that 'she has no son and her husband is old' (2 Kgs 4.14). In response to this revelation, Elisha, echoing the formula used by Abraham's guests announces: 'Next year at this time [כעת חיה] you will embrace a son' (v. 16).

The phraseological and thematic allusions of our chapter to Genesis 18 are fairly clear.[22] Not only does Elisha use a similar formula to that used by the three divine messengers in Genesis, but the Shunammite's incredulous response (v. 16) recalls both Abraham's and Sarah's response (Gen. 17.17; 18.12). Perhaps more significantly, the Shunammite's hospitality and generosity remind us of Abraham's famed traits. Like him she insists that her guest stop by her house and partake of her food, and like him she supervises the smallest details involving her guest's comfort. The enumeration of the ingredients of the festive meal and its preparation in Genesis 18 demonstrates Abraham's solicitousness, just as the detailed description of the furniture for Elisha's room speaks of the Shunammite's concerns with her guest's comfort. Both scenes imply that there is a causal link between the protagonist's righteousness and the birth of the son.

Yet the similarities in the characterization of Abraham and the Shunammite bring out all the more forcefully the significant differences between them. The Shunammite is a nameless woman who gives birth

---

22. Ariela Deem, *Zot ha-pa'am* (This Time) (Tel Aviv: Reuven Mas, 1986), pp. 103-12 (in Hebrew).

to a nameless son. Her admirable conduct leads to no enduring relation-ship with Yhwh. Structurally her role is restricted to a single narrative detailing how her only son was born and how he survived thanks to her initiative. Having performed the typical functions of maternity and maternality, she slips out of the narrative, letting the diegetic focus return to Elisha and his miraculous exploits. As in the case of the other mother-figures, the Shunammite's structural autonomy is restricted to the functions of maternity and maternality. Her independent actions and initiative lead first to her son's birth and later to his resurrection (2 Kgs 4.20-37), but as soon as the son's survival is ensured, the Shunammite disappears from the narrative scene. In this sense she shares much in common with Sarah and Rebekah who are whisked off the stage only after they have ensured the survival of their male heir.[23]

Nevertheless, it is undeniable that the nameless Shunammite out-shines Sarah, just as Hannah and Samson's mother outshine Rebekah and Rachel. How can we explain the fact that the latter three scenes attribute to their protagonists a moral stature they deny to the first three mother-figures? Why does the biblical narrative let relatively unimpor-tant mother-figures outshine the 'mothers' of the nation? I would like to suggest that it is precisely because the latter characters are accorded the high status of national progenitrices that they are deprived of the more impressive characterization of their counterparts in the latter scenes. By cutting the first three mother-figures down to size, the narrative 'com-pensates' for their high status. As the first progenitrix of the nation *and* a model of piety, Sarah would have been too positive, and from the standpoint of patriarchal politics too much like the first male progenitor, and therefore too threatening. By attributing such venerable character-istics as hospitality and piety to a nameless woman who gives birth to a nameless son, the biblical narrative does not risk as much. The omis-sion of proper names is yet another strategy whose function is to guard against a threateningly positive mother-figure. Despite their structural centrality and their mimetic impressiveness neither the Shunammite nor Manoah's wife are identified by proper names, but rather by the name of a town (Shunem) or through their marital relationship (Manoah's wife).[24] The omission of their proper names 'compensates' for the piety

---

23. Sarah manages to drive Hagar and Ishmael away (Gen. 21) shortly before she expires (Gen. 23.2). Rebekah disappears from the scene as soon as her protec-tive role is completed, allowing the literary focus to shift from Isaac to Jacob.

24. For a different reading of Manoah's nameless wife, see Adele Reinhartz,

and the special relationships they create with Yhwh's messengers. Unlike Hannah, who is given a proper name, Manoah's wife and the Shunammite are shown to hold discourses with Yhwh's angels and messengers. As we noted, Eli the priest can hardly compare with the angel who informs Manoah's wife of Samson's birth, or with Elisha who has the power to predict a birth as well as to resurrect a dead boy. Hannah is characterized as a resourceful and pious mother-figure, but her contact with the deity is one-sided: she prays to Yhwh and praises 'Him'. This may explain why, unlike the Shunammite and Manoah's wife, she is permitted to have a proper name.

Thus, while procreative contexts are the only contexts in which female characters are shown to have some form of dialogue with Yhwh, they nevertheless must comply with restrictive conditions. A mother-figure can *either* be an important spouse, *or* a morally impressive figure. She can *either* have a proper name, *or* be permitted to meet Yhwh's representative. The careful delimitation of traits and properties ensure that the valorization of the mother-figure remain within the limits of the 'proper' patriarchal boundaries.

As we have seen, the mother-figure in the annunciation type-scene is transformed from a peripheral character in the earlier narratives into a protagonist and a heroine in the later scenes.[25] This transformation parallels the gradual de-emphasis of the father-figure. This signals a growing valorization of mother-figures, or rather of their patriarchal responsibility to bear male heirs. The growing emphasis on the mother's righteousness creates an ever-stronger causal linkage between a woman's virtues and her ability to procreate. By interpreting a woman's procreativity as a divine reward, the annunciation type-scene

'Samson's Mother: An Unnamed Protagonist', in Brenner (ed.), *A Feminist Companion to Judges*, pp. 157-71. See also Yairah Amit, ' "Manoah Promptly Followed His Wife" (Judges 13.11): On the Place of Woman in the Birth Narratives', in Brenner (ed.), *A Feminist Companion to Judges*, pp. 146-56. For a different reading of the woman of Shunem, see Fokkelein van Dijk-Hemmes, 'The Great Woman of Shunem and the Man of God', in Brenner (ed.), *A Feminist Companion to Samuel and Kings*, pp. 218-30.

25. 'Protagonist' is a structural concept referring to the relations of a central character with most events and actions as well as characters described in a given narrative. 'Heroine' (or hero) is a mimetic concept referring to the human-like characteristics and traits attributed to a certain character who is either explicitly or implicitly judged in positive terms.

implies that barrenness is a kind of divine retribution, or an expression of moral deficiency. If a woman can overcome barrenness by being pious and virtuous then it is possible to hold her responsible for her inability to give birth. For if the ability to give birth is a divine compensation, then the inability to give birth may very well be a divine punishment. Barrenness thus becomes a moral as well as a physiological liability. The interpretation of a son's birth as a form of divine reward entails a stigmatization of barrenness as an expression of moral inferiority.

But if miraculous fertility is represented as a kind of divine reward, natural fertility is associated with a rather dubious array of characteristics, like foreignness, pridefulness, unattractiveness (from the husband's viewpoint). Three of the mother-figures discussed above are juxtaposed with naturally fertile mother-figures, all of whom are in one way or another devalued. Hagar, Sarah's Egyptian maid, is reported to become contemptuous of her barren mistress as soon as she conceives (Gen. 16.4). The naturally fertile Leah is not as pretty and well liked as Rachel (Gen. 29.17, 31). The naturally fertile Peninnah combines the characteristics of Hagar and Leah, as she is said to treat Hannah with cruelty and contempt, and to be Elkanah's less favored co-wife (1 Sam. 1.5-7). As the implications of the co-wives' contests are discussed in the chapter on the biblical wife, suffice it to say the increasingly dismissive treatment of the naturally fertile wife is a development that contrasts rather sharply with the development of the annunciation type-scene. Cast out into the wilderness by her irate mistress, Hagar wins the attention of Yhwh whose emissaries promise her that her progeny, the descendants of her son Ishmael, will become great (Gen. 16.7-14; 21.14-19). While Yhwh's attention to Hagar's plight is dramatized in two different and relatively detailed scenes, Yhwh's attention to Leah's plight is summarized briefly in a single verse: 'When Yhwh saw that Leah was unloved [שנואה], he opened up her womb, but Rachel [remained] barren' (Gen. 29.31). But if the second contest scene makes at least some reference to the plight of the unloved wife, the third one portrays her as hateful and completely undeserving of Yhwh's attention. Focusing on Hannah's plight, the text not only deprives Peninnah of Yhwh's attention, but it also deprives her of the reader's sympathy as it attributes to her a mean tendency to taunt and humiliate Hannah. Referred to merely as 'her [Hannah's] rival', the text states that Peninnah 'did indeed upset her [Hannah] because Yhwh had closed her womb' (1 Sam. 1.6). The text has nothing more to say about the naturally fertile mother.

But why should natural fertility be underestimated, even stigmatized? It would seem that the increasingly negative characterization of fertile mothers runs counter to the patriarchal interest in male progeny, for what can guarantee male progeny and patrilineal stability better than fertile mothers? On closer examination, however, the stigmatization of natural fertility parallels and complements the repeated presentation of mother-figures as naturally barren. Both patriarchal strategies undermine a mother's claim to or rights over her progeny. Both strategies justify the exclusion of mothers from biblical genealogies. By stigmatizing natural barrenness as well as natural fertility, the annunciation type-scene suggests that mothers give birth not because of but rather *despite* their natural deficiencies. The barren mother is deficient because she is an ineffective breeder.[26] As I suggested earlier, the increasing association of miraculous deliverances from barrenness with extreme devoutness and righteousness also implies that barrenness is a form of divine punishment. On the other hand, the repeated association of natural fertility with a mother's foreignness and moral defectiveness suggests in yet another way that women give birth *despite* their inherent shortcomings. By faulting both the procreative capabilities *and* the moral stature of mother-figures, the patriarchal text implies that male progeny belongs ultimately to Yhwh, but for all practical purposes to the father. By questioning the natural ability of mother-figures to give birth, and by questioning the moral stature of naturally fertile mothers, the text is questioning the rights and privileges that accrue to maternity. Complementarily, by denying male impotence and infertility, the annunciation type-scene contributes to the construal of fathers as the subjects and the true sources of male progeny.

This is not to contradict my analysis of the increasing valorization of mother-figures. It is only to emphasize that this valorization is not aimed at the mothers but rather at their instrumentality to the perpetua-

26. Using an anthropological-structuralist method of analysis, Nathaniel Wander points out the insistent 'doubts about the fertility, effectiveness, and identity of the matriarchs' in the book of Genesis. Though he is close to a feminist analysis, Wander is interested in analyzing what he calls the mytheme of the father's brother's daughter marriage. See his article, 'Structure, Contradiction, and "Resolution" in Mythology: Father's Brother's Daughter's Marriage and the Treatment of Women in Genesis 11–50', *JANES* 5 (1973), pp. 75-99.

tion of patriarchy. By containing the procreative powers of women and routing them in the 'right' direction, patriarchy legitimizes the political control of fathers over mothers. Mothers are clearly essential for the survival of patriarchy, but their essential role must not be given too much credit. The rights of fathers over their female counterparts as well as over their offspring are ensured by emphasizing the contingency of women's procreativity. Hence the repeated presentation of prospective mothers as naturally barren women. The emphasis on woman's *inability* to give birth complements the stigmatization of naturally fertile mothers. Both strategies undermine the potential political claims of mothers over their progeny, and mothers' potential claim to equity with and independence from the control of fathers. In other words, while affirming the institution of motherhood, that is, women's instrumentality to the perpetuation of patriarchy, the annunciation type-scene rejects the political claims implied by too ready an admission to the indispensability of maternity and maternality.

The Temptation Type-Scene

The protagonist of the temptation type-scene, like her counterpart in the annunciation type-scene, is a mother-figure who manages against the odds to give birth to a male heir. The major obstacle in the type-scene is the unavailability or indifference of prospective fathers. The mother-figure overcomes this obstacle by seducing the prospective father and giving birth to sons who continue his patrilineage. Like the annunciation type-scene, the temptation type-scene emphasizes that it is the mother rather than the father who desires male progeny. In the temptation type-scene, the mother-figure is naturally fertile, but she cannot fulfill her procreative duty because the father is either absent or unwilling to secure his own interest. By ascribing to the mother rather than to the father the patriarchal anxiety about patrilineal disruption, the temptation type-scene displaces the patriarchal interest in male progeny. The attribution of the anxiety to mother-figures denies the political interest that fathers have in the institution of motherhood and its product—the assured birth of male heirs. The focus on the mother-figure obscures one of the most vital interests of the patriarchal order. For it must be emphasized that the issue in both type-scenes is not merely the desire for children, but the perpetuation of the father's name and genealogy. As we shall see, the temptation type-scene does not merely valorize maternity and maternality. Rather, it approvingly recounts the exploits of mother-figures who risk their lives and reputations to secure the patrilineal continuity of an heirless father. In the annunciation type-scene, the heirless father is the prospective mother's husband. In the temptation type-scene, the heirless father is the prospective mother's father, or father-in-law. The annunciation type-scene valorizes the loyal wife who becomes a mother, while the temptation type-scene valorizes the loyal daughter-in-law (or daughter) who becomes a mother. A careful examination of successive temptation scenes reveals an increasing valorization of mother-figures that parallels the development noted in successive annunciation scenes.

The mother-figures in the first temptation scene (Gen. 19.30-38) are the nameless daughters of Lot. The elderly Lot is heirless. He is said to have lost his prospective sons-in-law who did not believe his warnings about the impending destruction of Sodom and Gomorrah (Gen. 19.12-14). Lot is also said to have lost his wife who had turned into a pillar of salt for having looked back on the burning cities (Gen. 19.26). Significantly, however, it is not Lot who is concerned about his progeny, but rather his daughters. All we know about Lot is that, traumatized by the destruction of Sodom and Gomorrah, he prefers to dwell in a cave in a mountain to dwelling in the city of Zoar, lest the latter be destroyed as well (Gen. 19.30). The initiative to secure Lot's progeny comes from Lot's elder daughter, who assumes erroneously that there are no more men in the world. Addressing her younger sister, she begins with two statements, the first statement seeming to correspond to the referential framework set up by the narrator. The second statement is based on misperception: 'And the first-born [daughter] said to the younger one: "Our father is old, and there is not a man on earth [בארץ] to come in to us after the manner of all the earth [הארץ]" ' (Gen. 19.31). The correct observation refers to the possibility that Lot's patrilineage will be disrupted. Since Lot is old, and since he has no sons, no one will remain to carry on his name. The daughter's misperception, on the other hand, refers to her concern about the survival of the entire human species. She is wrong to interpret the destruction of Sodom and Gomorrah as the destruction of the entire earth. The repetition of the word ארץ stresses that the source of her misinterpretation is precisely the fact that her understanding is confined to the boundaries of הארץ, in its literal and social sense. She is unaware that the destruction of Sodom and Gomorrah, which to her are the entire ארץ, originates in Yhwh's actions and in heaven (שמים, v. 24). Lot's daughter is wrong to presume that the fate of the entire human species is left in her hands. But she is right in predicting the possible disruption of Lot's patrilineage.

Lot's daughter's partly correct situation assessment is followed by a partly valorized plan for action: 'Come, let us make our father drink wine, and we will lie with him, to give life to our father's seed (זרא)' (Gen. 19.32). The means by which the elder daughter proposes to preserve זרא (lit. 'from our father') are surely questionable. They involve not only incest, but also deception. But this shockingly transgressive proposition is justified by the extenuating 'fact' that incest and deception seem to be the only means through which to achieve a justified aim. Since Lot would in all probability object to his daughters' plan, deception—and more specifically inebriation—are the only means through which to overcome his objection. The questionable actions proposed in the cohortative clause, seem to be justified by the final clause. The unselfish aim of preserving 'seed' from Lot seems to mitigate the first daughter's shocking proposal. This is not to say that the second statement ascribed to the elder daughter is morally less ambiguous than the first. Like the first statement, the second one is structured so as to balance the positive and negative aspects of the proposition.

The next three verses describe the actual performance of the plan, how the elder daughter inebriated her father and slept with him, how she proposed that her sister do the same, and how her sister did the same. Though the narrator could easily have stated that Lot's daughters carried out their plan, he prefers to describe it in some detail:

> So they made their father drink wine that night; and the first-born went in, and lay with her father, but he did not know her lying down or rising. And on the next day the first-born said to the younger one: 'Look, I lay last night with my father; let us make him drink wine tonight also, and come lie with him so we will give life to our father's seed.' So they made their father drink wine that night also; and the younger arose and lay with him; and he did not know her lying down or rising (Gen. 19.33-35).

One of the striking features of this scene is the absence of any explicit judgment of the clearly problematic acts it describes. The narrator describes the deceptive and incestuous crimes with a seemingly neutral voice, as if there was nothing at all wrong with them. But if an explicit evaluation is clearly missing from this description, an implicit judgment may be found in the very repetition itself. A brief and unspecific statement to the effect that Lot's daughter indeed carried out their plan would have been less condemnatory. The repetition of the 'fact' that the daughters colluded in the inebriation of Lot, and especially the repeated phrases 'and she lay with her father' and 'I lay last night with my father' instead of the more generalized prepositional pronoun 'with him' (which does occur in reference to the younger daughter), seems to serve as an implicit condemnation of the daughters' deceptive and incestuous initiative. In addition, the repeated emphasis on the 'fact' that the women both planned and executed their plan exonerates Lot of any responsibility for the action. But not content with the repetition of the 'fact' that Lot was drunk, the narrator adds that both times, Lot had no knowledge of what allegedly happened between him and his daughters. If the scene's use of repetition is to be construed as implicit judgment, it becomes clear that this judgment is mostly aimed at the mother-figures who have initiated and carried out an incestuous contact with an old, besotted man.

Nevertheless, the implicit evaluations we might tease out of the repeated details cannot deny the puzzling suppression of a more explicit criticism of the mother-figures' conduct. For, after all, in a way Lot's daughters are committing sexual perversions that remind us of the iniquities of the citizens of Sodom and Gomorrah. While the perceived lack of men functions as an ambivalent justification of the mother-figures' alleged actions, their goal, to give birth to male progeny, is by far the most powerful argument in their defense. What might explain the suppression of a more explicit indictment of Lot's daughters is their loyalty to the cause of patrilineal continuity, which they mistakenly interpret as identical with the survival of the human species. The successful results—the birth of male heirs—seem to justify the dubious means used by the mother-figures. The transformation of the daughters into mothers explains the narrator's reluctance to resort to more direct evaluative statements. The suppression of the narrator's explicit critique is in congruence with the formulaic 'happy ending' concluding both annunciation and temptation type-scenes. The successful birth of two male heirs signals implicit approval. Both mother-figures give birth to the progenitors of major nations: 'And the first bore a son and called his name Moab; he is the father of the Moabites to this day. And the younger one also bore a son and called his name Ben-ammi; he is the father of the Ammonites to this day' (Gen. 19.37-38).

The birth of male heirs is a formulaic expression of divine approval. We have seen in the annunciation type-scene that the birth of a male heir is the telos of the plot and the happy resolution of its central dilemma. This applies to the first temptation scene as well. The births of Moab and Ben-ammi signify the successful result of the mother-figures' efforts. Moreover, the male heirs of Lot are presented as progenitors of two great nations who continue to live 'to this day'. Yet, the happy ending of the temptation scene is stamped by the ambiguity that characterizes all its stages. For Moab and Ammon, the Transjordanian neighbors of the Israelites, are also their national enemies. Giving birth to Israel's national rivals is, to say the least, a highly ambivalent compliment.[27] The simultaneous affirmation and critique of the protagonists of the first temptation scene is its most distinctive characteristic.

The second temptation scene involving Judah and Tamar, his daughter-in-law, is less ambivalent in affirming the mother-figure's initiative. For one thing, the element of incest, which contributed more than anything else to the implicit indictment of the previous mother-figures is removed from this scene. Like her counterparts in the first temptation scene, Tamar is shown to be more concerned about the father in law's progeny than the father himself. And it is this concern for Judah's patrilineal continuity that redeems Tamar and valorizes her, despite her otherwise questionable conduct. But while the first temptation scene exonerates Lot of any responsibility for the incestuous intercourse with his daughters, the second temptation scene holds Judah equally responsible for the intercourse, though it too insists that the father-figure was unaware of the identity of the mother-figure.

Lot's daughters—notably the first-born—are shown to act partly on the erroneous assumption that the future of the human species depends on their initiative. In this sense, as I pointed out, their perception does not quite correspond with what the narrator presents as reality. Tamar, on the other hand, is right in assuming that she will not be able to ensure the patrilineage of her deceased husband, Er, and ultimately of Judah himself, unless she acts. Having lost Er, who 'was evil in Yhwh's sight' (Gen. 38.7), Tamar remains a childless widow. In order to 'raise seed' for Er, Judah orders his second son to perform the duty of a covenant brother (יבם) (v. 8). But realizing that the 'seed' will not be

---

27. By ascribing to Israel's enemies incestuous origins, the Israelite narrator uses this seemingly aetiological tale about ethnic etymology as a derisive critique. Compare Speiser, *Genesis*, p. 145.

his, 'Onan destroys [his semen] to the ground' during his intercourse
with Tamar (v. 9). This displeases Yhwh. Like Er, Onan is said to have
been 'evil in the sight of Yhwh' and consequently 'Yhwh killed him
too' (v. 10). Judah does not reveal to Tamar that he is reluctant to give
her Shelah, his third son, for fear of losing him as well (v. 11). Instead,
without revealing his fears and plans, he asks Tamar to return to her
father's house, and stay there as a widow, 'until Shelah my son grows
up' (v. 11). Tamar, however, sees through Judah's evasiveness. Unlike
her counterparts in the first temptation scene, Tamar's motivation is
based on insight and good judgment: 'For she saw that Shelah has
grown and she was not given to him as a wife' (v. 14). As Mieke Bal
correctly notes, Tamar is not only a focalizer, whose perspective orga-
nizes the narrated events, she is also the only one who 'sees' well, who
interprets the events correctly.[28]

Like other mother-figures in the first temptation scene, Tamar uses
deception in order to secure Judah's patrilineal continuity. Her deception is aimed at Judah, whose interest she is in effect serving. Lot's
daughters use the darkness of the night (vv. 33-35) and wine. Tamar,
upon hearing that her father-in-law is coming up to Timnah after the
sheep-shearing season, masquerades as a harlot and stations herself on
the road to Timnah: 'She put off her widow's garments, and put on a
veil, wrapping herself up, and sat at the entrance to Enaim, which is on
the road to Timnah; for she saw that Shelah was grown up, and she had
not been given to him as a wife' (Gen. 38.14). It is significant that
Tamar's justification actions follows the most disturbing element of her
deceptive behavior. Tamar deceives Judah because in a way he has
deceived her. Her action is compensatory as well as retaliatory. Not
only is she justified in her desire to give birth to a male heir, she is also
justified in deceiving Judah who has not kept his promise concerning
Shelah. It is also significant that the narrator prefers to give us a rather
detailed description of how Tamar disguises her identity to summariz-
ing briefly that she disguised herself as a prostitute, or a זנה. The
description of Tamar's changing her garments, and covering up her face
mitigates the potentially indicting implications of a briefer and more
direct but more incriminating statement. Instead of explicitly attributing
to Tamar the intention of seducing her father-in-law by masquerading

---

28. Mieke Bal, 'Introduction', *Poetics* 13 (1984), pp. 3-4. Special issue on 'Psychopoetics Theory', twinned with the special issue of style on 'Psychopoetics at
Work', p. 289.

as a זונה, the narrator spells out the meaning of Tamar's actions in the
following verse reporting what Judah sees, or rather misconstrues: 'And
when Judah saw her he thought her to be a harlot (זנה) for she covered
up her face' (Gen. 38.15). Tamar's deceptive identity as prostitute is
thus construed as part of Judah's misinterpretation.

Tamar's deception is less aggressive and less offensive than the one
attributed to her counterparts in the previous scene. Her deception consists of disguising her own identity rather than in blurring the vision of
her father-in-law. Judah is well aware of his actions. He is the one who
turns to the alleged prostitute: 'And he turned to her on the way and
said "Let me come in to you" ' (v. 16). While the previous scene
repeats several times that Lot's daughters intoxicated him with wine
and 'lay with him', this scene prefers to describe the transaction that
preceded the actual intercourse. In return for her sexual favors, Judah
promises to deliver a kid from his flock, and agrees to give her his staff,
cord and signet (vv. 17-18). These items will later prove to be crucial
for saving Tamar's life. For only after identifying these items as his
own does Judah realizes that he himself caused Tamar's pregnancy
(vv. 25-26). While it 'quotes' with some detail the pre-coital transactions between Judah and Tamar, this scene is rather elliptical and
euphemistic in describing the intercourse itself: 'And he came to her
and she conceived to him' (v. 18). While the previous temptation scene,
which contains no more than seven verses, uses the more explicit verb
'lie with' and attributes it to the female protagonists no less than seven
times, this scene is much more implicit and reticent in describing the
actual intercourse. Instead, a single verb summarizes the illicit action,
which is, in its turn, quickly followed by its desirable result: 'and she
conceived to him'.

Whereas the first temptation scene suppresses any explicit evaluation
of its female protagonists, the second scene is emphatic about exonerating Tamar of any guilt. The narrator attributes guilt to Judah, the victim
of Tamar's guiles, an unambiguous statement of rehabilitation. Judah's
rehabilitation of Tamar stands out in dramatic contrast to his willingness to condemn her to death upon hearing rumors that Tamar had
allegedly 'acted as a harlot [זנה]' and conceived through harlotry (זנונים)
(v. 24). The verse describing Judah's recognition of his personal para-
phernalia omits the direct object of the verb 'recognized' (ויכר), thus
expanding the meaning of the verb to include a more general recognition: 'And Judah recognized and said: "She is more righteous than I, for

I did not give her Shelah my son", and he did not know her any more'
(v. 26). By admitting his guilt, and by justifying Tamar's actions, Judah
rejects the interpretation of Tamar as a זוֹנָה who conceived through זְנוּנִים
as a false accusation. Coming from the man who was going to condemn
her to death, Judah's justification of Tamar is especially effective. Once
again, as in v. 14, the narrator repeats that Judah's fault was that he did
not give Shelah his son to Tamar. The repeated reference to Shelah
serves throughout the chapter as a justification of Tamar's actions.
Tamar acted as she did because, like Lot's daughters, she had no other
choice.

The valorization of Tamar's resourceful and courageous action is
also implied in the happy resolution of the scene. Tamar gives birth to
male twins (תּוֹאֲמִים), Peretz and Zerah. Like Lot's daughters, Tamar is a
foreigner, more specifically a Canaanite, but her offspring are considered legitimate successors of Judah.[29] The mother's foreignness has
special significance for biblical sexual politics. Peretz—who is said to
burst out of Tamar's womb before Zerah, who was positioned before
him (Gen. 38.29)—is given the special privilege of becoming one of
King David's ancestors (Ruth 4.18-22). Though Tamar herself will not
be considered as a genealogical link in the Davidic dynasty, she is
nevertheless shown to have enabled this felicitous turn of events. Her
vicarious association with the Davidic dynasty is itself an implicit
valorization of her audacious temptation of her own father-in-law.

But what exactly is it that this temptation scene valorizes? Although,
as we noted, Tamar's deprivation of her right to marry Shelah is
repeated three times in this scene (vv. 11, 14, 26), and although it is
presented as the main justification of Tamar's temptation, it is not
known whether Shelah ever marries Tamar. Even after Judah recog-
nizes that he was wrong in withholding Shelah from his daughter-in-
law, he is not shown to make up for his unjust treatment of Tamar. Why
does the narrative avoid the issue of Tamar's marriage to Shelah? The
reason seems obvious: despite the repeated references to Tamar's marriage, the issue at the heart of our narrative is the disruption of the

---

29. Tamar is given to Er, who is himself the son of a Canaanite mother, the
daughter of Shua, while Judah dwells by his Adulamite friend, Hirah. Her father's
house seems to be close to the Canaanite town, Timnah. On Tamar's foreign origins, see Athalya Brenner, *The Israelite Woman: Social Role and Literary Type in
Biblical Narrative* (Sheffield: JSOT Press, 1985), pp. 118-22. See also, Bal, *Lethal
Love*, pp. 89-103.

patrilineal chain. Once mended through the birth of Zerah and Peretz, there seems to be little justification for dealing with Tamar and Shelah. Having reached its telos—the birth of male heirs—the narrative comes to an end. A closer examination of Tamar's plan and actions reveals that her goal—in perfect congruence with patriarchal interests—is to give birth to male heirs, not to be married to Shelah. Had she been interested in marrying Shelah, Tamar could have embarrassed Judah into giving her Shelah. But she does not do it. The fact is that not only is Tamar risking her reputation and her life by seducing Judah, she also undermines the prospect of ever marrying Shelah. Indeed, the text states explicitly that even Judah himself 'did not know her anymore'. (v. 26) The marriage to Shelah is a displacement of the real telos of this temptation scene which, like the previous one, aims at valorizing the mother-figure who insures patrilineal continuity.

Some critics make the point that the conception of the son is the 'widow's right'.[30] Such an interpretation paraphrases the ideological displacement of the temptation type-scene. For after all, the scene focuses on the mother's struggles to preserve male progeny, while the father is depicted as a duped victim of his daughter-in-law's guiles. How does Tamar, or any mother, profit from supplying a father-figure with male heirs? At most, her profit is vicarious, for she herself will not become part of the patrilineal genealogy. The omission of further references to Tamar's marital status and her fate in general indicates that it is not her 'right' or her privileges that concern the narrator. Furthermore, it is precisely Tamar's selflessness, her alleged willingness to forget her right to Shelah and her relentless desire to fight for Judah's interest that are valorized in the temptation type-scene. The more explicit and detailed validation of the mother-figure in the second temptation scene validates the interests of motherhood as a patriarchal institution.

The story of Ruth is the story of a prospective mother who valiantly follows Naomi, her mother-in-law, and who stops at nothing in order to secure the genealogical continuity of her deceased husband's family. The man that Ruth will seduce is Boaz, her husband's wealthy relative. The detailed introduction which precedes the scene (Ruth 1), the 'chance' meeting between Ruth and Boaz (Ruth 2), as well as the legalistic conclusion (Ruth 4), function each in their own way as strategies

---

30. George W. Coats, 'Widow's Rights: A Crux in the Structure of Genesis 38', *CBQ* 34 (1972), p. 464.

of rehabilitation and valorization. The detailed plot notwithstanding, the temptation scene is the *peripeteia*, or the turning point, which insures the successful attainment of the story's telos, namely the birth of a male heir.[31] Like her predecessors in the first two temptation scenes, Ruth is introduced as a husbandless and childless woman. Mahlon, her husband, her brother-in-law Chilion, Orpah's husband, as well as Elimelech, her father-in-law, have all died without leaving behind them male offspring (Ruth 1.3-5). Unlike Tamar, who is compelled to stay in her father's house as a widow (Gen. 38.11), Ruth has no obligations to her husband's family. This is made clear in Naomi's speech, who dissuades both Orpah and Ruth from leaving their 'mother's home' in Moab, and following her to Judah (vv. 8-9). But unlike Orpah, who is convinced by her mother-in-law and returns to Moab (v. 14), Ruth refuses to disconnect her ties with her husband's mother. While Lot's first-born daughter assumes that there is 'no man left on earth to come [in] upon us', Ruth knows that she can, as Naomi put it, 'find peace...in her [new] husband's home' (Ruth 1.9). But Ruth refuses to disconnect her ties with Naomi, the last remnant and sole representative of her deceased husband. Her identification with her mother-in-law's fate, people, country and God is complete (Ruth 1.16-17). Ruth's loyalty to her husband's family is unprecedented, and her self-abnegation unparalleled by any other mother-figure.

Having established Ruth's lofty motivations, the introduction also avoids the slightest allusion to calculation or craftiness on Ruth's part. Chapter 2 makes it clear that Ruth came upon Boaz's field by chance: 'And she went forth and came and gleaned in the field after the reapers and she happened by chance [ויקר מקרה] upon the part of the field of Boaz of Elimelech's family' (Ruth 2.3). The repetition of the root קרה emphasizes that 'chance' or, as Campbell prefers, 'luck brought her' to Boaz's field.[32] It is also pure 'chance'—or rather Yhwh's design—that brings Boaz to that part of the field at just that right moment: 'And look [והנה] Boaz came from Bethlehem' (Ruth 2.4). In addition to conveying Ruth's point of view, the word והנה usually precedes an unexpected turn of events, or a focalizer's new perception.[33] The polite and cordial

---

31. Compare Shimon Bar-Efrat, 'Some Observations on the Analysis of Structure in Biblical Narrative', *VT* 30.2 (1980), pp. 156-57.

32. Edward F. Campbell, *Ruth* (AB; New York: Doubleday, 1981), p. 92.

33. On the function of והנה in the book of Ruth, see Adele Berlin, *Poetics and Interpretation of Biblical Narrative* (Sheffield: Almond Press, 1983), pp. 91-95.

dialogue that ensues between Boaz and Ruth makes it clear that Boaz is favorably disposed towards Ruth. By addressing her as 'my daughter' (בתי) (v. 8), encouraging her to glean in his field, and promising her his personal protection (vv. 8-9), praising her for her loyalty to her mother-in-law (v. 11), blessing her in the name of Yhwh (v. 12), and inviting her to partake of his meal (v. 14), Boaz indicates his interest in and respect for Ruth. The coincidental encounter between Boaz and Ruth prepares the way for the temptation itself and foreshadows its positive outcome. If Boaz favors Ruth in broad daylight and in front of his retinue, he will probably not reject her when she comes to him stealthily at night. The warm disposition Boaz publicly displays toward Ruth also suggests that unlike her predecessors, Ruth will not have to resort to deception in her attempt to seduce Boaz. While Lot's daughters and Tamar must disguise their real identities, this scene explains why, in Ruth's case, revealing her true identity will strengthen rather than hinder her cause.[34]

The legalistic description of the acquisition of Elimelech's field (קנה) and the acquisition (קנה) of Ruth by Boaz in 4.9-10 aim at emphasizing the legal and social propriety of the procedure.[35] The transaction described in this chapter has sparked much scholarly debate, notably around the legal meaning of קנה and the relationship of the procedure of 'redemption' (גאלה) described in Ruth and the law of levirate marriage binding a brother-in-law to marry the wife of a man who dies without leaving male heirs (Deut. 25.5-10).[36] It seems to me, however, that the most interesting question in this context is why did the narrator see fit to offer us a protracted description of legal transactions instead

34. On the central role of the motif of identity in the book of Ruth, see Ronald T. Hyman, 'Questions and Changing Identity in the Book of Ruth', *USQR* 39.3 (1984), pp. 189-201.

35. The verb קנה means 'to buy'. It is a transitive verb whose subject is Boaz, and direct objects are Elimelech's field and Ruth. For a different reading emphasizing the narrative subject positions of Ruth and Naomi, see Bal, *Lethal Love*, pp. 68-88.

36. See, e.g., D.R.G. Beattie, 'Ruth III', *JSOT* 5 (1978), pp. 39-48, and Jack M. Sasson, 'The Issue of *Ge'ullah* in Ruth', *JSOT* 5 (1978), pp. 52-64. See also Robert Gordis, 'Love, Marriage, and Business in the Book of Ruth: A Chapter in Hebrew Customary Law', in Howard N. Bream *et al.* (eds.), *A Light Unto my Path: Old Testament Studies in Honor of Jacob M. Myers* (Philadelphia: Temple University Press, 1974), pp. 241-64. See also Jack Sasson, *Ruth: A New Translation with a Philological Commentary and a Formalist-Folklorist Interpretation* (Baltimore: The Johns Hopkins University Press, 1979), pp. 115-47.

of briefly reporting that Boaz indeed 'bought' (קנה) Elimelech's field and Ruth? It would seem that the main effect achieved by the detailed description of the legal procedure is the confirmation that Boaz's alliance with Ruth is fully licit. Whether or not the described transactions correspond with what we know about the levirate from other sources, the fact remains that by acquiring Elimelech's field and marrying Ruth, Boaz means to 'establish the name of the dead in his inheritance, that the name of the dead may not be cut off from among his brothers and from the gate of his native place' (Ruth 4.10). The detailed description, the emphasis on the public forum, and the propriety of Boaz's actions mitigate the ambiguity of the temptation scene of the night before. The narrator refers to ten elders, the city gate (Ruth 4.1-2) and to Boaz's willingness to offer Mahlon's inheritance to the nameless גאל ('redeemer') (Ruth 4.3-5). The narrator emphasizes once again, lest the symbolic gestures of drawing one's sandal be lost on the reader, that Boaz is acting in full accordance with Israelite custom: 'Now this is how it was in former times [לפנים] in Israel on redeeming and exchanging; to confirm the transaction, the one drew off his sandal and gave it to the other, and this was the manner of attesting in Israel' (Ruth 4.7).

One could hardly imagine a more effective way of conveying to the reader that the relationship between Boaz and Ruth is in full agreement with the social order. As we have seen, the previous temptation scene justifies Tamar's initiative, but something is left unresolved. After Judah admits Tamar's righteousness, the text notes that 'he did not know her again' (Gen. 38.26). Still we are left with no explanations as to the meaning of Judah's decision to avoid further sexual contact with Tamar. Why does the narrator see fit to tell us that Judah avoided Tamar while remaining silent about Tamar's future? Why did the narrator avoid the issue of Shelah and Tamar? Does the note about Judah's sexual avoidance of Tamar aim at rehabilitating Judah or Tamar? Does it imply basically that they no longer repeated their transgressive behavior? But if there is a transgressive element in a woman's sexual relations with her father-in-law, what is it? Does it involve incest? Does it perhaps involve adultery, since Tamar was bespoken to Shelah? These questions remain largely unanswered. The problematic relationship between Judah and Tamar is only partially resolved, while her relationship with Shelah is not resolved at all. The second temptation scene is less offensive than the first one. To the extent that it involves incestuous and adulterous elements, it does so very subtly. The formulaic happy

ending of the second temptation scene is less ambiguous than the conclusion of the first one. Nevertheless, a certain ambiguity lingers over
the entire scene, which is not as completely resolved as it could have
been. The most obvious explanation for this ambiguity is that in view of
the attainment of the story's telos, namely the birth of two male heirs,
the narrator considered all the rest unimportant. This is not the case in
Ruth, which goes out of its way to rehabilitate both the prospective
mother and the prospective father. In contrast to Judah, Boaz publicly
offers Ruth to the גאל who is of closer kinship to Elimelech (Ruth 4.3-
6). It is only after the גאל publicly renounces Ruth ('less I destroy my
inheritance') and explicitly offers her to Boaz that Boaz marries her.

But perhaps the most obvious strategies of rehabilitation and justification are to be found in the description of the temptation scene itself.
Unlike Lot's daughters and Tamar, who plot and execute their plans,
the narrator makes it clear that the idea of seducing Boaz is not Ruth's
but rather Naomi's. Naomi, for her part, does not seem to be motivated
by self-interest, but rather by a concern for Ruth's welfare: 'Then Naomi
her mother-in-law said to her: "My daughter, should I not seek for you
a place of rest [מנוח] that will be good for you?" ' (Ruth 3.1). The
concern for Elimelech's patrilineage does not seem to play any role in
Naomi's motivations. Just as Ruth wishes to follow Naomi to Judah, so
does Naomi seem to be concerned by Ruth's welfare alone. The patriarchal stake in re-establishing the male-dominated genealogy is being
marginalized and downplayed. If Lot's daughters are openly concerned
about the survival of the species, and Tamar is concerned about her
marriage to Shelah, Ruth does not seem at all concerned about her well-
being. Rather it is her mother-in-law who encourages her to look out for
herself. Not only does Naomi select the right night, the night on which
Boaz is 'winnowing barley at the threshing floor' (Ruth 3.2), she also
picks the right moment: 'Do not let yourself be known to the man before he has finished eating and drinking' (Ruth 3.3). Athalya Brenner is
right in suggesting that both Genesis 38 and Ruth 3 are referring to the
impact of wine on the prospective father, for after all Judah goes up to
Timnah after the sheep-shearing season, a time that—like the winnowing of barley—calls for celebration. But what is more significant is the
fact that in the latter scenes wine is not mentioned explicitly. One might
assume that Judah goes up to Timnah to celebrate the sheep-shearing
season, an occasion that might have called for libation. But what is clear
is that Tamar (unlike Lot's daughters) is not the cause of what might be

construed as Judah's intoxication. In the case of Boaz, it is not at all clear whether his 'drinking' refers to an intoxicating beverage. The only possible allusion to such a possibility is the reference to Boaz's cheerful mood immediately after the description of his meal: 'And Boaz sat and drank and his heart was good and he came to lie down at the end of the heap' (Ruth 3.7).

In addition to picking the right place and the right time, Naomi instructs Ruth how to make herself attractive: 'Wash, anoint yourself, and dress up' (v. 3). Clothes fulfill an important role in the second temptation scene as well.[37] But while Tamar dresses up as a prostitute, to disguise her true identity, Ruth dresses up to make herself more attractive, to enhance her identity. There is no need for Ruth to disguise her identity and to use deception. While clothes function as a means of deception in the second scene, they are affirmed as a means of seduction in the third scene.

Having established the necessary preparatory stages of Ruth's seduction, Naomi goes on to discuss the heart of the matter: 'And when he lies down [שכב], find out [ידע] the place where he lies [שכב]; then go and uncover his feet [מרגלתיו] and lie down [שכב]; and he will tell you what to do' (Ruth 3.4). While the first temptation scene repeatedly uses the verb שכב in the sense of intercourse, this scene repeatedly uses the verb in its literal, non-sexual sense.[38] The verb שכב is used in this sense in the description of the couple's encounter on the threshing floor: 'And Boaz ate and drank and his heart was good, and he came to lie down [שכב] at the end of the heap, and she came in quietly [בלט], and uncovered his feet [מרגלת], and lay down [שכב].' The same use of the verb appears in Boaz's invitation to Ruth to stay with him till the morning: 'Lie [שכב] here until the morning. And she lay down [שכב] by his feet' (Ruth 4.13-14). The repeated use of שכב in its non-sexual sense contrasts rather dramatically with its use in the first temptation scene, where as we have seen, the emphasis on שכב in its sexual sense is attributed to the female protagonists. This is not to say that the sexually charged terms שכב and מרגלת (designating both 'feet' and 'sexual organs') lose

---

37. Compare, Brenner, *The Israelite Woman* (Sheffield: JSOT Press, 1985), pp. 118-22.

38. See Nelly Furman, 'His Story Versus Her Story: Male Genealogy and Female Strategy in the Jacob Cycle', in Collins (ed.), *Feminist Perspectives on Biblical Scholarship*, pp. 107-16.

their euphemistic effectiveness.[39] The point is that our scene only alludes to what the previous scenes describe rather explicitly. The narrator understates and refines the events as much as possible. Though the
second temptation scene is much less insistent in its description of the
mother-figure's sexual performance, it nevertheless makes it clear that
Tamar's seduction led to intercourse. In the third temptation scene,
there is no reference to intercourse at all. All we are told is that 'she lay
[שׁכב] by his feet till the morning, but arose before one could recognize
the other, and he [Boaz] said: "Let it not be known that a woman came
to the threshing floor" ' (Ruth 3.14).

Boaz, rather than Ruth, is concerned about appearances. In this
respect, he faintly resembles Judah, who is concerned lest he be the
objective of public derision when it is found out that he used the sexual
services of a prostitute (Gen. 38.23). But while the text in Genesis 38
admits that Judah has indeed 'misbehaved', our text suggests that Boaz
is concerned lest people misconstrue Ruth's presence in his threshing
floor. More importantly, Ruth is completely exonerated of the slightest
hint of deceptiveness. Ruth steals out of the threshing floor because
Boaz advises her to do so. In a similar way, Ruth steals into the threshing floor strictly upon Naomi's instructions: 'And she [Ruth] said: "All
that you say to me, I will do" ' (Ruth 3.5). Thus Ruth is exonerated of
the deceptive guiles attributed to the female protagonists of the first two
temptation scenes.

I noted earlier that Tamar's seduction is less aggressive than the one
attributed to Lot's daughters. The third temptation scene is even more
insistent on the mother-figure's consideration and gentleness. Upon
Naomi's advice, Ruth does nothing but uncover Boaz's feet. Exposed
to the cold of the night, Boaz 'was startled and turned over [והנה] a
woman by his feet' (Ruth 3.8). While in the second temptation scene, it
is Tamar who asks the questions and determines the results of her
encounter with Judah, here it is Boaz who dominates this dialogue.
Unlike Tamar who demands a price and a pledge for her sexual services, Ruth implores Boaz: 'Spread your wing upon your maidservant,
for you are a גאל' (Ruth 3.9). Though, as noted, the sexual element is
there, Ruth appeals to Boaz's sense of duty and moral sensitivity. She
does not impose herself on him—but rather begs him to act on her

---

39. On the use of *leitwort* or the heuristic function of repeated words in the
book of Ruth, see Edward F. Campbell, *Ruth* (Anchor Bible, NY; Doubleday, 1981)
See also Alter, *The Art of Biblical Narrative*, pp. 88-113.

behalf. Boaz's detailed and solemn response (Ruth. 3.10-13) contains
not only an affirmative answer, but also an indirect evaluation of Ruth
whom he praises as 'a woman of valor' (אשת חיל) (v. 11).

Like her predecessors', Ruth's efforts are crowned with success. The
narrative makes a point of stressing the features of the happy ending.
There is a clear correlation between the imagery of emptiness and death
in the beginning of the narrative and the imagery of plenty at the end.[40]
In addition to becoming a mother, Ruth becomes Boaz's wife, a special
reward which distinguishes her from her predecessors. Yet, it must be
noted that Ruth, like Tamar, is by no means motivated by a selfish concern for her own fate. Such a concern would in fact disagree with her
valorization as a biblical heroine, who thrives on selflessness and
loyalty to her husband's family. As in the case of Tamar, marriage or
the fate of the mother involved is incidental to the product—the male
son. As noted, the mother-figure is not valorized for her interest in her
own security, but rather in the stability of a patrilineal genealogy.
Hence, Ruth's marriage is mentioned briefly as one in a series of events
(Ruth 4.13). By contrast Obed, her son becomes the center of attention,
as Naomi's source of pride and comfort (Ruth 4.14-17), and as one of
King David's progenitors (4.18-22).

In many ways, the story of Ruth is an apotheosis of the temptation
type-scene.[41] One can hardly imagine a more strenuous validation of its
central mother-figure, Ruth, as well as of Naomi, who is shown at the
end to become a kind of surrogate mother: 'Then Naomi took the boy,
and put him in her bosom, and became his nurse [אמנת]' (Ruth 4.16).
Yet the narrative's celebration of Ruth and Naomi makes it all the more
puzzling to find no mention of their names in the genealogical list that
concludes the book. The genealogical list enumerates the names of the
fathers only: 'And these are the generations [תולדות] of Perez: Perez
caused the birth [ילד] of Hezron, and Hezron caused the birth [ילד] of
Ram, and Ram caused the birth [ילד] of Aminadab, and Aminadab
caused the birth [ילד] of Nahshon, and Nahshon caused the birth (ילד)
of Salmon, and Salmon caused the birth (ילד) of Boaz, and Boaz caused
the birth [ילד] of Obed, and Obed caused the birth (ילד) of Jesse, and

---

40. Compare Trible, *God and the Rhetoric of Sexuality*, pp. 181-87.

41. D.F. Rauber, 'The Book of Ruth', *Literary Interpretation of Biblical Narratives* (Nashville: Abingdon Press, 1974), pp. 163-76. See also Trible, 'A Human
Comedy', in *God and the Rhetoric of Sexuality*, pp. 166-70; 195-96.

Jesse caused the birth [ילד] of David' (Ruth 4.18-22). Though rather awkward in English, the phrase 'cause the birth of' is closer, literally, to the hiphil form of ילד 'to give birth', which is why I prefer it to the figurative 'beget', suggested by Campbell, and to the unlikely literal translation 'bore' suggested by J. Sasson.[42] While scholars have been preoccupied with the fact that Boaz rather than Mahlon appears in this genealogical list, nobody has been disturbed by the incongruity between the narrative, which clearly focuses on the mother-figure(s) and the egregious omission of their names from the genealogical list.[43] My guess is that this question has not been raised, since most if not all genealogical lists in the Hebrew Bible consist of the names of fathers. The repetition of all-male genealogical lists has rendered natural, valid and unproblematic the omission of the names of mothers from genealogical lists in general and the name of Ruth from this list in particular. This testifies to the effectiveness of formulaic repetition as a literary and political strategy. But it does not justify the general oblivi-ousness to its patriarchal functions. The various genealogies in the Hebrew Bible have specific purposes, both poetical and political.[44] It seems to me that a much overlooked function of all-male biblical genealogies is to *validate the idea that though mothers are admittedly important participants in giving birth, 'the fruit of their womb' belongs to the fathers.*

Thus, when it comes to generational continuity (תולדות), women's role is first understated, and later denied. By repeating the all-male formula in the beginning and the end of various narratives, the biblical text validates this denial. Repetition and the omission of necessary explanations naturalizes and sediments the patriarchal construction of generational history. While the early genealogical formulas make more frequent references to mothers and daughters (Gen. 4.17-26; 5.1-32; 10.1-32; 11.10-32), especially where pre-Israelite genealogies are involved (Gen. 22.20-24; 25.1-28), there is, beginning with Jacob, an

---

42. See Campbell, *Ruth*, p. 170, and Sasson, *Ruth*, p. 178. The RSV obviates the problem by resorting to the noun 'father', i.e. 'Perez was the father of Hezron', etc.

43. For a summary and further arguments in support of the view that the genealogy is original, not a mere appendix to the book of Ruth, see Sasson, *Ruth*, pp. 178-90.

44. Marshal D. Johnson, *The Purpose of the Biblical Genealogies* (London: Cambridge University Press, 1969), pp. 3-84.

increasing tendency to omit mothers and daughters from the generational lists. Thus, while most of the male descendants of Shem are said
to have 'given birth' (ילד) or 'caused the birth' of 'sons and daughters'
(ובנות בנם) (Gen. 11.10-32), Jacob fathers twelve sons and only one
daughter, Dinah. While the biblical text admits the role of mother-
figures in the framework of specific narratives and scenes, it denies
them a place in the genealogical chains that constitute both compositional and referential linkages, tying together various literary episodes
and historical periods. Thus, the second annunciation scene is preceded
by the following statement: 'These are the generations of Isaac, the son
of Abraham, Abraham caused the birth [הוליד] of Isaac' (Gen. 25.19).
This statement emphasizes that, despite the admitted importance of
Sarah who gave birth to Isaac, and despite the valorization of Rebekah
as a bride in ch. 24, we must remember that 'Abraham caused the birth
of Isaac'.[45]

The geneaological list at the end of Ruth is an ideological statement.
One of its aspects refers to the relationship of women to generational
continuity. The all-male geneaology repeats once again that no matter
how righteous and deserving, mothers must not be included in generational or dynastic lists. The political function of the conclusion of the
book of Ruth is not only to 'bolster David's claim to the throne' as
agreed by various scholars, it is also to bolster the exclusive claim of
fathers to their descendants, to generational continuity, to history. The
omission of mothers from genealogical lists is complemented by the
male-centered inclusio pattern, beginning—as is the case in the book of
Ruth—with reference to the father and ending with reference to the son.
All this is not to deny the valorization of the mother-figure in Ruth.
Rather it is to point out that this valorization has specific political functions, and that it is well suited to the needs of the patriarchal order.
Mother-figures are to be valorized when they go out of their way to re-
establish patrilineal disruption. They may not, however, lay claim to the
privilege and authority of fathers who are the only legitimate claimants
of tribal or dynastic headship.

45. The association of historical continuity with masculinity is revalidated in a
recent book celebrating the contribution of biblical literature to Western culture.
See Herbert N. Schneidau, *Sacred Discontent: The Bible and Western Tradition*
(Berkeley: University of California Press, 1976), pp. 174-247.

The Patriarchal Function of 'Motherhood'

I have noted in my analysis of the annunciation type-scene that the repeated presentation of mothers as barren women functions as an implicit denial of the political rights of mothers. If mothers are naturally barren, they have no right to their offspring. The unfailing fertility of fathers endows them implicitly with rights denied to mothers who are so often barren, and who need some miraculous intervention so as to perform their procreative duty. I also noted that fertile mothers are both affirmed and stigmatized as either foreigners, as neglected or less loved in comparison to their barren counterparts, or as morally inferior to the latter. Lot's daughter, Tamar, and Ruth are presented as naturally fertile mothers, and in this respect their characterization is congruent with the characterization of the fertile contestants we discussed earlier. All three mother figures are 'foreign', in that they do not belong to the Abrahamite line. Much has been written about the Moabite identity attributed to Ruth.[46] If, however, we keep in mind the association of fertility and foreignness, we shall notice that Ruth is said to be Moabite, for the same reason that Hagar is said to be an Egyptian, and Tamar a Canaanite. As a foreigner, and especially as a foreigner who is willing to disavow her national identity (like Ruth), a woman is permitted to become a mother of Israelite male heirs, and even to give birth to the prospective ancestors of King David. But women must not figure as subjects in the patrilineal chains linking various episodes, and historical periods together. The attribution of foreignness to major mother-figures resembles in terms of its patriarchal function the attribution to them of natural barrenness. Though both barrenness and foreignness are defects that are often ultimately 'redeemed'—barren mothers become fertile and foreign mothers are absorbed through their male offspring—both characteristics imply a fundamental inferiority, an otherness that justifies their exclusion from patrilineal genealogies, and deprives them from the authority and privilege of fathers.

Foreignness, however, is only one of the characteristics attributed to naturally fertile mother-figures. As already noted, moral imperfection is another characteristic commonly attributed to naturally fertile mother-figures. The repeated presentation of the temptation type-scene, like the repeated presentation of the annunciation type-scene stigmatizes—

---

46. See Sasson, *Ruth*, p. 232.

however subtly—the mother-figures involved. No amount of apology can completely erase the 'fact' that in all three temptation scenes it is the mother-figure who seduces the father-figure. The narrative of Ruth is a case in point, just because of its elaborate justification of its epony-mous heroine. After all, in view of Boaz's positive disposition towards Ruth in ch. 2, it is unclear why Ruth, encouraged by Naomi, should find it necessary to 'tempt' or seduce Boaz at all. The function of the woman's temptation is clear in the first and second scenes where the prospective father would be uninterested in cooperating with the pro-spective mother. Much as Ruth is valorized, she does not completely transcend the parameters of patriarchal motherhood. Subtle as the temp-tation scene may be, it nevertheless leaves its stigmatic impact on the naturally fertile mother-figure, an impact which complements the attri-bution of her foreignness.

The subtle—and I cannot overemphasize this qualifier—stigmatiza-tion of the naturally fertile mother is congruent with the suppression of explicit references to Yhwh's intervention in the temptation scene. As noted earlier, procreative contexts are the only contexts in the Hebrew Bible where mother-figures are shown to interact directly with Yhwh or 'His' messengers. But Yhwh does not appear as an active participant in temptation type-scenes involving naturally fertile mothers. In the book of Ruth, Yhwh appears in this capacity only once: within the frame-work of Ruth's transition to fertility (Ruth 4.13). This is not to deny that the text is implicitly alluding to Yhwh's 'presence behind the scenes' especially behind the 'coincidental' encounter of Ruth and Boaz, or the 'productive' encounter of Tamar and Judah. There is, how-ever, a significant difference between this implicit and circuitous pre-sentation and the far more explicit presentation of Yhwh's role in the annunciation type-scene. Unlike Rebekah who addresses Yhwh through an oracle and is answered by 'Him', unlike Manoah's wife who meets Yhwh's angel and speaks with him, and unlike the Shunammite who has a direct contact with Elisha the prophet, the protagonists of the temptation type-scene are neither addressed nor *explicitly* noticed by a divine agency. Nor do the protagonists address Yhwh or pray to him, as, for example, Hannah does. Genesis 38 notes that Yhwh is displeased with Er and Onan, but it does not note that 'He' is pleased with Tamar or intends to help her out of her plight. Similarly Yhwh is mentioned by several characters in the book of Ruth, among them by Ruth herself in her vow to Naomi (Ruth 1.17), but as already noted 'He' does not appear as an active participant in the plot until the happy moment of Ruth's conception.

On the other hand, both annunciation and temptation type-scenes focus on a prospective mother's *inability* to give birth. Both types of nativity narratives thus question maternity as a source of female power. Most nativity scenes are suspended between the mother's recognition of her inability to perform her procreative duty and the happy reversal of events, occasioned, explicitly or implicitly, by divine intervention. As noted in the beginning of the chapter, the emphasis in biblical nativity narratives is on *prospective* mothers, who for one reason or another cannot yet perform their procreative duty. This may explain why such short shrift is given to the moment of maternity, or the event of giving birth. Verses reporting about successful births usually emphasize Yhwh's role, noting that the latter 'remembered' (זכר/עכד) the woman (Gen. 21.1; 30.22; 1 Sam. 19), or that He responded to the husband's prayer (Gen. 25.24). While nine months of pregnancy are encapsulated in a fraction of a verse, reports about maternity tend to dwell on the perfect 'fit' between the 'actual' birth and the date predicted by Yhwh or 'His' messenger (as in the cases of Sarah [Gen. 21.2], and the Shunammite [2 Kgs 4.17]). In the case of Tamar, the emphasis is on the newborns, the parturition taking up only half a verse: 'When the time of her delivery came, behold [הנה] twins in her womb' (Gen. 38.27), and just as in the case of Rebekah, the mother is left behind while the next two verses go on to describe which twin came out first (Gen. 38.29-30; Gen. 25.24-26). Another common strategy of evasion is the concatenation of events related to conception and/or parturition. The concatenation strategy minimizes the significance of maternity. Thus, for example, in the case of Manoah's wife, only one-fourth of a verse reports about the act of giving birth, while naming the son, his growth and his blessing by Yhwh take up the remaining three syntactic segments (Judg. 13.24). In Ruth 4.13, we find a combination of an emphasis on Yhwh as the author of conception, as well as a rather crowded list of events: 'And Boaz took Ruth, and she became his wife, and he went in to her, and Yhwh gave her conception, and she gave birth to a son.' The conciseness of this crowded and busy report is typical of biblical description of maternity. It reveals a certain dis-ease with admitting woman's procreative role. Lumped together with other 'facts', maternity and the act of giving birth become a single item in a list of equally significant events.

The sketchy descriptions of maternity complement the elimination of the mother-figures after their son's births. The report about a successful parturition usually precedes the last reference to the mother-figure in the nativity narrative. As soon as she has fulfilled her procreative role, the mother-figure is whisked off the stage. Though most mother-figures 'die' diegetically, by simply not being mentioned after the birth of their sons, some nativity narratives prefer mimetic deaths, whereby mother-figures are said to have died shortly after the birth of their sons. Thus, for example, having given birth Isaac (Gen. 21.1-2) and having secured his position as Abraham's true and only heir (Gen. 21.10), Sarah is reported to have died (Gen. 23.1-2). Sarah dies 'conveniently' having performed the roles of maternity and maternality. Nothing intervenes between Hagar's expulsion on Sarah's orders, and the latter's death at the ripe age of 127. By contrast, Abraham is shown to regret the expulsion of Hagar and Ishmael and magnanimously provides them with water for their journey in the wilderness (Gen. 21.11-14), to establish a peace treaty with King Abimelech and Pichol his officer (Gen. 21.22-34), and to be willing to sacrifice Isaac at Yhwh's request (Gen. 22.1-19). Though Sarah is not shown to participate in any significant events after she secures Isaac's superiority over Ishmael, the text interpolates the above stories about Abraham and Isaac before reporting on Sarah's death. This renders the relationship between Sarah's death/elimination from the text and Isaac's birth less obvious. By contrast, Rachel is reported to have died right after the successful birth of her last son, whom she names Ben-oni ('the son of my sorrow') and whom Jacob renames Benjamin. Significantly, none of the mother-figures studied here dies before she accomplishes her procreative duty. Even the exceptionally perfect Ruth does not break this rule. Ruth is not mentioned again after the report about the birth of Obed.

The elimination of the mother-figure after the birth of a son complements the male-dominated inclusio pattern mentioned above. Despite the focus of nativity narratives on mother-figures, most of them begin and end with references to fathers and sons. Thus, for example, though Hannah is clearly the protagonist of 1 Samuel 1, the narrative opens with a reference to Elkanah: 'There was a man from Ramathaim-zophim from the hill country of Ephraim, and his name was Elkanah, the son of Jeroham, son of Elihu, and son of Tohu, son of Zuph, an Ephraimite' (1 Sam. 1.1). The genealogical enumeration of Elkanah's forefathers constitutes the linkage of the narrative to the 'broader' male-controlled frame of reference. In the same way, the conclusion of the nativity narrative with the birth of a son links the nativity narrative to what follows.[47]

Unlike the annunciation type-scene that opens with a reference to the mother-figure's husband, the temptation type-scene opens with a reference to the husband's father. Genesis 38, for example, begins with a reference to Judah, though Tamar is the clear protagonist of the narrative: 'And it was at that time that Judah went down from his brothers, and turned in to an Adullamite, whose name was Hirah' (Gen. 38.1). Similarly, the narrative centering on Ruth begins with a sentence whose subject is Elimelech: 'In the days when the judges ruled there was a famine in the land, and a man from Bethlehem [in] Judah went to live in the Fields of Moab [שְׂדֵי מוֹאָב], he and his wife and his two sons.' (Ruth 1.1) The introductory statement focusing on the father-figure parallels the concluding statement focusing on the son. The male-centered inclusio confines the mother-figure to her proper literary place, which never transcends the limit of a single, well-delimited, short narrative, or the 'isolated tale'.[48] It also facilitates the transition of the diegetic focus from the female protagonist of the isolated tale to the male protagonists whose lives begin at the point of the mother's mimetic or diegetic death.

All this is not to deny the increasing validation of mother-figures traced throughout both the annunciation and the temptation type-scenes. Rather, it is to point out that the validation serves specific purposes, and that validating strategies must be studied in conjunction with restrictive and stigmatic strategies. Only by examining the interaction of these apparently contradictory impulses shall we be able to comprehend the ideology that shapes nativity narratives. For a narrative like Ruth, for example, is as strenuous in its exoneration of the mother-figure as it is in its emphatic denial of the father's investment in his patrilineage. The narrative displaces the male interest in male progeny not only by pre-

47. The traditional explanation is that the valorization of Ruth the Moabitess served as a polemic against nationalistic critiques of 'mixed' marriages. More recently, Harold Fisch suggested that the marriage of Boaz, the Judahite and Ruth the Moabitess represents the mending of the separation between Lot and Abraham (Gen. 19), which was partially mended through the relationship of Judah (Gen. 38). See, 'Ruth and the Structure of Covenant History', *VT* 32.4 (1982), pp. 425-37.

48. For a detailed exemplification of the male-centered inclusion pattern of the annunciation type-scene, see Fuchs, 'The Characterization of Mothers'.

senting Boaz as the passive and innocent object of the mother's seduction, a ploy used by all temptation scenes. By investing Naomi with the father's authority and anxiety over patrilineal disruption, the narrative denies that men are the primary beneficiaries of as exemplary a devotion as Ruth's to the interest of patriarchy. While the temptation type-scene rejects the idea that fathers are interested in patrilineal continuity, the annunciation type-scene rejects the idea that fathers can be sterile. Only mothers are eager, even desperate, to maintain patrilineal continuity, and only mothers are barren. Consequently, the best prize mothers can hope for is the act itself of giving birth to sons, while fathers are 'naturally' entitled to other awards, such as the exclusive control over these sons and representation in genealogical chains. Mother-figures are unquestionably the most valorized gynotypes in the Hebrew Bible, but, as noted previously, this valorization has very specific goals. What is celebrated in nativity narratives is the mother's successful attempt to give birth to male heirs, not her procreative powers. Those powers are rather marginalized or even denied. Mother-figures are indeed 'positive' characters, but we must not forget to ask 'positive' from whose point of view, and for what purposes, and above all, what *are* 'mothers' according to the biblical narrative?

It is tempting to identify the affirmation of a certain female gynotype with a pro-female or even feminist stance. Phyllis Trible argued for the following interpretation:

> He [Boaz] has patriarchal power, but he does not have narrative power. He has authority within the story but not control over it. The story belongs to Ruth and Naomi—and to chance, that code for the divine... As a whole, this human comedy suggests a theological interpretation of feminism: women working out their own salvation with fear and trembling, for it is God who works in them. Naomi works as a bridge between tradition and innovation. Ruth and the females of Bethlehem work as paradigms for radicality. All together they are women in culture, women against culture, and women transforming culture.[49]

Trible's distinction between Boaz's 'authority within the story' as opposed to his lack of 'control over it' ignores the fact that by their very nature fictional characters never have 'narrative power'. The power to interpret reality or create myths belongs to a particular hegemonic ideology whose mouthpiece is the narrator. In this respect the 'story

---

49. Zvi Adar, *The Biblical Narrative* (trans. Misha Louvish; Jerusalem: Department of Education and Culture of the World Zionist Organization, 1959).

belongs to Ruth and Naomi' even less than it belongs to 'chance' or to 'God'. The careful orchestration of literary strategies in the Ruth narrative as well as in other nativity narratives demonstrates that very little in the biblical narrative is left to 'chance', least of all the presentation of a male 'God' as the true source of female fertility. The meekness and obedience of Ruth and the devotion of Naomi to the cause of patrilineal continuity and their recourse to 'feminine' ploys to attain the political goal of their male counterparts hardly support their interpretation as 'paradigms of radicality'. If anything, the traits and actions attributed to these mother-figures are symptomatic of a patriarchal ideology that never fails to praise what it values most in women.

But just as it is misleading to interpret the affirmation of mother-figures as a 'theological interpretation of feminism', it is misguided to ignore the ideological functions of what the Bible presents as the mother's goals. Coming from a different angle, Athalya Brenner, who unlike Trible notes the ambiguous characteristics attributed to Ruth and Tamar, then ultimately agrees that these narratives represent a remarkable shift from the Bible's 'conventional morality'. Brenner summarizes the apparently paradoxical affirmation of 'temptresses' like Ruth and Tamar thus:

> In short, the reader gets the impression that deeds attributed to these mothers of great men are recounted with relish rather than with an intention to moralize. They celebrate the matriarch's achievement to such an extent that the dubious means she employs are considered tokens of her resourcefulness and determination. The question is: What are the features in each story that enable the authors to rise above conventional morality and record the exploits of the Temptress without censure?... Women who risk whatever little social status they have, and possibly their lives, in order to perpetuate the continuity of Judahite leader stock display a rare kind of courage. Therefore and despite the fact that they are foreigners, the authors who record their tales are on their side.[50]

Brenner is right in insisting on the mother's abnegation and desire to 'perpetuate the continuity of Judahite leader stock' as the primary reason for the puzzling validation of the foreign 'temptress'. What she fails to consider, however, is the complicity between the mother's

50. Brenner, *The Israelite Woman*, p. 108. Similarly, Ilana Pardes sees the story of Ruth as 'Idyllic Revisionism'. See her *Countertraditions in the Bible*, pp. 98-117.

'positive' motivation and the political concerns of patriarchy. For, as demonstrated in this chapter, it is precisely the alleged desire to perpetuate patrilineal continuity that defines and validates the protagonists of the temptation type-scene, and for that matter all biblical mother-figures. The 'relish' with which the 'authors' recount these tales is directly related to the 'intention to moralize'. There is a perfect fit between the details they emphasize and the interest of patriarchy. The absence of explicit commentary does not mean that there is no intention to moralize. The valorization of mothers devoted to patriarchy is itself a form of moralizing. Far from rising 'above conventional morality', biblical narratives about mother-figures are well within the conventional boundaries of biblical sexual politics.

It has been argued that the biblical insistence on patrilineage is a demythologizing and liberating concept. Linked with historical evolution it has been extolled as the Bible's highest achievement.[51] The question feminist critics should pose is liberating for whom? *Cui bono*? What are the interests served by the annunciation type-scene, the temptation type-scene and by nativity narratives in general? If the answer is the father's and the son's interests, then surely we are right in questioning the ideology in the text and the androcentric reader that strives to validate this answer as the manifestation of an absolute or divine principle.

Motherhood is indeed extolled in the Hebrew Bible, but it is extolled to the extent that it validates the father's authority and consolidates the son's right to security and prosperity. The mother is a means to an end, she is necessary and therefore validated. But her validation functions ultimately as the validation of the patriarchal hierarchy.

51. Schneidau, *Sacred Discontent*, pp. 241-42.

Chapter 4

THE BRIDE AND BIBLICAL BETROTHAL TYPE-SCENES

The Shrinking Role of Brides in Successive Betrothal Type-Scenes

A careful examination of successive narratives and type-scenes dealing with wife-figures reveals a development pointedly opposite to the one underlying the presentations of mother-figures. Whereas mother-figures emerge as increasingly predominant in relation to their male counterparts, especially in the context of annunciation type-scenes, wives appear to undergo an opposite evolution, progressively losing in status, integrity and impact relative to their male counterparts.[1] What has come to be known as the betrothal type-scene best dramatizes this significant development.[2]

Three times in the Hebrew Bible, a prospective wife and husband meet at a well (Gen. 24.1-58; 29.1-20; Exod. 2.16-21). Despite considerable variation in the characterization of the participants and the literary construction of the particular scenes, the three narratives contain identical motifs and are based on an identical progression of events. All three encounters lead to the betrothal of the woman and the man. The two meet by the well; the prospective bride draws water from the well, and then hurries to tell her family about the stranger. This leads to the stranger being invited to a meal by the woman's family, and then to a betrothal agreement.

The threefold repetition of the betrothal scene was explained by some

---

1. The status of the bride as a woman in transition between father and husband is especially precarious. Mieke Bal explains the havoc wreaked on some brides in the book of Judges as a result of an implicit transition from an ideology of patrilocal marriage to one of virilocal marriage. See *Death and Dissymmetry*, pp. 81-93.

2. The term betrothal type-scene is taken from Alter, *The Art of Biblical Narrative*, pp. 47-62.

as the result of the oral transmission of the stories.[3] An interpretation of the repeated thematic and structural cluster as a type-scene and a more detailed analysis of the betrothal type-scene in particular is offered by Robert Alter, who perceives it as a foreshadowing technique. According to Alter, each type-scene signals the groom's 'emergence from the immediate family circle...to discover a mate in the world outside', while the well symbolizes fertility or even femininity.[4] By contrast to the groom, the bride fulfills a rather limited role in this scene.[5] The bride is described as a treasured object: she is a virgin and she is physically attractive.

In what follows, I will argue that the progressive permutations in the presentation of the bride provide an effective hermeneutic key to the patriarchal ideology that structures and informs conjugal narratives in general and the betrothal type-scene in particular. Yet despite the significance of the permutations, 'stable' motifs and structures are important as well. If we are right in speculating that the betrothal type-scenes have foreshadowing functions, what do they 'presage' about the power relations of respective couples?

The first betrothal type-scene is the longest and most elaborate one. Taking up the entire chapter of Genesis 24 (if we consider vv. 1-9 as an introduction to the scene), it relates with great detail the circumstances surrounding the betrothal of Isaac and Rebekah, through the mediation of Abraham's servant. A factor halting the pace of the scene's development is the repetition of phrases, the detailed description of action and the repeated 'quoting' of monologue and dialogue. Thus, for example, Rebekah's act of offering water to the servant and watering his camel is repeated four times. It first appears as a provisional act in the servant's prayer to Yhwh (Gen. 24.14), then described as a performed action (vv. 18-20). For the third time it appears as a reported provisional act, in the servant's dialogue with Rebekah's family (vv. 43-44), and finally as a reported performed act in the same dialogue (vv. 45-46). One function of the fourfold repetition is to allude to the providential element in the servant's auspicious encounter with Rebekah. The perfect 'fit' between the servant's prayer and Rebekah's response implies that their

3.   See Robert C. Culley, 'At the Well', in *Studies in the Structure of Hebrew Narrative* (Philadelphia: Fortress Press, 1976), pp. 41-43.
4.   'The well at an oasis is obviously a symbol of fertility and, in all likelihood, also a female symbol.' Alter, *The Art of Biblical Narrative*, p. 52.
5.   Williams, *Women Recounted*, p. 46.

meeting and its aftermath only appear to be coincidental. But while the narrator avoids mentioning Yhwh as an active participant in the encounter, he allows the servant to make this intervention more, though not entirely, explicit. In his solemn and detailed address to Laban and Bethuel (vv. 35-49), the nameless servant mentions the names of God five times (vv. 40, 42, 44, 48). Though these references to Yhwh emphasize explicitly the link between Abraham and Yhwh, they also imply that a refusal to 'give' away (נתן) Rebekah will amount to a rejection not only of Abraham, but also of Yhwh's plan.

The fourfold repetition of Rebekah's hospitable act, however, serves as a technique of characterization as well as an evaluative strategy.[6] One clear function of the various modes of repeated description in this context is to bring out Rebekah's generosity and kindness. Yet, the subtle differences between the various repeated moments require attention.

The servant's prayer expresses a request for less than Rebekah eventually gives:

> Let the girl [נער] to whom I shall say, 'Please, lower your jar that I may drink,' and who will say 'Drink, and I will water your camels too', let her be the one you choose for whom thou hast shown steadfast love to my master (Gen. 24.14).[7]

Described as performance, Rebekah's response is reported thus:

> And the servant ran towards her and said: 'Pray, give me a little water to drink from your jar.' She said, 'Drink, my lord,' and she hastened to let down her jar upon her hand, and let him drink. When she had done letting him drink, she said, 'I will draw for your camels also, until they had done drinking.' So she hastened to empty her jar into the trough and ran again to the well to draw, and she drew for all his camels (vv. 17-20).

The difference between these two versions demonstrates that Rebekah did better than fulfill the servant's hopes. Whereas he planned to ask her only to 'tilt' or 'lower' (הטי) her jar, and proceeded to ask her only

---

6. On the different forms and functions of repetition in the biblical narrative, see Meir Sternberg, 'The Structure of Repetition in Biblical Narrative' [Hebrew], *Hasifrut* 25 (1977), pp. 110-50. See also Yair Hoffman, 'Between Conventionality and Strategy: On Repetition in Biblical Narrative' [Hebrew], *Hasifrut* 28 (1979), pp. 89-99. See also Alter, *The Art of Biblical Narrative*, pp. 88-113.

7. The RSV's omission of וגם ('and also') (Gen. 24.14) misses the emphasis of the text on Rebekah's generosity as envisioned by the servant.

for 'a little water' (מעט־מים) to drink or sip (הגמיאיני), 'she hastened to let down her jar upon her hand, and let him drink'. Rebekah is quick to respond to the stranger's request (ותמהר) and answers with politeness and gentility, calling the stranger 'my lord'. She spares no effort in her response to the stranger's request, and instead of merely tilting her jar to let him sip a little water, she actually takes it down, and instead of handing it over to him, holds it in her hand, lets him drink and waits until he is satiated. In addition, she not only offers some water to the servant's camels, but 'hastens' to draw and provide water for *all* (לכל) his camels, and waits until they have all been satiated.

Another factor that slows down the described progression of events is the repetition in reporting and reported speech.[8] Dominating the scene from this point of view is Abraham's servant in his prayer to Yhwh (vv. 12-14), his dialogue with Rebekah (vv. 17-28), and his reporting speech to Bethuel and Laban (vv. 33-49). In the latter speech, by far the longest in the scene, the servant essentially repeats information conveyed to the reader in the introduction to the scene (vv. 1-9). The reason for this repetition stems essentially from his will to persuade Bethuel and Laban of the divine nature of his encounter with Rebekah and to convince them that it is Yhwh's will that Rebekah should follow him to Canaan as Isaac's future bride. The speech then is rhetorical rather than informative; instead of propelling the plot, it slows it down. In this respect, the servant's discourse differs remarkably from that assigned to Rebekah. Her succinct speech acts are always informative and normally introduce a turn of events. Her speeches might be described as predicative in opposition to the servant's descriptive ones.

Thus, for example, her responses to the servant's request first for water and later for hospitality are succinct, but both introduce a series of major actions and events. Her first response (vv. 18-19) is a preface to a busy series of events involving physical exertion on her part, since she had to draw and provide water for the man and his camels, and her second response (vv. 24-25) is a preface to a busy series of hospitality gestures from the family. Her third response: 'I will go' (v. 59), the shortest of all her responses, rendered as one word in the original (אלך), is a preface to a long journey from Aram Naharayim to Canaan. All three speech acts amount to affirmative responses signifying a willingness to accept her divinely designated role as Isaac's future wife.

---

8.   See Polzin, *Moses and the Deuteronomist*, pp. 18-19.

Her fourth speech act: 'Who is that man yonder walking in the field towards us?' is the only one represented in the interrogative mode, but that too precedes a significant act, namely her encounter with her bridegroom Isaac. Rebekah's speech acts are predicative not only because they introduce a series of actions, but also because they amount to actions; on the illocutionary level they reflect acceptance and receptivity, which implies on the perlocutionary level that Rebekah is in fact the bride chosen by Yhwh for Isaac.[9] Insofar as they generate actions, the servant's speeches can also be defined as predicative, but they take up a much broader textual span than Rebekah's concise enunciations. On the other hand, it is noteworthy that Rebekah's speech acts are mostly gestures of receptivity, acquiescence, obedience and positive responsiveness rather than gestures expressive of autonomy, independence and initiative. Rebekah is not asked whether she agrees to the betrothal but whether she consents to follow the servant immediately (vv. 56-58). In this respect she fits well within the category of favorable biblical heroines.[10] Despite her important role in this scene, she does not deviate in essence from the normative parameters of female discourse in the biblical narrative, which typically curtail women's discourse in general, and especially narrating discourse. Female characters in general seldom narrate a story, and when they do it is usually very brief. To narrate significant events presupposes a measure of authority unless the text itself raises a question in reporting that someone in the story narrates something.[11]

Thus even Rebekah, who is the most talkative bride in the biblical betrothal type-scenes is not assigned a narrating discourse. Describing Rebekah's hastening back home to tell her family of her encounter with Abraham's servant, the text offers only a diegetic summary: 'Then the maiden ran and told her mother's household about these things' (v. 28), and an indirect content paraphrase: 'Thus the man spoke to me' (v. 30), rather than allowing Rebekah to narrate the events through direct discourse.[12]

---

9.   'Illocution' here refers to the intended meaning(s) of the speech act; 'perlocution' to the unstated implication(s) of the speech act.

10.   On obedience and submissiveness as primary hallmarks of biblical heroines, see Esther Fuchs, 'Female Heroines in the Biblical Narrative', *Mankind Quarterly* 23 (1982), pp. 149-60.

11.   Williams, *Women Recounted*, p. 39.

12.   For a survey of different styles of speech representation, see Brian McHale,

Rebekah's obedience and receptivity do not entail passivity. The verbs 'hasten' (מהר) and 'run' (רוץ) are each ascribed to her twice in the narrative, once in the context of her encounter with the servant and later as she runs home. The quick succession of verbs describing her energetic and eager activity at the well also characterizes her as dynamic and active as well as generous and hospitable. In this context it is instructive to compare Rebekah's actions to those of her brother, Laban. While Rebekah is shown to provide water to someone she perceives as a stranger without expecting any rewards, Laban acts upon learning that the man in question is wealthy and therefore worthy of attention: 'When he saw the ring and the bracelets on his sister's arms...he said: "Come in, blessed of the Lord; why do you stand outside? For I have cleared the house, and made room for the camels" ' (vv. 30-31). The temporal clause preceding Laban's sententious welcome establishes an unmistakable causal link between his ulterior motives and his show of hospitality. Furthermore, whereas Rebekah invites the servant by assuring him that: 'We have both straw and provender enough and room to lodge in' (v. 25), Laban stresses that room had to be made for the guest and his retinue, thus implying that this effort should not go unrewarded; he especially emphasizes that it was he who cleared the house and made room for the camels.[13]

To a large extent, it can be said that both the servant and Laban function as foils in the characterization of Rebekah, their conduct and discourse highlighting hers. What is perhaps most obtrusive, however, is the absence of Isaac, the bridegroom who appears only at the end of the scene, and even here not as the subject of purposeful action but rather as a participant in an apparent coincidence that is in fact the product of divine orchestration: 'And Isaac went out to meditate in the field in the evening; and he lifted up his eyes, and he looked and behold [והנה], there were camels coming' (v. 63). At this point the narrative focus shifts back to Rebekah who is shown to 'fall' [נפל] or alight from the camel upon seeing the stranger advancing towards them. Having learned from the servant that this is his 'master' she covers herself with her veil. Only in the final verse does Isaac emerge as an active subject, or rather a recipient of a highly prized object, which is the best way to

'Free Indirect Discourse: A Survey of Recent Accounts', *Poetics and Theory of Literature* 3 (1978), pp. 249-87.

13. RSV misses this emphasis by rendering *piniti et habayit* as merely 'I have prepared the house'.

define the role of Rebekah at this point: 'Then Isaac brought her into his mother Sarah's tent, and took Rebekah, and she became his wife; and he loved her. So Isaac was comforted after his mother's death' (v. 67). In this context Rebekah appears as the direct object of three transitive verbs (brought, took, loved) ascribed to Isaac, and the subject of a single intransitive verb designating the transformation of her status in relation to Isaac. The final verse also omits any reference to Rebekah's attitude or feelings, focusing on her function within the framework of Isaac's life.

The concluding statement notwithstanding, Rebekah plays a far more central and significant role than Isaac in this betrothal type-scene. It has been suggested that Rebekah's central role in the scene foreshadows her important role as 'the shrewdest and most potent of the matriarchs, and so it is entirely appropriate that she should dominate her betrothal type-scene'.[14] Considered in this light, the ceremonial blessing Rebekah receives from her family (v. 60) may serve as an anticipatory motif of the paternal blessing she will later procure for her favored son, Jacob. Similarly, her bustling activity by the well may seem to foreshadow her hurried preparation of her husband's preferred food as part of her effort to pass Jacob off as Esau, Isaac's favored son. By the same token, Isaac's minimal participation in the betrothal scene intimates his status as the least active and significant of the patriarchs. We shall see later, however, that the elaborate description of the first betrothal type-scene not only functions as a foreshadowing technique, but also as a strategy of ideological legitimation. In many ways, the first betrothal scene introduces for the first time patriarchal concepts of marriage. What the elaborate and solemn scene hides is the concept of patrilocal marriage, the notion that a bride is to leave her family and move to her husband's place of birth, or, more precisely, to the residence of her husband's father.

The second betrothal scene introduces the concept of polygyny, another basic patriarchal institution. The first introduction of such concepts and institutions is the most detailed one. The second betrothal type-scene involving Jacob and Rachel also includes an encounter at a well, the drawing of water, a hurried reporting of the news, and a betrothal agreement. Yet it differs markedly from the first one. For one thing it is far more limited in terms of narrative span, taking up 17

14. Alter, *The Art of Biblical Narrative*, p. 54.

verses compared to the 57 dealing with the first scene. The factor of narrative space is highly significant within the framework of the biblical narrative, with its typical tendency toward economy and condensation. The short span of the second betrothal type-scene then may be interpreted as an index of its relatively more limited importance. The elaborate introduction to the first betrothal type-scene, featuring Abraham's dialogue with the senior servant of his household (זקן ביתו) (Gen. 24.2) about Isaac's future bride and the proper procedure for concluding the betrothal is another indication of the relative importance of this type-scene. The second type-scene is not prefaced by any introduction relating directly to it. While the former is preceded by a pact between Abraham and his servant, the latter is preceded by a pact between Yhwh and Jacob (Gen. 28.13-15). Jacob vows allegiance to Yhwh contingent upon His continued protection and providence (Gen. 28.20-22). The following betrothal type-scene, then, is only one of a series of events indicating Yhwh's special interest in Jacob. It also constitutes only part of what can be seen as the internal cycle (Gen. 29–31) within the broader cycle of the Jacob stories (Gen. 25.19–35.22).[15] This is in congruence with the emphasis on Jacob as the focalizer and protagonist of the second betrothal scene. As the object of Jacob's interest, Rachel performs a less important role than her counterpart in the first scene. This shift in focus from bride to bridegroom is, for our purposes, the most important transformation in the presentation of the betrothal type-scene.

As in the first scene, the narrator in the second is anxious to point out that the events are orchestrated by Yhwh, although here the participants may not be aware of it. Just as Rebekah appears on the scene as soon as the servant completes his prayer to Yhwh (Gen. 24.15), so does Rachel appear just as Jacob interrogates the shepherds about her father, Laban. But unlike the servant who runs (רוץ) toward Rebekah requesting her to give him some water (Gen. 24.17), Jacob, when told that Rachel is coming with the sheep, continues to talk with the shepherds by the well (Gen. 29.6) until she approaches. Only when he sees Rachel and her flock does Jacob discontinue his dialogue with the shepherds: 'Now when Jacob saw Rachel, the daughter of Laban, his mother's brother, Jacob went up and rolled the stone from the well's mouth, and watered the flock of Laban, his mother's brother' (Gen. 29.10). Only later do we

---

15. For a detailed analysis of the Jacob cycle, see Michael Fishbane, *Text and Texture: Close Readings of Selected Biblical Texts* (New York: Schocken Books, 1979), pp. 40-62.

learn what it is in Rachel's appearance that inspired Jacob to single-handedly roll a heavy stone which required the collaboration of numerous shepherds to move (Gen. 29.2-3). Instead of pausing at this point to introduce Rachel, as it does in the first betrothal type-scene (Gen. 24.16), the text continues to focus on Jacob's actions: 'Then Jacob kissed Rachel and wept aloud. And Jacob told Rachel that he was her father's kinsman, and that he was Rebekah's son; and she ran and told her father' (Gen. 29.11-12). While Jacob dominates the scene in action, discourse and emotional expression, Rachel is allowed to act essentially only as mediator between Jacob and her father. All we know about Rachel at this point is her familial status as Laban's daughter and Jacob's kin, and her occupation as shepherdess, facts that are repeatedly mentioned in the course of the scene. Only later do we learn that she is 'beautiful and lovely' (Gen. 29.17), which serves more as an explanation for Jacob's preference for her over Leah, her elder sister, rather than as part of her own characterization. Rachel's beauty explains Jacob's love for her, but it does not do much to illuminate her character, no more than do her silence and lack of distinctive action.

Whereas Rachel's beauty and Jacob's consequent love for her are the only things that commend Rachel, Rebekah is implicitly praised for her generosity, diligence, sensitivity, hospitality, politeness, obedience, as well as her good looks and unquestionable virginity (Gen. 24.16). In contrast to her dynamic predecessor, who is shown to draw water for both herself and others, Rachel allows Jacob to draw water for her. In a sense her passivity and helplessness highlight Jacob's strength and resourcefulness. The text stresses that the heavy stone upon the well requires the collaboration of several shepherds to be removed (Gen. 29.2-3, 8). (Alter suggests the stopped-up well is symbolic of Rachel's barrenness.) It is possible that the sight of Rachel inspires Jacob to remove the stone singlehandedly, just as his love for her will later inspire him to work for her father for 14 years (Gen. 24.20, 19), but she herself is not shown to undertake any action, or express any thought or feeling about him. A vagrant escapee from Esau's wrath, Jacob arrives empty-handed at the well. Unlike Abraham's servant, he has no jewels to give or wealth to promise to his prospective bride. Yet, he outclasses his predecessor with his physical strength and willpower. It is he who helps Rachel water the herd. The power-structured relations this scene establishes between Jacob and Rachel allude to her future as a barren co-wife, a frustrated rival of her sister, a beloved wife who is nevertheless rebuked by her husband, and finally to her death giving birth to her second son.

Jacob supersedes Rachel in both referential and compositional terms. Not only is he described as the strong and muscular initiator of the scene's major action sequence, he is also the protagonist and focalizer of the scene. The events are shown from his point of view. While Jacob dominates the scene, Rachel is not allowed to dominate even one entire verse, tucked—as it were—into combined and subordinate clauses (Gen. 24.6, 9, 12, 16, 17), or referred to as direct or indirect object (vv. 10-12, 18-19). The three intransitive verbs she controls as subject are 'come', 'run' and 'tell', which befit the role of a messenger.

And indeed Rachel functions essentially as intermediary between Jacob and Laban. As soon as Laban appears on the scene, she disappears. The focus shifts from Jacob and the shepherds to Jacob and Laban. It is true that Rebekah too does not participate in the betrothal treaty concluded between Abraham's servant and her family, yet she is at least summoned up when the servant insists he must leave with the bride immediately: 'They said, "We will call the maiden and ask her" ' (Gen. 24.57). In the second betrothal type-scene the bride's father and her prospective bridegroom conclude a betrothal treaty without so much as consulting or even informing the bride. In the ensuing treaty between Jacob and Laban, Rachel emerges as little more than a prized object. Later, both Rachel and Leah will be given by their father to their bridegroom in return for his services.

Rachel is not only overshadowed by her future bridegroom and her father, but also by her sister, Leah. When she does appear as the object of Jacob's attention, she is presented in conjunction with Leah: 'Now Laban had two daughters; the name of the older was Leah and the name of the younger was Rachel' (Gen. 29.16). Informationally, this verse does not add anything to what the reader has already gathered from the previous references to Rachel as Laban's daughter (vv. 6, 9-10, 12-13). Its impact is strategic; it points out that Rachel is not the only daughter, although she has benefited from the text's exclusive attention up to this point. The following references to Rachel are relative and comparative: 'Leah's eyes were weak, but Rachel was lovely and beautiful' (Gen. 29.17).[16] The introduction of Rachel as part of a unit of two daughters foreshadows her status as only one-half of a unit of two wives. She may

---

16. The Hebrew original refers to Leah's eyes as רכות which can be rendered as either 'weak' or 'delicate'.

be the beloved bride, and later the preferred co-wife, but she will never

be the exclusive wife, a fact that will deeply affect her literary presentation. Her actions will constantly be introduced in juxtaposition with those of her sister, denoting unflagging competition for their mutual husband. Furthermore, unlike Rebekah who will have a say in the fate of her sons, and who will supersede her husband's judgment in this context, Rachel, like Leah, will appear mostly as a reproductive means rather than as an autonomous character, a wife, or even a mother. She will be shown as a jealous and exasperated barren co-wife (Gen. 30.1) and a frustrated reproducer of children. Both her life and death are closely related to her reproductive function. Her most important achievements revolve around her indirect help in the conception of Dan and Naphtali (Gen. 30.3-8) and her giving birth to Joseph (Gen. 30.22-24), while her death is said to be occasioned by the birth of her second son, Benjamin (Gen. 35.16-20).

The third betrothal type-scene involving Moses and Zipporah reflects a further reduction in the status of the bride, as well as in the status of the betrothal scene in general. The third betrothal scene is shorter and more compact than the previous one, taking up a mere five verses (Exod. 2.16-21), compressed within the story of Israel's oppression by Pharaoh and Moses' preparation for national leadership. The limited narrative span that this betrothal type-scene takes up within the context of the Moses cycle reflects the peripheral role of wife and marriage in the leader's life (Zipporah is important in Exod. 4.22 and a cause of concern in Num. 12).

Like the previous type-scene, this one manipulates the conventional motifs for two major purposes: (1) to intimate Yhwh's continued interest in the hero, and (2) to justify this interest by presenting the heroic features of the divinely designated man. Like Jacob, who flees from the wrath of Esau, Moses flees from the wrath of Pharaoh. The apparently coincidental encounter by the well of the hero with his future bride, signifies in both cases the beginning of a reversal in the status of the hero from a vagrant fugitive, to a master of his own household. The conduct of the heroes by the well intimates that they are divinely empowered. Jacob singlehandedly rolls an enormous and heavy stone from atop the well, while alone Moses faces a whole group of inimical shepherds who interfere with the attempt of Reuel's daughters to water their father's flock: 'The shepherds came and drove them

away; but Moses stood up and rescued them, and watered their flock'
(Exod. 2.17). Moses' intervention on behalf of the helpless girls is consistent with his intervention on behalf of the Hebrew underdogs as
described in the preceding episode (Exod. 2.11-14). It also foreshadows
his successful confrontation with Pharaoh as the leader of his oppressed
people, especially through the verbs 'rescue' (וַיּוֹשִׁעָן) and 'deliver'
(הִצִּילָנוּ) ascribed to Moses in this scene, first by the narrator (v. 17) and
again by Reuel's daughters (v. 19). While Moses' success intimates that
God supports him, his initiative reflects a refined moral sense as well as
a good measure of courage, namely the constitution of one who deserves
divine support and the role of a leader. The text represents Moses' heroic
characteristics by detailing the different stages and aspects of his action;
Moses is said to 'stand up', 'rescue' the girls and 'water' Reuel's flock.
While the verb 'rescue' conveys the general significance of the action,
the verb 'rise up' intimates that Moses was still sitting as the scuffle by
the well erupted, and that he could have avoided action by simply ignoring the situation. By stating that Moses had to rise up, the text stresses
that Moses was not content with merely enabling the girls to do their
job, but proceeded to water their flock. This is repeated for emphasis in
the girls' report to their father when asked why they returned home so
early: 'They said, "An Egyptian delivered us out of the hand of the
shepherds; and he even drew water for us and watered the flock" '
(Exod. 2.19). Whereas the first description refers to Moses watering the
sheep with a single verb וַיַּשְׁקְ, the girls' report uses two different verbs
each referring to a different stage of the action, namely the act of drawing water (דלה) and the act of watering the herd (וַיַּשְׁקְ). Their report
highlights this act further by using the intensive form of the verb דָּלָה
דָּלָה, which repeats the verb through infinitive and conjugated form,
which can be approximated in English by 'he even drew' or 'he also
drew'. Unlike Jacob, who musters the strength to remove the stone from
the well upon seeing Rachel, whom he knows to be his kin, Moses is
shown to help complete strangers. Precisely by not singling out any of
the girls as attractive, the text establishes that Moses' act was not
inspired by any ulterior motives, that what propelled him was altruism
rather than eroticism. The selfless gesture on Moses' part reflects one of
the central characteristics of the leader who will later be shown to dedicate his entire life to a cause and to a collective group rather than to any
particular person or to his own interests.

But the scene's persistent focus on the character of the bridegroom visibly diminishes the role of the bride. Although Moses is a vagabond

and an empty-handed foreigner, he is by far more powerful than the daughters of the respectable native priest, Reuel. The girls are not only shown to be physically powerless and helpless, they also lack the resourcefulness typifying their predecessors in the previous scenes. Unlike Rebekah and Rachel, who both hurry home to report to their families of their encounters with strangers at a well, Reuel's daughters fail to either thank the stranger or to volunteer any information once they return home. It is only after their father questions them that they tell him about their mysterious deliverer, at which point the priest scolds them for their ingratitude and lack of tact: 'He said to his daughters, "And where is he? Why have you left the man? Call him, that he may eat bread" ' (Exod. 2.20). While the previous scenes present the bride's custodians, specifically her brother or father in a somewhat ambiguous light, this type-scene foregrounds the potential father-in-law at the expense of his daughters, thus prefiguring his important role in Moses' career in contrast to that of his future wife. The scene all but ignores the relationship between bride and bridegroom and proceeds to deal with the relationship of the bridegroom and his future father-in-law: 'And Moses was content to dwell with the man, and he gave Moses Zipporah his daughter' (Exod. 2.21). Unlike the previous scene that emphasized Jacob's desire for Rachel as the primary motivation for the betrothal, here the betrothal is more a product of the men's mutual trust and friendship. Zipporah's feelings and thoughts, even her appearance or the feelings she might have evoked in Moses are unknown. The scene does not distinguish her from her other sisters by noting her conduct or looks, neither does it explain why Reuel chose her rather than any of her other sisters. The bride's existence is predicated on her name only. Her function is little more than that of an object, delivered from one man to another in a gesture of goodwill. Immediately following this transaction Zipporah is shown to perform her most important function: 'She bore a son, and he called his name Gershom…' (Exod. 2.22). It is true that in the previous cases, the wife's reproductive role appears shortly after the conclusion of the betrothal, yet in the first and second scenes a narrative interval is allowed to intervene between a woman's conjugal status and reproductive function. In the third type-scene, by contrast, there is no effort to camouflage the close relationship between the betrothal and the conception of sons. The verse relating to the birth of Gershom immediately follows the verse that describes her transference from her father to her future husband.

Rebekah and Rachel are introduced as prized objects; Zipporah does not earn even this status. Just as Rebekah's important role in the story of her betrothal foreshadows her active intervention in and impact on the life of her husband and children, so is Zipporah's minor role in her betrothal consonant with her peripheral role in Moses' career.[17] In the book of Exodus, she will be mentioned only twice more: first in conjunction with her son's circumcision (Exod. 4.25) and later as she and her two sons rejoin Moses in the desert (Exod. 18.2). Only in the first instance, rendered in a highly opaque and mystifying fashion, does she emerge as an independent subject, taking initiative on behalf of her husband and son, and in the process saving Moses' life. Encountering the angel 'who sought to kill him' (Exod. 4.24), Zipporah 'took a flint and cut off her son's foreskin and touched Moses' feet with it and said: "Surely you are a bridegroom of blood to me" ' (Exod. 4.25).[18] The concise description of Zipporah's action is not only difficult to interpret, it is doubly mystifying because no reference is made in the encounter between Yhwh and Moses to the need for Gershom's circumcision. What we might conclude, however, is that Zipporah interferes successfully on behalf of her husband and son, and that in this capacity she emerges as an independent character. But when we encounter Zipporah again, much later, she emerges once again as a mute item of exchange offered to Moses by Jethro. Just as in the betrothal scene, Jethro is shown to give (נתן) Zipporah to Moses in matrimony, so he is here to 'take' (לקח) Zipporah and her sons, and bring them back to Moses: 'Now Jethro, Moses' father-in-law, had taken Zipporah, Moses' wife, after she had been sent away...' (Exod. 18.2) and 'came with his sons and his wife to Moses in the wilderness' (Exod. 18.5).

Like the previous reference to Zipporah, this one too raises more questions than answers. For one thing, nowhere prior to this reference does the text suggest that Zipporah has been sent away, and that she and her sons had been living with Jethro rather than with Moses. Furthermore, it is not clear whether Moses sent Zipporah back to her father, or whether the latter reclaimed her. In any case, it is unknown why this

---

17. For a different reading of Zipporah, see Pardes, 'Zipporah and the Struggle for Deliverance', in *Countertraditions in the Bible*, pp. 79-97.

18. The verse is difficult and given to many interpretations. See Greenberg (*hatan damim lamulot*).

happened. Nevertheless, the text does not find it necessary to fill in this informational gap. The fact of Zipporah's separation from Moses appears in a temporal clause, subordinated to the main sentence dealing with Jethro's action.[19] While Zipporah is barely mentioned in passing, Jethro emerges as a major character in Exodus 18. This reflects the dismissive attitude of Moses to his wife in contrast to his high esteem for his father-in-law, a situation already prefigured in the type-scene. When Moses hears of the arrival of Jethro, his 'wife and her two sons' (Exod. 18.6), the text notes that: 'Moses went out to meet his father-in-law, and bowed down and kissed him. And they asked each other of their welfare and went into the tent' (Exod. 18.7). Moses is not shown to extend any welcome to his bride. There is no indication that he paid any attention to her. While Jethro goes on to occupy a major role in Exodus 18 as an advisor to Moses, Zipporah is almost consigned to oblivion, except for her appearance in Numbers 12. Her return to Moses signals no change in her peripheral status. The short shrift given to Zipporah may reflect, in addition to Moses' attitude to her, the narrator's point of view as well. The opaqueness of the references to Zipporah are, to a large degree, products of her dismissive treatment by the narrator. Had he considered her important, more information concerning her state and actions would appear, thereby forestalling the ambiguity of the verses dealing with her. The dismissive treatment of Zipporah in the third betrothal type-scene then is highly characteristic of her treatment as Moses' wife.

The diminishing emphasis on the bride-figure can be interpreted as a literary strategy of an ideology whose goal is to minimize the power of women as prospective wives. While as a prospective mother, a woman ensures patrilineal continuity and thus performs an important role within the patriarchal frame of reference, as a wife her contribution is questionable. 'Good' prospective wives, like Rebekah, Rachel and Zipporah learn how to recede into the background as soon as their link to their prospective male partner has been established. De-emphasizing the status of the bride-figure is also valuable for an ideology that sanc-

19. In Hebrew this information is encapsulated by two words, a temporal adverb and a noun, whereas in most English translations it takes up at least a full temporal clause. The RSV 'after he had sent her away' does not convey the connotation of the Hebrew term שלוחים, which is open to several interpretations. Most importantly, it is not clear why Zipporah was sent back to her father and whether she was forced to leave Moses or departed voluntarily.

tions the coupling of several brides with a single groom. The decreasing narrative span of the betrothal type-scene, its shrinking into all but few verses reporting the mere 'fact' about the marriages of judges like Gideon and Samson and of kings like Saul, David and Uriah implies that betrothal as an event in the careers of biblical male heroes is not particularly important. The illusion of narratives about betrothal implies that they might not be worthy of the narrator's attention. The acquisition of a bride increasingly becomes an act taken for granted and one whose importance is eclipsed by other narrated events. By the same token the increasing emphasis on the groom's character signifies that the betrothal has no autonomous importance but as an incident in the hero's represented biography, while the growing stress on his power versus that of the bride prescribes the power relations that ought to prevail between them.

Perhaps the most important implication of the structural transformations we have observed refer to the function of the betrothal type-scene as the dramatic foreshadowing of the marital relations between the characters involved. As noted above, the greater role played by Rebekah in comparison to Isaac, foreshadows their marital relations, where she will be the major mastermind behind Jacob's career, in accordance with Yhwh's plans. Concomitantly, Rachel's impact on her husband is described as much more limited than that in the first betrothal type-scene of her predecessor on her husband. The gradual disappearance of the bride from later books makes the later obliviousness to the fates of women as wives seem natural. The shorter shrift marriage and wife-figures in general receive in the biblical narrative serves the ideology of male dominance in much the same way as the growing emphasis on the figure of the mother as the producer of male offspring does.

Does Ruth fulfill a role similar or analogous to the bridegrooms we mentioned? It has been suggested that the story of Ruth contains sketches of the betrothal type-scene, as here too are found the term נערה ('maiden'), the motif of water drawing (by Boaz's servants), and that of a festive meal.[20] The differences between Ruth and her male counterparts are so instructive, that Jacob and Moses move toward autonomy and independence. Both are shown to arrive at their future brides' lands empty-handed, just like Ruth, they are shown to work (both as shepherds) and finally to be able to free themselves of their economic

---

20. See Alter, *The Art of Biblical Narrative*, pp. 58-60.

dependence on their respective fathers-in-law and to leave for their

original place of birth with their wives and children. Ruth, by contrast, is shown to move toward an ever-increasing economic dependence on Boaz: gleaning the discarded sheaves of his reapers (Ruth 4.10). The water-drawing motif that serves in the second and third type-scenes to dramatize the strength and ability of the prospective bridegrooms, serves here as testimony for Boaz's protectiveness and Ruth's helplessness: 'Have I not commanded the young men not to molest you? And when you are thirsty, go to the vessels and drink what the young men have drawn' (Ruth 2.9). By the same token, the meal to which Ruth is invited is not the happy occasion of concluding a betrothal agreement between herself and Boaz, as it is in the case of the first and third type-scenes, but once again an additional indication of Boaz's generosity and Ruth's neediness: 'And in the meantime Boaz said to her: "Come here, and eat some bread and dip your morsel in the vinegar"...and she ate until she was satisfied' (Ruth 2.14). The meal described here is not a symbolic enactment of mutual trust, but the charitable donation of the wealthy to the poor; Ruth eats because she is poor and hungry, not because she symbolically seals a mutual transaction. The role reversal that accords a woman the status of hero does not change the underlying power-structured relations between the sexes as presented in the previous scenes. Jacob and Moses, despite their foreignness and poverty are shown to supersede their prospective brides in both physical strength and initiative; not only do they not beg their brides for help or food, they are shown to supply their future wives with water, warding off different impediments on the maidens' way. By contrast, Ruth's subordination to Boaz in terms of economic and social status is unmistakable. She is shown not only to depend on him for physical survival, but also to solicit his protection through his marrying her (Ruth 3.9). Ruth does not hesitate to beg for Boaz's help and protection, and often refers to herself as his 'maidservant'. If betrothal motifs can be found in the story of Ruth, they help substantiate the bride's subordination to her bridegroom, rather than extol woman's independence and self-determination.

But more importantly, despite the preponderance of the betrothal theme in Ruth, the narrative lacks the distinctive structure of the betrothal type-scene. For one thing the encounter at a well and the ceremonious drawing of water by the bride or bridegroom are missing here. Part of the reason seems to lie with the story's emphasis on the bride's efforts to secure herself a husband. Whereas the propitious, apparently coincidental encounter of the potential couple by the well dramatizes the unawareness of both bride and bridegroom of their future mutual bond, the book of Ruth emphasizes Ruth's deliberate and well-thought-out effort to 'hook' Boaz and thus bring an end to her and her mother-in-law's plight. A coincidental encounter by a well may create the erroneous impression that Ruth's pursuit of Boaz is inspired by selfish or sensual interests, rather than by her loyalty to her dead husband, which is precisely what the narrative extols. Furthermore, since the story is intent on dramatizing Ruth's utter poverty, helplessness and total dependence on Boaz, a meeting by the well, casting Ruth in the role of a girl drawing water will undermine the impression that the story has worked to achieve in the exposition. The verb 'run' (רוץ), characteristic of previous scenes, is missing here due to the absence of a paternal figure whose attitude to the encounter is urgently decisive for its impact and result. Above all, the story of Ruth does not serve one of the most important functions of the normative betrothal type-scene, namely to dramatize Yhwh's involvement in the fate of His chosen heroes, and as a dramatization of the heroes' heroic traits. In the first type-scene the success of Abraham's servant dramatizes Yhwh's commitment to Abraham and Isaac, just as the apparently coincidental encounter of Jacob and Moses with their future brides signals Yhwh's involvement in and approval of their action. At the same time, the betrothal type-scene (especially the latter two), also reflect the heroic features of the divinely appointed characters, serving as indirect justification of God's choice.

While in the case of the patriarchs and Moses, the betrothal type-scene is only one in a series of episodes confirming Yhwh's commitment to and care for them, in the case of Ruth, the betrothal is not just the central but the only event recounted about her. It is only because Ruth is female that the story about her revolves around what leads to her successful betrothal. The betrothals of male heroes are never allowed to control the major focus of their narratives. The betrothals of the male heroes constitute stages on their road toward greater accomplishments, while the heroine's betrothal is her ultimate goal. Indeed, as soon as Ruth is married and gives birth, she disappears from the narrative scene, the plot having reached its telos. It can be said that the betrothal is Ruth's *raison d'être*; she exists for the betrothal, not vice versa. Since Ruth's most important function is to bring about her be-trothal with Boaz, any heroic characteristics or even her power superi-ority over her future husband would in fact jeopardize the prospect of her betrothal. After all, as the biblical narrative makes clear even in the case of Rebekah, one of the bride's essential properties is obedience, both to her family (her father or brother) and to her future husband. To dramatize Ruth's generosity, pride or courage would serve no patriar-chal purpose in terms of the betrothal, or in terms of Ruth's non-existent future career, her submissiveness and gratitude. The story of Ruth obviously reflects Yhwh's design and intervention (as does every biblical story for that matter), but the purpose of this intervention is not to signify continued commitment to the heroine, but divine interest in the continuity of the patrilineal succession from Perez to King David, via Ruth's son Obed. It is Ruth's role as a means (reproductive agent) to an end (patrilineal continuity) that underlies her transformation from the heroine she is shown to be in chs. 1–3 into the chattel—the passive object of Boaz's economic and social transactions—she is portrayed to be in ch. 4. The point is that despite her heroic status and central role in the narrative and although she appears to be performing a role normally reserved to the bridegroom of the typical betrothal scene, Ruth performs in essence the role of the bride as seen in the previous scenes. The narrative is controlled by the gender of the heroine, rather than by the distinctive structure of the typical betrothal scene. It is true that she travels to her future bridegroom's country as do the bridegrooms, but unlike them, she stays there. The betrothal scene signifies a temporal hiatus in the career of the bridegroom staged in his bride's native land, by the end of which he will return to his own country with his wife and children. This is not the case in the story of Ruth, a fact of paramount importance in the framework of the Bible's normative patrilocal mar-riage. It is also true that Ruth rather than Boaz takes the initiative to bring about her betrothal with Boaz, but it is important to remember that she is inspired by loyalty to her late husband and his mother, rather than her own attraction to Boaz. In the final analysis she does not take or receive Boaz as Jacob receives Rachel and Moses receives Zipporah, but vice versa. She is taken—or rather purchased—by Boaz.

It is not coincidental that the book of Ruth presents as heroine a childless widow rather than a beautiful virgin like Rebekah, or a maiden in love like Michal. Ruth is shown to act in the interests of her father-in-law and her deceased husband. No female character is shown to approach a man she loves, or to suggest that she be wedded to him. The only case in which a woman is said to love a man is that of Michal, Saul's daughter (1 Sam. 18.20). But unlike Shechem who gains his father Hamor's cooperation in negotiating for Dinah (Gen. 34.4) and unlike Jacob who approaches Rachel's father, Michal is not shown to approach her father and request that she become David's bride. The biblical text offers no information on or insight into Michal's reaction to her father's subsequent decision to take her away from David and give her to another man, Palti, the son of Laish (1 Sam. 25.43), just as it remains silent about her attitude to David's taking her away from Palti for himself (2 Sam. 3.15-16)—an act of political maneuvering rather than love.[21] Even in the exceptional case of Michal, whose feelings for her future husband are recorded, a woman's desire is not shown to have any impact on the events narrated in the text. On the whole, a woman's emotional attitudes to her potential or actual mate, both in betrothal scenes and other relevant narratives, are not so much as mentioned, let alone presented as motivating factors leading to the conclusion of a betrothal agreement.

Passive, Obedient, Inscrutable:
The Characterization of Brides and the Economic Factor

All betrothal type-scenes, as well as brief reports about betrothal events, are framed by references to male initiative. In the betrothal scenes surveyed, the primary actors who bring about a successful betrothal agreement are always male. In the first scene, it is the bride's father-in-law, in the second it is the prospective husband, and in the third the bride's father. What remains constant in all these scenes is the exclusion of a female character as the primary initiator of the marriage contract. This configuration reinforces the status of the bride as an object of male desire and interest. Naomi and Ruth collude in a scheme to 'snare' Boaz into marriage; neither of them is shown to propose it to Boaz.

While the betrothal scenes tell us little about a bride's inner world, they show us the groom at significant turning points that highlight both

---

21. David asks for Michal after the death of Saul as part of a broader strategy aimed at securing control over Israel. On the political aspect of David's marriages, see Jon D. Levenson and Baruch Halpern, 'The Political Import of David's Marriages', *JBL* 99 (1980), pp. 507-18. See also Adele Berlin, 'Characterization in Biblical Narrative: David's Wives', *JSOT* 23 (1982), pp. 69-85.

his career and character. For the bridegroom, the betrothal type-scene normally signals an initiation into adult independence and autonomy. The scenes preceding the betrothal type-scene present the bridegrooms as youths. Prior to the first betrothal type-scene, Isaac is shown to be Abraham's son, dependent for life or death on his father's will (Gen. 22). Prior to the second betrothal, Jacob is shown as Rebekah's son, obeying her advice and following his father's orders (Gen. 28.1-5), while Moses is shown as rather brash, acting on impulse, and almost risking his life in his confrontation with the Egyptian taskmaster and the Hebrew slave (Exod. 2.11-15). As Rebekah enters the scene shortly after Sarah's death, she helps Isaac be 'comforted after [the death of] his mother' (Gen. 24.67). By specifying that Isaac introduces Rebekah into his mother's tent (Gen. 24.67), the text alludes to Rebekah's substitutive function: by replacing Sarah, Isaac moves from bereavement to a promise of a new future.[22] In the cases of Jacob and Moses, the betrothal type-scene signals a transition from alienation and vulnerability to relative economic stability and autonomy.

In all three betrothal type-scenes the encounter with the future bride signals divine providence, for the groom or his representative. This is particularly clear in the first betrothal scene, which emphasizes the 'fit' between Abraham's servant's prayer and Rebekah's response. The quick succession of the divine response after the request also implies divine providence, for Rebekah appears immediately upon the completion of the servant's prayer. With Jacob, the encounter with Rachel occurs following the vow he makes to pay allegiance to Yhwh if He gives him 'bread to eat and clothing to wear' (Gen. 28.20). The betrothal with Leah and Rachel in the wake of which Jacob receives shelter, sustenance and later wealth signifies the divine response to Jacob's vow. Moses' betrothal to Zipporah does not follow any explicit vow, but since it provides Moses with temporary shelter, sustenance and a family of his own, the implication is that the real author of the propitious events is Yhwh, who has a special stake in Moses as the future leader of the Israelites.

But what does the betrothal signify for the bride? Since the biblical narrative gives us no information on either of the brides prior to the betrothal type-scene, it is difficult to judge if for them too the betrothal

22. The Hebrew text reads literally 'and Isaac was comforted after his mother' without specifying the word 'death'. This convey the narrator's reticence to use this term in this context explicitly, or better yet, Isaac's emotional attitude to the event.

dramatizes a transition to a better situation. All one can deduce from the

betrothal scenes is that some transition from one male's custody to another's seems to be taking place. The betrothal type-scenes do not expand on the legal or economic aspects of this transition; in point of fact, they seem to mask them to some extent.[23]

The veiled expressions referring to the bride as chattel consist in the verbs 'take' (לקח) ascribed usually to the groom, and 'give' (נתן) usually ascribed to the father. In the first scene, these terms appear in Laban's and Bethuel's response to the servant's bid: 'Then Laban and Bethuel answered... "Behold, Rebekah is before you, *take* her and go, and let her be the wife of your master's son, as the Lord as spoken" ' (Gen. 24.50-51; emphasis mine). While the bridegroom's representative here 'takes' (לקח) (Gen. 24.37, 38, 51), her father (and brother) 'gives' (Gen. 24.41) the bride to him. These terms recur in all the betrothal narratives, whether they appear as brief reports, or as full-fledged scenes.[24]

Laban too uses the term 'give' in his agreement with Jacob (Gen. 29.21). The role of the bride's father is even further emphasized here, as he is shown to manipulate both his daughters and his son-in-law by replacing the desired daughter with the other. While the text records Jacob's anger and dismay at Laban's machinations, it remains silent

---

23. The few laws that explicitly refer to the status of a bride 'in transition' portray her as chattel. A father had the right to give his daughter to a prospective husband in return for monetary compensation. The father was to be compensated by the rapist of his daughter (Deut. 22.23-27). In case a father sold his daughter as concubine or slave, she could not be resold (Exod. 21.7-11). A husband could not sell his wife, but he could divorce her at will, whereas she could not divorce him. The daughter does not inherit from her father, except for cases where there is no male heir (Num. 27.8); neither does a wife inherit from her husband. A vow made by an unmarried woman needs the consent of her father just as one made by a married woman requires that of her husband (Num. 30.4-17). Legally both the unmarried and the married woman remained minors all their lives, with no legal authority over their own lives. If widowed, a woman often returns to her father's house or remains under the authority of her father-in-law. For further details on the legal status of the Israelite woman as daughter or bride, see de Vaux, *Ancient Israel*, I, pp. 24-40. See also Bird, 'Images of Women', pp. 41-88.

24. Compare also the Philistine father who 'gives' his daughter to his friend instead of Samson (Judg. 15.2). Saul is reported to promise to 'give' his daughter Merav to David, and ends up giving her to another man (1 Sam. 18.17-19). Saul is later reported to 'give' him Michal, his second daughter (1 Sam. 18.27).

about Leah's or Rachel's reaction to the manipulation by their father. Leah serves as direct object of her father's actions (as he 'takes' and 'brings' her to Jacob [Gen. 29.23], just as much as Rachel does: 'then Laban *gave* him his daughter Rachel as a wife' [v. 28]). The third betrothal type-scene also presents the bride as a valued object transferred from father to prospective husband: 'and he [Jethro] gave Moses his daughter Zipporah' (Exod. 2.21). If the betrothal means for the father 'giving' and for the bridegroom 'taking', for the bride it signifies being transferred from one male to the other. Nevertheless, the betrothal type-scenes refrain from stressing the economic nature of the betrothal transaction, which is not to say they eliminate it altogether.

In contrast to brief episodes describing fathers offering up their daughters as prized objects, the betrothal type-scenes make only veiled references to the economic value of the bride.[25] The value of the biblical bride is measured by androcentric terms: she is desirable if a virgin and if good-looking. While nothing is said about the looks or virginity of Isaac and Jacob, both Rebekah and Rachel are presented as attractive virgins (Gen. 24.16; 29.17). The bride's potential as a good worker is only hinted at. In all three betrothal type-scenes the brides appear first as tending their fathers' herds. Though this element has often been interpreted as a bucolic detail in an idyllic picture, it may very well imply that in addition to her sexual merits, the bride in question will also turn into an important source of income for her husband.

There seems to be a direct correlation between the money paid for the bride and her prized qualities. Rebekah's good looks, intact hymen and good manners are rewarded by the precious gifts bestowed on her and her family by Abraham's servant. The text does not fail to register the impact these gifts produce on Laban, Rebekah's brother (Gen. 24.30). Assuming that the perceptive servant has noticed the impact the jewels have made on Rebekah's family, it is safe to believe that by describing the great wealth of Abraham, he alludes to the lucrative aspect of the proposal he offers the Nahor clan: 'The Lord has greatly blessed my master, and he has become great. He has given him flocks and herds, silver and gold, menservants and maidservants and camels and asses' (Gen. 24.35). Thus all appears to be perfect, Rebekah is a pretty object of desire and Isaac has ample means to purchase her.

---

25. Caleb is reported to have promised his daughter, Achsa, to the man who would capture Kiriath-Sepher (Josh. 15.16, Judg. 1.12). Saul gives Michal to David in return for 200 slain Philistines (1 Sam. 18.27).

Though equally veiled, the financial element appears in the second type-scene as well. Here, however, the means are not as ample, the groom finds it necessary to offer labor in exchange for the beautiful Rachel. As he puts it to Laban: 'I will serve you seven years for your younger daughter, Rachel' (Gen. 24.8). The references to the financial benefits of the marriage transaction are even more veiled in the third betrothal type-scene. Moses, having arrived in Egypt empty-handed, is fortunate to acquire both a livelihood as a shepherd and a respectable Egyptian wife. Like Jacob, Moses will return to Canaan a man of means and the master of a wife. In important ways, the characterization of the bride as passive, obedient and object-like serves the patriarchal interpretation of prospective wives as chattels.

What is most significant, however, is the decrease in the narrative attention given to the bride-figure, which complements the gradual decrease in the groom's enthusiasm about his prospective wife. While the betrothal pact between Isaac and Rebekah is carefully planned by Abraham, Jacob finds his mate as if by coincidence. The ceremonious speeches of Abraham's servant are replaced by Jacob's laconic expression of interest in Rachel, and by Moses' complete silence in regard to Zipporah. Whereas Jacob labors for 14 years in exchange for Rachel, Moses does not seem to expend any effort at all to procure his prospective wife. The gradual diminishment in the groom's (or groom's representative's) interest in his prospective wife complies with the growing conciseness of the betrothal scenes themselves. As prospective mates, it would seem that women do not and should not command too much attention.

Critical Affirmations of the Betrothal Type-scene

Some treatments of the biblical characterization of brides do not pause to point up the implicit universalization of the bridegroom's point of view. Rebekah is said to pass the test she is put to with 'flying colors'.[26] And yet the very notion that the woman must pass a test to prove herself worthy of the bridegroom is itself a patriarchal requirement. Indeed, why is the bridegroom not tested to see if he is adequate to the bride's expectations and desires?

Even when the 'otherness' of the prospective bride is acknowledged, it is taken as 'archetypal expressiveness', as a literary or stylistic con-

26. Sternberg, *The Poetics of Biblical Narrative*, p. 137.

figuration.[27] The symbolic function of the bride as a womb, a well, a source of wealth for the groom is taken for granted. Her role as an enabler and mediator is at times mystified and dignified by mythological interpretations of her role as enabler and mediator between the male hero and the world.[28] By construing the marginality of female characters as part of a broader narrative scheme, as part of an archetypal, universal frame of reference we risk endorsing and validating patriarchalism. The various strategies used by modern critics to 'explain' the art of the biblical narrative reinscribe ancient constructions of power relations between men and women by implicitly justifying as universal and eternal narrative modes produced by a male-centered imagination.

27. Alter, *The Art of the Biblical Narrative*, p. 52.
28. Williams, *Women Recounted*, pp. 46-47.

Chapter 5

THE BIBLICAL WIFE:
STRUCTURE AND SETTING IN CONJUGAL NARRATIVES

Biblical laws subordinate wives to their husbands. They prescribe the
wife's dependence on her husband, depriving her of economic independence and turning her into his economic asset and exclusive sexual
property.[1] Laws pertaining to betrothal and marriage, divorce, inheritance, vows, cultic and religious observances construct the wife as
chattel, along with a man's other wives, concubines, children, servants
and livestock. The interest of the husband is identified as the interest of
the entire household. What is permitted the husband is not tolerated for
the wife. A woman's sexuality belongs exclusively to her husband; a
wife's sexual contact with another man is considered one of the most
severe sins and is punished by death (Lev. 20.10; Deut. 22.22). A husband can subject his wife to a most humiliating and traumatic ordeal by
drinking 'curse bringing waters' (מים המרים) if there is evidence that
she had intercourse with another man, or if a 'spirit of jealousy passes
over him' (Num. 5.14, 30). This ordeal does not incur any penalty for
the husband if the 'curse bringing waters' prove the woman innocent
(Num. 5.11-31). According to biblical law, the husband could have
unlimited access to any number of unmarried women. No penalty is
recorded for a man who has sexual relations outside the framework of
marriage, as long as he does not intrude into another man's preserves.

---

1.   For a detailed study of Israelite marriage laws, see J. Pedersen, *Israel: Its
Life and Culture* (London: Oxford University Press, 1926), I, pp. 61-71; de Vaux,
Ancient Israel, I, pp. 24-40; Phyllis Bird, 'Images of Women', pp. 41-88. On
woman's status as her husband's property, see also Carolyn Pressler, 'Sexual Violence and Deuteronomic Law', in Brenner (ed.), *A Feminist Companion to Exodus
to Deuteronomy*, pp. 102-12. See 'The Subject of the Law', in Fewell and Gunn
(eds.), *Gender, Power, and Promise*, pp. 94-116. Brenner, *The Intercourse of
Knowledge*, pp. 110-35.

The laws stigmatize as adultery (נאף) only a married woman's sexual attachment to another man. A man, whether married or not, could by contrast engage in sexual relations with additional wives, concubines and prostitutes, and even rape an unattached virgin, as long as he took it upon himself to compensate the virgin's father.[2] That man would, however, be punished in various ways, including death, had he dallied with a married woman. It is thus safe to speculate that from a legal point of view a wife was perceived largely as a man's possession. There are no laws requiring a husband to consult with his first wife about taking a second one, or taking into account the point of view of the raped woman and her willingness to marry the man who assaulted her. Neither is the woman who is subjected by her husband to a public ordeal by water compensated in any way if found innocent of her husband's suspicion.

Biblical laws reveal a patriarchal perspective to the extent that they identify justice with a man's point of view. These laws construct the female body as her husband's possession. In this respect they dovetail with biblical narratives about adultery. Scholars usually agree that legal and narrative materials differ in their approach to women.[3] To what extent and how do biblical narratives resist or withstand the patriarchal ideology inspiring biblical law? To what extent and how do biblical narratives about marriage and conjugal relations strengthen or weaken the fundamental premises of patriarchal ideology?

In this chapter, I would like to examine the imprint of androcentric and patriarchal thinking on the biblical narrative. My argument is that

2.   According to Exod. 22.15-16, the rapist has an option not to marry the victim. According to Deut. 22.28-29, the rapist is not permitted to 'send away' (*šlḥ*) the victim for the rest of his life. Calum M. Carmichael perceives the Deuteronomistic law as protective of the woman involved. See Calum M. Carmichael, *Women, Law and the Genesis Tradition* (Edinburgh: Edinburgh University Press, 1979), pp. 33-42. For a different opinion, see Judith Ochshorn, *The Female Experience and the Nature of the Divine* (Bloomington: Indiana University Press, 1981), pp. 200-17. See also, especially, Bird, 'Images of Women', pp. 48-57. I disagree with the opinion that the source P, the Priestly Code which is concerned with laws presents women differently from the source J as Ilana Pardes argues. See her book, *Countertraditions in the Bible*, pp. 56-59.

3.   Carmichael's *Women, Law and the Genesis Traditions* argues that the biblical law writer, specifically, the Deuteronomist, was inspired by the stories of Genesis and other biblical stories and sought to provide solutions for legal questions about the status of women raised by these narratives.

the patriarchal double standard was not only legalized and perpetuated through biblical marriage laws, but also through conjugal narratives, namely narratives about husbands and wives. Plot construction, point of view, characterization, dialogue, denouement, recurrent motifs and progressive transformations of type-scenes will be here examined not as aesthetic structures, or literary conventions, but as patriarchal strategies.

Specifically, I will focus in this chapter on two major conjugal type-scenes, the adultery type-scene and the contest type-scene, although I shall make occasional digressions into other conjugal narratives for comparative purposes. The adultery type-scene featuring one wife and two husbands is a mirror image of the contest type-scene featuring two wives and one husband. In harmony with the legal stance on adultery, the adultery type-scene ends with the removal of one man and the unification of the wife with only one husband. In complementary congruence with the biblical stance of polygyny, the contest type-scene ends with the stabilization of the initially explosive relations between two wives and one husband. In both scenes, the patriarchal interest is shown to complement the monotheistic and national interest.

As we shall see, the justification of the male-dominated arrangements often combines the Bible's patriarchal ideology with its national and monotheistic ideology. Adultery, as we shall see, is not only a 'private' sin against a husband, but also a threat to the genealogical continuity of the Israelite nation. By contrast, the polygynous setup is shown to secure not only the interest of the husband but primarily the patrilineal interest, as God is always shown to side with the husband rather than the wife. In the contest type-scene, as we shall see, Yhwh encourages the victimized wife to return to the polygynous setup and, in harmony with the husband's interest, what He promises her is progeny, not redemption from an oppressive marriage. What follows is a closer examination first of the adultery type-scene and next of the contest type-scene.

The Adultery Type-Scene

What I define here as the adultery type-scene is a scene that presents a husband, a wife and a powerful king who either threatens to or actually succeeds in appropriating to himself another man's wife. The apparent victim in all the adultery type-scenes is the original husband, who is either redeemed or vindicated by Yhwh. The powerful king is either threatened by Yhwh or actually punished for his interest in the forbidden wife. The wife is ultimately united with only one lawful husband: she is either restored to her original husband or transferred to her new husband. The first adultery type-scene in Genesis presents Abram as the victim-husband, Sarai as the coveted wife and Pharaoh as the powerful king (Gen. 12.10-20). Severe drought in Canaan compels Abram to go down to Egypt. On the way, Abram asks Sarai, his beautiful wife, to present herself as his sister, for fear that the Egyptians will kill him. The reputation of Sarai's beauty indeed reaches Pharaoh and he takes Sarai to his palace. Subsequently, Yhwh inflicts great plagues on Pharaoh and his household. The king realizes he has committed a sin and, after rebuking Abram, restores his wife to him and sends him away with the rest of his possessions.

In the second scene only the identity of the king is changed: here it is Abimelech, the king of Gerar, who plays the role of contender for the beautiful Sarah, Abraham's wife (Gen. 20.1-18). Having been presented as Abraham's sister, Sarah is taken by Abimelech. The latter is subsequently rebuked by God, who proceeds to plague the king's wives with temporary barrenness. Abimelech hastens to return Sarah to Abraham, and although he chastises Abraham for misleading him, he nevertheless gives him money and gifts in compensation for his temporary loss.

In the third scene the identity of the king remains the same. It is once again Abimelech, the king of Gerar who plays the role of the potential adulterer, while the husband is Isaac and the wife Rebekah (Gen. 26.1-12). Isaac presents Rebekah as his sister, but when Abimelech notices the couple together, he realizes that Isaac has lied to him and chastises him for his lie. Isaac explains that he feared for his life, and Abimelech grants the couple full security in his kingdom.

The fourth adultery type-scene features David as the powerful king, Uriah as the victimized husband and Bathsheba as the coveted wife (2 Sam. 11–12). King David takes Bathsheba and has intercourse with her while Uriah is fighting in the battle against Ammon. When he learns that Bathsheba has conceived, he invites Uriah to Jerusalem and tries repeatedly to send the latter home. When Uriah refuses to go home, David orders Joab to send Uriah to the most dangerous battle, after which Uriah is killed and David proceeds to marry Uriah's wife, Bathsheba. David is subsequently sharply rebuked by Nathan the prophet and punished by Yhwh.

The Genesis adultery scenes have been identified by scholars as the wife–sister narratives.[4] To my mind, although the motif of presenting a wife as one's sister indeed appears in all three narratives, it is only one of the motifs that make up the story. It does not justify entitling all three narratives as wife–sister narratives only on the basis of this motif. It must be remembered that Abram/Abraham, and Isaac present their wives as sisters only as an excuse, as a deception by which they hope to save their lives. The motif of the wife–sister is compositionally part of the larger subject of adultery, or rather adultery which is narrowly avoided through divine intervention. Much has been written about these narratives in an effort to both explain the dubious conduct of the husband-figures in our type-scene as well as in order to account for the repeated appearance of the same cluster of motifs and plot structure.[5] The problems involved in our type-scene address not only the husband's cowardice, deceptiveness, willingness to sacrifice his wife for his own security and the allusions to incest, but also the failure of God to censure the husbands' conduct. For God in all these scenes appears to side unequivocally with the husband, although the latter's conduct is not quite up to par with one's expectation of a man singled out by God for preferential treatment.[6]

4.   For a survey of traditional scholarship on this story, see Exum, 'Who's Afraid of the "Endangered Ancestress?" ', *Fragmented Women*, pp. 148-69. None of the traditional modern discussions discuss the wife's perspective and her own responses to the unfolding events. Examples include: James G. Williams in *Women Recounted*, pp. 46-47; see also Culley, *Studies in the Structure of Hebrew Narrative*, pp. 34-41.

5.   E.A. Speiser suggests that the recurrent motif of the wife-sister alludes to the ancient Hurrian institution of a wife who was also invested with the status of a sister. What the Genesis narratives refer to, according to this explanation, is not an incestual marriage with one's sister or half-sister, but rather to a historical-social institution. See E.A. Speiser, 'The Wife-Sister Motif in the Patriarchal Narratives', in Alexander Altmann (ed.), *Biblical and Other Studies* (Cambridge, MA: Harvard University Press, 1963), pp. 15-28. See also Sarna, *Understanding Genesis*, pp. 102-104. Speiser explains that the various versions correspond to different sources and different authors. But as Robert C. Culley remarks, these explanations do not clarify why the different versions of the story were included in the final edition of the text. See Culley's *Studies in the Structure of Hebrew Narrative*, pp. 40-41.

6.   Taking issue with the critical evaluations of the husband's questionable conduct in relation to his wife, Robert Polzin argues that all the versions, including the first one (Gen. 12), are equally 'sensitive to ethical issues' ('The Ancestress of Israel in Danger', *Semeia* 3 [1975], pp. 81-98 [84]). Polzin bases his argument on the fact that Abram receives wealth but not progeny following the adulterous affair

In part at least, the repeated versions of the story can be explained as the results of an apologetic rewriting.[7] It should be noted that only the first scene alludes to the fact that the monarch has actually committed adultery with the wife, although even here the text remains rather ambiguous. The phrase 'and the woman was taken to the house of Pharaoh' (Gen. 12.15) is a rather euphemistic description of actual adultery. Similarly the verse: 'And Yhwh plagued Pharaoh and his house with great plagues because of Sarai, Abram's wife' (v. 17), does not clarify precisely what happened to 'Sarai, Abram's wife'. Nevertheless the scene does allude to the possibility that actual adultery took place. The second scene, by contrast, quite emphatically precludes the possibility. Although the text admits that 'Abimelech, king of Gerar, sent, and took Sarah' (Gen. 20.2), it makes it clear that 'Abimelech had not come near her' (Gen. 20.4). In the third scene, the wife is not even taken into the monarch's house. Isaac, like Abram/Abraham claims that his wife is his sister (Gen. 26.7), but this does not lead to the separation of husband and wife. Abimelech finds out that Isaac lied about his wife. Looking out of his window, he sees 'Isaac playing with Rebekah his wife' (Gen. 26.8).

What we are observing then is a progressive shift from a scene in which adultery is an implied possibility to a scene where husband and wife remain united despite a potential threat to their marriage. Each

of Sarai and Pharaoh, whereas he receives both when actual adultery is prevented (Gen. 20). The problem with this argument is that when adultery is prevented in the second version, it is not Abraham who prevents it from taking place, but God. It is therefore unclear why Abraham should be rewarded with both wealth and progeny for a sin he could have committed by encouraging his wife to commit adultery, were it not for the propitious intervention of God. In all three versions, the husband is shown to be fully prepared to give his wife up for adultery, and the ethical problem this raises is not solved but further exacerbated by the reward he receives, both in the form of wealth and progeny. For a different reading of Abram's role in Gen. 12, a reading that rejects his interpretation as a sympathetic victim, see Fokkelien van Dijk-Hemmes, 'Sarai's Exile: A Gender-Motivated Reading of Genesis 12.10–13.2', in Brenner (ed.), *A Feminist Companion to Genesis*, pp. 222-34.

7. Cheryl Exum offers a psychoanalytic approach to the Genesis narrative. According to Exum the repetition reveals a desire for a beautiful woman and fear of the death she may cause. See *Fragmented Women*, pp. 148-69. On David's relations with his wives, see also Shulamit Valler, 'King David and "his" Women: Biblical Stories and Talmudic Discussions', in Brenner (ed.), *A Feminist Companion to Samuel and Kings*, pp. 129-42.

subsequent scene denies with greater vehemence the mere possibility that the husband should allow his wife to be taken away from him by another man. But it is also possible that the repeated appearance of the story is a didactic strategy, not only an apologetic ploy. The threefold repetition of the adultery scene in Genesis implies among other things that polyandry, a wife's sharing more than one husband, is absolutely unacceptable as a marital arrangement. It makes it clear that the reverse of polygyny is a grave sin; it is the unpardonable sin of adultery. The presentation of God as an interested party in the adultery scenes makes the patriarchal message loud and clear. God is shown to intervene in all adultery scenes in Genesis as well as in 2 Samuel, which dramatizes the graveness of the issue. The graveness of the sin is also dramatized by its potential national repercussions. Short of God's intervention on behalf of the husband, Sarai/Sarah and Rebekah could have conceived and given birth to another man's offspring. This would have jeopardized the 'integrity' and 'purity' of the national origins of Israel, as the identity of the fathers of the nation would not be as easily ascertainable.

The structure of the adultery type-scene hinges to a large extent on the patriarchal concept of adultery and on the didactic opprobrium which it implies. The fact that the adulterer is a powerful monarch indicates that a husband's authority over his wife could only be compromised *in extremis*, namely, when a powerful rival encroaches on her preserves. By casting the adulterer in the role of a monarch the scene explains how adultery could have taken place at all. It takes a gross disparity in power relations between two men to undermine the 'normal' power relations between husband and wife. In the Genesis scenes, the husband's vulnerability is increased by his temporary sojourn in the land of the foreign monarch. Abram/Abraham and Isaac find themselves in a territory controlled by powerful monarchs, and in many ways they are the subjects of Pharaoh and Abimelech, just as Uriah is King David's subject. It is the husband's vulnerability that leads to the destabilization of the ideal order, namely, one in which the husband's control over his wife is uncompromised by outside intervention. The destabilization of the ideal patriarchal order is dramatized in the adultery scenes through a series of objective correlatives, beginning with drought in the land of Canaan (Gen. 12.10; 26.1) and ending with a political war against the Ammonites (2 Sam. 11.1). The reinstitution of the proper conjugal relationship, namely the wife's re-enclosure within the control of her proper husband, be he her original partner or a new one, is accompanied by such objective correlatives as increased wealth (Gen. 20.14-16; 26.12-14), and military victory (2 Sam. 12.27-31). Thus the literary structure of the adultery scenes confirms the patriarchal notion that uxorial monogamy is the proper and natural order, and that any deviation from this order might result in serious consequences.

Although the adultery type-scene dramatizes the destabilization of the patriarchal marriage institution, it never questions the latter's underlying premises. It is never doubted that the wife should in fact belong exclusively to her husband. The husband who is shown to part with his wife does it under extreme circumstances. Abram/Abraham and Isaac are willing to give up their control over their wives out of fear for their lives, while Uriah is not so much as aware of his wife's adultery. The idea that other societies may be less stringent about uxorial monogamy is proven to be a wrong hypothesis on the part of the husband. Having discovered the true identity of Sarai, Pharaoh rebukes Abram thus: 'What did you do to me? Why did you not tell me that she was your wife? Why did you say she is my sister so that I took her to be my wife?' (Gen. 12.18-19). Abimelech, the king of Gerar, also appears to agree that uxorial polygamy, namely adultery, is a grave sin: 'Then Abimelech called Abraham and said to him: "What did you do to us? And how have I sinned against you that you have brought on me and my kingdom a great sin? You have done to me deeds that must not be done"' (Gen. 20.9). But if Pharaoh's and Abimelech's protests may be construed as fearful reactions to God, rather than sincere opinions, the third scene makes it clear that the foreign monarch genuinely believes that adultery is an odious sin, for Abimelech here rebukes Isaac before God had a chance to intervene: 'And Abimelech said: "What did you do to us? One of the people might have easily lain with your wife, and you would have brought guilt on us"' (Gen. 26.10). When David commits adultery he knows he is sinning. His desperate attempt to cover up the deed by sending Uriah to sleep with Bathsheba is indicative of his fear. When confronted by Nathan the prophet, he confesses: 'And David said to Nathan: "I have sinned against Yhwh"' (2 Sam. 12.13).

The adultery type-scene thus stresses that adultery, the act of taking a wife from her husband, is agreed by all parties to be a sin. Both the husband and the monarch confirm through speech and behavior the fundamental objectionability of adultery. Both husband and monarch find the notion of one man's sexual access to another's wife repellent, and what leads both of them to abrogate this principle are external constraints, not a volitional rebellion against the principle itself. It is particularly noteworthy that the foreign monarchs agree with this principle, thus creating the impression that adultery as defined in the Bible is regarded as a grave sin. The husband in the Genesis type-scene is shown to be wrong in surmising that a foreign society may have different notions about adultery. The explicit verbal admission on the part of all monarchs in the adultery scenes that their potential or actual desire to share another man's wife is sinful, also implies that *no one*, not even a powerful monarch, can permit himself to commit adultery. The repeated intervention of God on behalf of the husband and the involvement in the act of key national figures lend additional forcefulness to this patriarchal message.

The 'real' victim in the adultery type-scene is the husband. His political weakness and vulnerability is highlighted by the immense power of his rival, the monarch. The husband is a foreigner in his rival's country, Abram in Egypt, Abraham and Isaac in Gerar and Uriah the Hittite in Judea. The husband's political weakness explains why he could not repel his rival's interest in his wife. It also explains why nothing short of divine intervention could set things aright, for although the monarchs may agree that adultery is sinful, their conviction may not stop them from trying to abuse their power. All the Genesis scenes make it clear that the husband hides his conjugal relationship with his wife out of fear. Yet, a closer examination reveals that each subsequent scene presents the husband in a slightly more positive light.

The first scene permits Abram to explain his motives for lying about his wife in his speech to Sarai: 'Now, I know that you are a beautiful woman. And if the Egyptians see you they will say, "this is his wife" and they will kill me and let you live' (Gen. 12.11-12). The second adultery type-scene, however, invests more effort in justifying the husband's conduct. Whereas the previous scene quotes him as saying he fears for his life, this scene links his fear for his life with a distrust of a place where the fear of God is not known. Thus Abraham is quoted as saying to Abimelech: 'Because I thought: "Surely, there is no fear of God in this place and they will kill me because of my wife" ' (Gen. 20.11). Whereas the first scene implies that Abram tells an outright lie about his fraternal relationship to her, the second scene mitigates this impression by putting the following words in Abraham's mouth: 'And moreover she is indeed my sister, but not my mother's daughter, and so she became my wife' (Gen. 20.12). This implies that Abraham told only half a lie concerning Sarah's identity. In the third scene the husband spreads the deceptive rumor about his wife, only in reaction to the queries of the local inhabitants about his wife: 'And the men of the place asked him about his wife; and he said, "She is my sister," for he feared to say "My wife," lest the men of the place should kill me for Rebekah, for she is very good-looking" ' (Gen. 26.7). Unlike Abram-Abraham, Isaac lies about Rebekah, not before but after the inhabitants' interest in his wife becomes evident. In addition, his fear is given additional credence by presenting it as part of the evaluation of the omniscient narrator. Whereas Abram claims he fears for his life in his speech to Sarai, and while Abraham claims the same in his explanation to Abimelech, in the case of Isaac, it is not the protagonist himself but the narrator who affirms that 'he feared to say "My wife"'. This authorial presentation implies that Isaac's fear was truly his motive for lying. Isaac's motive is presented from an authorial rather than figural point of view, which gives it greater credibility. In addition, the third scene allows Isaac to explain himself once again in his speech to Abimelech: 'Because I said: "Lest I die because of her" ' (Gen. 26.9).

The fourth adultery scene, however, is the most sympathetic in its treatment of the husband. Here the husband, Uriah, neither lies nor compromises his integrity in any other way. Unlike his predecessors he does not collaborate in any way in the adulterous act, which is committed in his absence and unknown to him. Uriah is the epitome of the noble, innocent husband, whose courage and uprightness contribute to his victimization.

If the husband in the adultery type-scene is the victim, the monarch is the victimizer. Yet the Genesis scenes do not portray the monarch as an outright villain. His actions are not only explained but to some extent justified. He is shown to act out of ignorance rather than malice. It is implied that he takes another's wife because he is misinformed about her uxorial status. Not only the husband but the monarch too is given a chance to express his thoughts and feelings in rather detailed speeches. The monarch is given an opportunity to express his point of view in the protest he lodges with the husband. Pharaoh says to Abram: 'What did you do to me? Why did you tell me that she was your sister?' (Gen. 12.18). The formula 'What did you do to me?' reappears in the outraged castigation of Abimelech, king of Gerar, and is addressed to Abraham (Gen. 20.9-10) and to Isaac (Gen. 26.10). Despite the monarch's role as actual or potential adulterer, he does not emerge as a villain. The fact is that, like the husband, he is shown to be misguided and ignorant rather than evil. While the husband is ignorant about the laws and customs of the indigenous population of the foreign land, the foreign king is shown to mishandle the situation because he is unaware of the wife's true identity.

The last adultery scene is less sympathetic toward the king; here the circumstances are less extenuating.[8] The power relations between husband and monarch reveal an unambiguous imbalance. Uriah is not merely a powerless man sojourning in a foreign land, but the king's subject and one of his faithful fighters. The text makes it clear that David does not mistake Bathsheba for an unmarried woman, but rather sends for her after being informed that she is Uriah's wife (2 Sam. 11.3). While the Genesis adultery scenes describe for the most part potential adultery acts, here it is made patently clear that adultery takes place (2 Sam. 11.4). Whereas in the Genesis scenes, the husband is partly responsible for the problem, having deceived the monarch about his wife's identity, here the husband is shown to be not only completely innocent, but also noble, fiercely loyal to the king and self-sacrificing. When called up from the front by David, who encourages him to 'go down' to his house 'and wash' his 'feet' (v. 8), Uriah prefers to spend the night 'at the door of the king's house with all the servants of his lord' (v. 9). When the deceptive and pusillanimous David tries to send Uriah to the wife he himself impregnated, Uriah's patriotic response is 'The Ark and Israel and Judah dwell in booths; and my lord Joab and the servants of my lord are camping in the open field; shall I then go to my house, to eat and to drink, and to lie with my wife?' (2 Sam. 11.11).[9]

In the Genesis scenes, it is the husband who deceives the monarch,

8.   For a reading of David's affair with Bathsheba as a story of rape, see J. Cheryl Exum, 'Raped by the Pen', in *Fragmented Women*, pp. 170-201. Exum stresses the suppression of Bathsheba's point of view and sees it as literary rape in addition to the adulterous rape she suggests transpired between David and Bathsheba.

9.   It has been suggested that the text calls for more than one interpretation of Uriah's refusal to go down and see Bathsheba when he is called up from the battlefield to Jerusalem on David's orders. Since the text does not clarify whether or not Uriah knows of the king's affair with Bathsheba, his response to the king can be taken either as an expression of unmitigated loyalty, or as an ironic allusion to the king's actions and intentions. See Menakhem Peri and Meir Sternberg, 'The King Through Ironic Eyes', *Hasifrut* 1 (1968), pp. 263-92 (Hebrew).

whereas here it is the monarch who deceives the husband, by trying unsuccessfully to cover up the truth about his adulterous affair. David's treacherousness emerges as all the more reprehensible when juxtaposed with Uriah's loyalty, innocence and magnanimity, which ultimately lead to his murder by proxy, as orchestrated by the exasperated David (vv. 14-17). The last adultery scene leaves no doubt as to the husband's innocence and victimization by the monarch.

Nevertheless, even here, although the monarch's actions are far from justified, neither are they completely arbitrary. David is not shown to take another man's wife out of spite, by availing himself of what is inaccessible to the common man, nor is he shown as breaching the laws against adultery. Although the narrative does not justify David's actions, it nevertheless attempts to explain them. It does not content itself with a summary report indicating that David takes another man's wife. Rather it dramatizes in detail the scene which has caused the king to commit the crime: 'It happened, late one afternoon when David arose from his bed and was walking upon the roof of the king's house, that he saw from the roof a woman bathing; and the woman was very beautiful' (2 Sam. 11.2). The scene uses David's perceptual and psychological point of view.[10] Not only does it follow David's gaze, detailing what he sees, but it also describes David's mood. Referring to the protagonist as 'David' rather than 'the king', the scene reveals him as an ordinary and fallible man, vulnerable as any man would be to a woman's temptations.[11] The exposition to the scene clarifies that both the general state of affairs and the particular condition in which David was found were ripe for a private entanglement with a woman. For one thing, David is unpreoccupied with the ongoing war against the Ammonites since Joab, his able officer, is in charge of the military situation, and as his men

10. 'Perceptual point of view' refers here to one's visual perception, 'psychological point of view' refers to intellectual and emotional perception of the character involved. On point of view in biblical narrative, see Berlin, *Poetics and Interpretation of Biblical Narrative*, pp. 43-82. Berlin offers a slightly different definition of the above terms. See also Meir Sternberg, 'The Truth vs. All the Truth: The Rendering of Inner Life in Biblical Narrative', *Hasifrut* 29 (1979), pp. 110-46 (Hebrew).

11. David is referred to as 'king' when Uriah's point of view is introduced: 'And Uriah went out of the king's house, and there followed him a present from the king' (v. 8). This is also the case in the context of Joab's message (v. 20). On the function of naming as indicator of point of view in the biblical narrative, see Berlin, *Poetics and Interpretation of Biblical Narrative*, pp. 59-61.

seem to reap victory: 'and they ravaged the Ammonites and besieged Rabbah' (2 Sam. 11.1).[12]

After a brief siesta, 'David arose from his couch and was walking upon the roof of the king's house' (v. 2). The text follows the king's gaze as his eyes encounter what appears to be an unexpected and irresistible sight. The woman he sees is not only naked, but in the process of bathing herself. Not only is the object of desire fully exposed, her bathing motions are probably as seductive as her nakedness as she makes herself cleaner and even more appealing to our voyeuristic protagonist. The text notes that the woman was not only good-looking, but 'very beautiful'. This compact description makes it amply clear how great was David's temptation, and how difficult it must have been for him to overcome his passion. The purposeful succession of actions following this description ('and David sent and inquired', 'David sent messengers and took her') indicates that David is driven by passion, not by reasoned malicious calculation. This does not mean that the story vindicates but rather that it attempts to explain David's action, by detailing his perceptual and psychological point of view.

As in the Genesis adultery scenes, both victimizer and victim, that is monarch and husband, are allowed to express their point of view, and the actions of both are fully motivated. It is true that the adulterer in the final scene emerges as more culpable than his predecessors, just as the husband emerges as unambiguously innocent and victimized, unlike his counterparts in the Genesis scenes. Yet the husband's role as victim and the adulterer's as victimizer remain the same in all adultery scenes. The conflictual situation, positing a defenseless but 'right' husband over against a politically powerful but 'wrong' adulterer, remains unchanged, and so does the plot progression featuring the (potential or actual) act of adultery as the complicating moment, and the punishment of the adulterer (and in Genesis the compensation to the husband) as the resolution of the problem. The underlying definition of adultery as one man's act of stealing another man's wife also remains constant throughout the type-scene, as in all cases, the adulterer is shown to 'take' (לקח) the husband's wife. By dramatizing God's intervention in the adultery

12. See Peri and Sternberg, 'The King through Ironic Eyes', pp. 269-71. See also their 'Caution: A Literary Text! Problems in the Poetics and Interpretation of Biblical Narrative', *Hasifrut* 2 (1970), pp. 608-63 (Hebrew). See also Boaz Arpali, 'Caution: A Biblical Story! Comments on the Story of David and Bathsheba and on the Problems of Biblical Narrative', *Hasifrut* 2 (1970), pp. 580-97 (Hebrew).

type-scene, the message is conveyed that this act is a severe crime. The adulterer's punishment by God and his characterization as the 'wrong' party in the conflict give a moral legitimation to the legal terms of the adultery laws. The conflictual situation pitting husband against adulterer is consistent with the underlying principles of the biblical adultery laws, which define the criminality of the act of adultery not in sexual terms, but in terms of property rights. The adulterer is in the wrong not because he gains carnal knowledge of a woman but because he avails himself of another man's property.

By contrast, scenes portraying a woman taking a married husband away from another woman do not involve divine intervention in the wake of which the former is punished and the latter rewarded. The fact is that no scene in the Bible deals with an event or a situation featuring a woman taking or threatening to take another woman's husband. Such scenes would lack ideological meaning. After all, what would be the didactic value of such a scene? Given the legal liberty of any man to avail himself of several women, a scene showing women contending for a single man would be void of dramatic tension. There would be no conflict between fact and aspiration, between law and action, because only a male's aspiration and action have meaning. A narrative recording the point of view of an abandoned wife, or of two women contending for the same man, would be lacking in both plausibility and emotional charge. For one thing, in an androcentric context woman is not perceived as capable of such emotions. The portrayal of such emotions would be not only implausible but worthless, as the existence of such emotions would not have any moral or theological meaning to justify their literary inscription.[13] From a patriarchal perspective, a narrative about a husband's adulterous affair with a strange woman would be meaningless and unedifying, whereas a wife's adulterous affair with a strange man is an incident worth telling and repeating. It is the encroachment of one man upon the preserves of another that endows the adultery type-scene with its moral pathos. At work is not a religious

---

13. In her article about the relationship between ideology and literary form, Nancy K. Miller points out: 'If no maxim is available to account for a particular piece of behavior, that behavior is read as unmotivated and unconvincing'. See 'Emphasis Added: Plots and Plausibilities in Women's Fiction', *PMLA* 96 (1981), pp. 36-47 (36). For a detailed discussion of literary conventions and cultural-ideological consensus, see Elizabeth Ermarth, 'Fictional Consensus and Female Casualties', in Heilbrun and Higonnet (eds.), *The Representation of Women in Fiction*, pp. 1-18.

principle, a 'human' or 'universal' moral code, nor the eternal impulses of jealousy or love, but rather a patriarchal legal code, which perceives a wife as her husband's property.[14] This becomes clear when we consider the fact that none of the adultery scenes features a situation where the husband is illicitly claimed by another woman. As we shall see, when two women are shown to contend for the same man, as for example in the contest type-scene, they do not fight for an exclusive right over the man but for the right to give him male offspring. Accordingly, God does not intervene to restore a man to his lawful wife but rather to help his barren wife conceive. Neither woman in the contest type-scene is 'right' or 'wrong', and neither is punished or rewarded for having sexual access to another woman's husband. What determines the plot structure as well as the characterization in the adultery type-scene is the patriarchal ideology that defines a wife as her husband's property. This is particularly salient in the scene's portrayal of the wife.

Although the wife is the cause of the central conflict in the adultery type-scene, her point of view is consistently suppressed. Whereas both the husband and the adulterer are endowed with a unique point of view, revealed through the narrator's interpolations or in the characters' dialogues or actions, the wife in the adultery type-scene lacks a point of view of her own, both in the perceptual and the psychological sense. We are not told what she feels or thinks before, during and after her encounter with the adulterer. Her transference from her husband to the adulterer and back is reported through the male participants' viewpoints

14. Robert Briffault notes that sexual jealousy and the notion of the husband's exclusive sexual rights over his wife have evolved from economic arrangements in hunting societies. His monumental study on marriage institutions in primitive societies challenges the idea that male jealousy or the need to possess a woman exclusively stems from a primordial 'male instinct'. As he points out: 'Claims to exclusive sexual possessions have developed, and developed somewhat tardily, in relation to the consolidation of the economic association between sexual partners, and jealousy throughout the more uncultured races has no reference to exclusive sexual possession, but precisely to the economic loss resulting from the dissolution of the association by desertion or abduction.' See Robert Briffault, *The Mothers: A Study of the Origins of Sentiments and Institutions* (3 vols.; New York: Macmillian, 1927), I, p. 608. On the relationship between economic developments in ancient society and the institution of marriage, see also Frederick Engels, *The Origin of the Family, Private Property and the State* (ed. and introduction Eleanor Burke Leacock; New York: International Publishers, 1972). On the institution of motherhood, see Rich, *Of Woman Born*. See also Fuchs, 'The Characterization of Mothers', pp. 117-19.

as they perform the roles of, respectively, dispatcher and recipient. In the first scene Abram is allocated three verses to voice his anxieties, concerns and reasons for presenting Sarai as his sister (Gen. 12.11-13), whereas Sarai remains a mute addressee.

> And then when he came near to entering Egypt, he said to Sarai his wife: 'Now I know that you are a beautiful woman. And so if the Egyptians see you, they will say, "This is his wife", and they will kill me and let you live. Please say that you are my sister so it may be well with me thanks to you, and I may live because of you' (Gen. 12.11-13).

The progression of the plot suggests that Sarai follows her husband's request, but it gives no indication as to her wishes or fears. It is not clear whether Sarai obeys her husband willingly or resentfully. Neither is there any information about her experiences at Pharaoh's house. Whereas the monarch is allowed two verses in which to vent his frustrations, prove his innocence, protest, complain and recriminate against Abram, Sarai is not allowed a single word through which to express her frustration with or disappointment at her husband, her fear of the king, her humiliation when added to his harem, or her relief once returned to her husband. The text is not interested in Sarai's psychological point of view, or in her verbal utterances. Lacking a voice of her own, she is presented as Abram's addressee as he asks her to cooperate with him in his attempt to save his life. But Sarai's role as Abram's addressee reveals very little about her own motivations. What it does instead is allude to her husband's sense of vulnerability and defenselessness, which inspire him to opt for deception as a means for survival.

In the second scene, Sarah appears as Abimelech's addressee. Once again, however, the speech reveals more about the speaker than about the party spoken to. Abimelech informs Sarah that he has given Abraham a large sum of money to clear himself of blame and to compensate the couple 'And to Sarah he said: "Here I gave your brother a thousand pieces of silver, here this is for you a compensation and before all you are righted" ' (Gen. 20.16). The king reveals himself as an innocent character, if not a righteous one. In fact, all of Abimelech's dialogues in the scene contribute to his exoneration and exculpation, just as Abraham's dialogues justify *his* actions. Sarah's silence as well as her role as addressee do not add much to her characterization or to the explanation of her point of view.[15]

---

15. In his dialogue with God, Abimelech quotes Sarah as confirming Abraham's

In the third adultery scenes, the wife does not even appear as a mute interlocutor. Neither Isaac nor Abimelech addresses Rebekah, who seems to be unaware of Isaac's deception. Unlike the first matriarch she is neither consulted nor informed of the plot involving her. Her status as Isaac's wife is clarified in the interchange between Isaac and Abimelech (Gen. 26.9-11).

Unlike the last adultery scene in Genesis, comprising in all six verses, the adultery scene in 2 Samuel, taking up 27 verses, is much more detailed, especially in its presentation of David's and Uriah's dialogues. While it is true that Uriah's dialogues are ambiguous, leaving room for disparate interpretations, and while the informational gaps in the narrative may invite the reader to reconstruct them as an ironic critique of King David's point of view, the text nevertheless uses the participants' words as reflectors of their psychological and moral perspectives, in a highly subtle and suggestive manner.[16] What the text fails to allude to, even circuitously, is Bathsheba's point of view.[17] It is not known what she feels when summoned by David, whether or not she attempts to object to the king's intentions, what is her part in the king's decision to persuade Uriah to join her, what she feels once Uriah appears in Jerusalem and refuses to come down to his house and see her, how she reacts to Uriah's death, how she reacts to her son's death, and what her attitude is to David who marries her after the son's death. The only words Bathsheba is allowed to utter throughout the entire scene are informative and factual, they reveal nothing about her feelings or motiva-

lie: 'Did he not himself say to me: "She is my sister"? And she, even she herself said: "He is my brother." In the integrity of my heart and the innocence of my hands I have done this' (Gen. 20.5). Although it is the only instance in the Genesis adultery scenes of a recording of the wife's words, this is but the exception that proves the rule. For one thing, Sarah's alleged two words are reported by Abimelech, not by the narrator, which brings into question their authoritativeness, or credibility. Secondly, even if they are to be believed, these words do not add anything to the illumination of the matriarch's point of view, she who is here presented as a deceiver without offering her the opportunity to justify herself. It should be noted that Sarah is presented as a liar in the annunciation scene as well (Gen. 18.15).

16. See Peri and Sternberg, 'The King' (n. 5) and 'Caution: A Literary Text!'.

17. Whereas Peri and Sternberg consider at great length information and evaluative gaps concerning David's thoughts about Uriah, Joab's thoughts about David, the messenger's thoughts about Joab and David, and Uriah's thoughts about David and Bathsheba, they do not consider the paucity of information about Bathsheba's thoughts. See Boaz Arpali, 'Caution, A Biblical Story!' (p. 590 n. 11).

tions: 'And the woman conceived; and she sent and told David and said: "I am pregnant" ' (2 Sam. 11.5). These are the only words (*hārâ 'ānokî*) she is allotted throughout the scene. These words move the plot forward rather than revealing Bathsheba's character or point of view. Bathsheba is the only wife in the biblical adultery scenes allowed to use dialogue, but even this minimal verbal expression conveys nothing about her point of view, character or inner life.

Dialogue in the biblical narrative, as in all narratives, serves as an effective means of indirect characterization and one of the most common techniques of representing a perceptual, psychological or ideological point of view.[18] From this perspective the biblical narrative behaves like most literary narratives. Yet, in addition to its function as a literary device, dialogue in the Bible is also symbolic of power. God is said to have created the world through words: the human capacity to use words entails an ability to share in this divine faculty.[19] Speech signifies power. By naming different creatures, including his wife, Adam is shown to assert his authority over the rest of creation (Gen. 2.19-20, 23). The use of dialogue in the biblical narrative indicates a certain hierarchy of significance and power, with reporting speech (a speech act that narrates an event) taking precedence over reported speech (a speech act quoted in another's speech).[20] The omission of the wife's speech in the adultery type-scene not only avoids an opportunity to characterize her but also reflects her relative powerlessness in this context. The wife's silence indicates that she has neither power nor authority vis-à-vis the men who contend for her ownership. Her point of view is irrelevant in the context of marital relations. By eliminating her words, the type-scene indicates that the wife herself is of marginal significance in the framework of a story about proper and improper conjugal relations. The orchestration of dialogue in the adultery type-scene reflects not only a male perceptual and psychological point of view, but also a patriarchal ideology. Right and wrong in the context of marriage is to be arbitrated by men and for men.

The wife's silence in the adultery type-scene is analogous to the bride's silence in the betrothal type-scene. As we have observed, the

18. On the function of dialogue in the biblical narrative, see Shimon Bar-Efrat, *The Art of the Biblical Story* (Tel Aviv: Sifriat Poalim, 1979), pp. 88-99; Berlin, *Poetics and Interpretation of Biblical Narrative*, pp. 33-42.

19. Alter, *The Art of Biblical Narrative*, p. 182.

20. Williams, *Women Recounted*, pp. 38-39.

bride is given the privilege of speech in the presence of her groom's servant. She becomes mute as soon as her future husband enters the scene. By manipulating dialogue in scenes involving husbands and wives, the biblical narrative establishes a gender-related, power-based and hierarchical propriety. By eliminating the wife's speech, the biblical narrative virtually nullifies the wife's independent point of view. For the most part she is presented not as an autonomous being but as her husband's adjunct.

Naming in the adultery type-scene is yet another indicator of the underlying perception of the wife-figure as her husband's adjunct. The recurrent reference to the wife not through her proper name, but through her relationship to her husband reveals the point of view of the participants and especially of the narrator. In the first adultery scene, for example, Sarai's name is always qualified by the apposition 'Abram's wife' (Gen. 12.17) or by the possessives 'his wife' (v. 11) and 'your wife' (vv. 18-19). Otherwise she is referred to as 'the woman' or 'the wife', designated by the same Hebrew word אשה (vv. 14-15). With few exceptions, this is also the case in the second adultery scene in regard to Sarah's name (Gen. 20.2, 3, 7, 11-12, 14) and in the third scene involving Rebekah (Gen. 26.7, 9-11).[21]

In the fourth scene, the wife is referred to as 'the woman' or 'Uriah's wife' (2 Sam. 11.2-3, 5, 11, 26). The name Bathsheba occurs only once in the scene (v. 3), as David's messengers identify the mysterious bathing nymph for the enchanted king. The messengers identify Bathsheba as 'Eliam's daughter the wife of Uriah the Hittite'. Establishing

---

21. The rare references to the wife by name are never made by God or by her husband. The second adultery scene uses Sarah's proper name in conjunction with Abimelech's address. This use serves as an indicator of Abimelech's attitude toward Sarah. For example, when he first sends for Sarah, he does not yet realize that she is Abraham's wife. The use of Sarah's private name (Gen. 20.2) is indicative of Abimelech's ignorance of Sarah's conjugal status. The second time Sarah's name appears in the context of Abimelech's address occurs after it becomes clear to the monarch that she is Abraham's wife (Gen. 20.16). The narrator's use of Sarah's proper name and Abimelech's reference as Abraham as Sarah's 'brother' seem to imply that the ruler refuses to accept the truth about Sarah's marital status. At the same time, however, it is also possible to read these references to 'Sarah' and her 'brother' as an ironic evocation on the part of the deceived monarch of the couple's original self-presentation. This ironic usage enables Abimelech to express his criticism of the couple's behavior while making conciliatory gestures intended to compensate them for the discomfort he has inadvertently caused them.

Bathsheba's conjugal relationship with Uriah is essential for the proper understanding of the plot and the proper evaluation of David actions. After all, what incriminates David is not merely his sexual interest in a woman, but in *another man's* woman. The use of the possessive suffix of 'wife' in the last scene, as well as in the adultery type-scene in general, indicates the wife's status as her husband's property, and consequently serves as a constant reminder of the impropriety of the actions of the monarch who attempts to possess another man's property. The scene does not treat the wife as a character, but uses her as the means whereby the sin of adultery is shown to be committed. The wife's point of view is irrelevant to the adultery type-scene. It would introduce an unnecessary digression from the main course of events and from the center of attention, which is the actions of the men involved. The omission of the wife's speech and the repeated references to her as her husband's wife are necessary in order to maintain her status as the *means* of the calamity and as the *cause* of the sin of adultery.

The wife's actions in addition to her silence further reinforce her status as a non-subject. At best she is an agent whose will is not to be distinguished from the volitional motives ascribed to the other characters. The wife in the adultery scenes is never shown to act on her own initiative or wishes, but on the desires of either her husband or the monarch. Just as Sarai/Sarah obeys unhesitatingly her husband's plan, so does Bathsheba follow the orders of King David.[22] The wife functions as the indirect or direct object of the male participants' actions, not as a subject, or what we might refer to as a full-fledged character.[23] The first two scenes present the wife as both an indirect object—as she is spoken to by her husband (Gen. 12.11-13), and a direct object—as she is taken by the monarch to his house (Gen. 12.15; 20.2). The two later scenes

22. Although Bathsheba, like her counterparts in the first two adultery scenes, is said to be taken by the monarch ('And David sent messengers and took her'), hers is the only case in which an active verb is used, indicating an ever-so-limited extent of independence. Yet this serves as an implicit incrimination of Bathsheba. The verse describing the king's actions goes on to say: 'and she came to him, and he lay with her' (2 Sam. 11.4). The verb 'to come', attached to the married woman, may imply a hint of willingness, even eagerness on the part of Bathsheba to do the king's bidding. See also Arpali, 'Caution! A Biblical Story', p. 590.

23. This definition of characters as subjects versus objects is inspired by Tzvetan Todorov's application of grammatical categories to narrative. See 'The Grammar of Narrative', in *The Poetics of Prose* (trans. Richard Howard; Ithaca, NY: Cornell University Press, 1977), pp. 108-19.

present the wife as a direct object only. Rebekah functions simultaneously as the object of the monarch's gaze and of her husband's erotic
attention: 'and Abimelech looked out of the window and saw, and
behold, Isaac was playing with Rebekah his wife' (Gen. 26.8).[24]
Bathsheba is the object of David's voyeuristic gaze before he takes her
and lies with her (2 Sam. 11.2, 4). The verb 'take' (לקח) recurs in all
but the third adultery scene, and in all cases the object of the verb is the
wife, as she is first taken by the monarch (Gen. 12.15; 20.2; 2 Sam.
22.4), and later taken back by her husband (Gen. 12.19), or returned to
him by the monarch (Gen. 20.14).[25]

The wife's role as her husband's adjunct and possession is in compliance with the biblical understanding of the wife's legal status. Without
this implied understanding the adultery type-scenes would be devoid of
meaning and pathos. What makes the transference of the wife from her
lawful master (בעל) to another man so objectionable and odious is the
unstated notion that she is her husband's exclusive property. Endowing
the wife with an independent point of view, a will and a moral sense of
her own would unnecessarily complicate the narrative, which is primarily concerned with the threat posed by a powerful man to a husband's exclusive rights over his wife. As Nathan's parable makes clear,
the issue in the adultery type-scene does not pertain to sexuality but to
property rights. Bathsheba is presented as Uriah's one and only

> little ewe lamb, which he had bought and reared; and it grew up together
> with him, and with his children. It ate of his morsel, and drank of his
> own cup, and lay in his bosom, and was unto him as a daughter (2 Sam.
> 12.3).[26]

24. The original מצחק ('amuse, play') has sexual connotation, which explains
the outraged reaction of Abimelech to the scene he witnesses. The Hebrew word
functions as a euphemism. See, for example, Gen. 19.4 (the case of Lot's sons-in-
law) and Gen. 39.14, 17 (the case of Joseph and Potiphar's wife).

25. The expression used by Pharaoh, 'here is your wife take [her] and go' (Gen.
12.19), is similar to that used by Laban and Bethuel in conjunction with Rebekah's
betrothal: 'Here is Rebekah before you take [her] and go' (Gen. 24.51).

26. It should be noted that all the adultery scenes present the victimized husband as monogamous. A husband possessing many wives would not make for a
convincing victim. The presentation of a polygamous husband may also expose the
sexual double standard inherent in the biblical context of adultery. The presentation
of a monogamous husband, by contrast emphasizes the reprehensibility of the adulterous act, just as the presentation of the ewe lamb's owner as poor heightens the
moral repulsiveness of the rich man's act.

Nathan stresses the intimate relationship between the poor man and his ewe lamb rather than the fact that the animal was the poor man's only source of income. Nevertheless, the point is not lost on David, who angrily orders that the rich man ought to compensate the poor man 'fourfold' for his loss (2 Sam. 12.6). The ewe lamb's intervention in the parable as an independent subject protesting, for example, against its unjust slaughter would be just as implausible, futile and irrelevant as the wife's protest against *her* fate in the adultery type-scene. The anthropocentric perspective of the parable focusing exclusively on the problem of the human subject parallels the androcentric perspective of the adultery type-scene with its exclusive focus on the male subject.

Endowing the wife with the status of an autonomous human being with a moral capacity to judge right from wrong might have suggested that she rather than he is the victim.[27] Had she been allowed to protest against her husband's attempt to use her for his benefit or against the monarch's attempt to appropriate her, *she* might have emerged as the real victim in the scene, manipulated and exploited by both her husband and her claimant. But this would not have served the purpose of the type-scene, whose focus is the husband as victim. The emphasis on the hero as victim serves not only the patriarchal ideology of the type-scene, but also the monotheistic and national ideologies underpinning the biblical narrative. The presentation of the hero as just but vulnerable, and the introduction of the monarch as powerful but unjust highlight Yhwh's stature as the only hero who is both just *and* powerful. Yhwh is more powerful than the sinning monarch, and more just than the husband. Yhwh leaps out of the most desperate and entangled situations to mete out justice, protect the vulnerable, punish the transgressor, forgive his erring protegés, and re-establish order so that the genealogical continuity and national integrity of his chosen people will not be jeopardized. The adultery type-scenes demonstrate that the genealogical

---

27. The stories of David's relationships with Michal and Abigail may also imply adultery. See Regina Schwartz, 'Adultery in the House of David: The Meta-narrative of Biblical Scholarship and the Narratives of the Bible', *Semeia* 54 (1991), pp. 35-55. On David's relations with his wives, see Danna Nolan Fewell and David M. Gunn, 'In the Shadow of the King', *Gender, Power, and Promise*, pp. 141-63. See also Shulamit Valler, 'King David and "his" Women'. On Abigail, see Alice Bach, 'The Pleasure of Her Text', *The Pleasure of Her Text: Feminist Readings of Biblical and Historical Texts* (Valley Forge, PA: Trinity Press International, 1990), pp. 25-44.

chain, from Abram to Jacob and from David to Solomon, is based on
Yhwh's providence, and not necessarily on the moral integrity of Israel's
patriarchs, matriarchs or political leaders.

The adultery type-scene, like the betrothal type-scene, signals the
hero's initiation into a higher stage of maturity and moral responsibility. Like the betrothal type-scene it too dramatizes Yhwh's concern for
the hero. In the former this concern is expressed through the successful
appropriation of a suitable bride; in the latter it is revealed through the
reappropriation of the wife. Both female types act essentially as prized
objects. In the betrothal type-scene as in the adultery type-scene God's
special concern for the hero is also reflected in the transition from
instability and precariousness to security. What symbolizes the hero's
precarious position in the Genesis type-scene is the drought in the
promised land, which forces the hero into foreign territory (Gen. 12.10;
26.1). What signals the shift to greater stability is the hero's accumula-
tion of great wealth and eventual return to Canaan (Gen. 12.16; 20.14-
15; 26.12-14). While the Genesis type-scene uses economic imagery to
convey the hero's transition to security, the last adultery scene uses
martial imagery. David's adultery is preceded by a description of a state
of war with the Ammonites (2 Sam. 11.1), and the narrative ends with a
description of David's victory over Rabbah (2 Sam. 12.29-31).[28] What
does matter in the presentation of the wife in the adultery type-scene is
her status as prized object. She is beautiful and submissive, as is the
bride in the betrothal type-scene, and like the latter she is shown to be
transferable from one male to another. Her transference from her father
to her groom in the betrothal type-scene functions in a similar way as
her restoration to her husband in the adultery type-scene. It reflects
Yhwh's continued loyalty to her husband (in the case of Bathsheba, to
her future husband). She is the means by which God shows his favor to

28. Although ch. 11 describes the adulterous act and its consequences, the
adultery type-scene is not quite completed until the end of ch. 12, which describes
God's punishment of David and the latter's repentance. On the problem of literary
delimitation in the story of David and Bathsheba, see Uriel Simon, 'An Ironic
Approach to a Bible Story: On the Interpretation of the Story of David and
Bathsheba', *Hasifrut* 2 (1970), pp. 598-607 (Hebrew). Simon argues against Sternberg and Peri's presentation of ch. 11 as an autonomous literary unit, as does Boaz
Arpali in 'Caution! A Biblical Story'. Sternberg and Peri explain in their response
that literary segmentation is determined by the critical concern of the reader. See
their response in 'Caution! A Literary Text', pp. 631-32.

her mate. Her significance lies not in her point of view, but in her liaison with her potential or actual husband, in what this liaison means for him, and in how it affects him.

Two Digressions on the Inferiority of the Wife-Figure

In this sense the adultery type-scene is paradigmatic of all conjugal narratives, namely narratives involving a wife–husband relationship. I would like to argue that even in narratives that are not necessarily concerned with an adulterous affair, the wife-figure, namely the female character performing an uxorial rather than a maternal role, functions almost without exception as a means through which the narrator illuminates the husband's predicaments, failures and victories. Most, if not all, conjugal narratives are dominated by the husband's point of view. In most conjugal narratives, the wife-figure serves either as a prized object, the acquisition of which signals the husband's political success or his special relationship with Yhwh.

Representationally, in most conjugal narratives the wife-figure serves either as a catalyst in the plot or as a foil highlighting her husband's character. To exemplify this point, let me digress from my focus on the adultery type-scene to other relevant conjugal narratives. The example I would consider is David's relationship with Michal, his first wife. The reason why I have chosen Michal as our primary example is that she, more than any other wife-figure in the biblical narrative, seems to defy the stereotype of the submissive wife and even of the typical woman. Adele Berlin points out that Michal behaves and is treated by David more like a man than a woman.[29] But if it is true that Michal remains childless, and that she is never said to be beautiful, as Berlin rightly points out, she is nevertheless a secondary character whose primary role is to catalyze major events in David's career, to signal different stages in David's development toward fully established monarchy and to highlight Yhwh's favorable attitude towards him.

In his discussion of the characterization of Michal and her relationship with David, Robert Alter justifiably points out the numerous literary gaps that leave open such important questions as: Did David marry Michal for love or for reasons of political expediency? What happened to Michal during her marriage to Paltiel the son of Laish? Why did David claim her back? Did Michal remain childless because of David's

---

29. Berlin, *Poetics and Interpretation of Biblical Narrative*, pp. 24-25.

sexual neglect of her or because she was barren?[30] Alter remarks that the tantalizing gaps leave room for the reader's speculation, and invite him or her to fill the missing gaps. The Bible's reticence in regard to characters' motivations is a form of literary art as well as an expression of the biblical conception of human beings as 'unknowable and unforeseeable'.[31]

Although I agree with Alter's observations regarding the techniques of biblical characterization, I would like to argue that when it comes to the characterization of women—notably of wife-figures in conjugal narratives—the biblical narrative becomes especially reticent. I would like to suggest that the biblical narrator leaves gaps in Michal's story because as a wife-figure her story does not matter as much as her husband's story. The narrator erases Michal's story even as he reports it. He also explains why Michal was unfit to inherit from her father and become queen in her own right. The narrative does, however, provide information about what it considers important, namely, the development of David's military and political career and his progress from an obscure young man to the royal throne of Israel. A careful consideration of the contexts in which Michal appears reveals that she is mentioned whenever a significant development occurs in David's political career. She first appears, without previous introduction, when the narrative describes David's first important contact with the royal family: 'And Michal, Saul's daughter, loved David; and they told Saul, and it pleased him' (1 Sam. 18.20). This piece of information explains not only how David manages to become part of the royal family, but also how David manages to survive Saul's hostile plot to kill him (1 Sam. 19.11-17). The reference to Michal's love for David is crucial because otherwise her valiant intervention on his behalf, her shrewd manipulation of Saul's henchmen, and her willingness to risk her life for him would be left unexplained. Yet as soon as Michal performs what will become her most important role in the biblical narrative, namely saving David's life, she disappears from the narrative.

She resurfaces in the context of David's attempt to gain political control of the nation after the death of Saul and Jonathan:

---

30. Alter, *The Art of Biblical Narrative*, pp. 114-30. On the Bible's avoidance of fixed descriptions of character, see Bar-Efrat, *The Art of the Biblical Story*, pp. 110-11. See also Sternberg, 'The Truth vs. All the Truth'.

31. Alter, *The Art of Biblical Narrative*, p. 127.

> And David sent messengers to Ishbosheth, Saul's son, saying: 'Deliver me my wife Michal, whom I betrothed for a hundred foreskins of the Philistines.' And Ishbosheth sent, and took from her husband, from Paltiel the son of Laish. And her husband went with her, weeping as he followed her to Bahurin. Then Abner said to him: 'Go, return', and he returned (2 Sam. 3.14-16).

The description of Michal's transference from her devoted husband, Paltiel, the son of Laish, who follows her crying, omits any reference to Michal's own feelings as she departs from her second husband and becomes reunited with David, her first husband. It also omits any reference to David's emotional attitude to Michal. This implies that David is not motivated by love for Michal, but by the pragmatic and political benefit of reappropriating King Saul's daughter.[32]

But if Michal's first appearance signals David's first steps toward the throne and if her second appearance signals his furthering his royal authority, her last appearance reflects David's final political victory as Israel's unchallenged ruler and as Yhwh's chosen leader. A juxtaposition of Michal's first and last appearances also dramatizes a transition from Michal the determined princess to Michal the demoted wife, complemented by an opposite shift from a vulnerable and persecuted David to a strong and secure David.

The window that appears in both the initial and final presentations of Michal focuses this shift through its metonymic function.[33] In the first presentation Michal 'lowers David through the window', thus saving his life (1 Sam. 19.12). In the final presentation, Michal is said to 'look out through the window' (2 Sam. 6.16) and see David 'leaping and dancing before Yhwh'. Here Michal is the passive observer of David's actions, whereas in the former scene she is the active subject who saves David's life. The conjugal scene presents David's response to Michal at the end of their dialogue, leaving Michal with no suitable answer to his remarks. What the text does reveal is that Michal dies childless (2 Sam. 6.23). In

32. Michal exemplifies the role of all of David's wives as political means in his gradual move to securing greater political power and authority. See Levenson and Halpern, 'The Political Import of David's Marriages', pp. 507-18. See also David Gunn, *The Story of King David: Genre and Interpretation* (Sheffield: JSOT Press, 1978 [1978]), pp. 88-100. Compare Cheryl Exum's discussion of Michal in *Fragmented Women*, pp. 42-93.

33. On the window as symbol of escape and oppression, see Nehama Aschkenazy, *Woman at the Window: Biblical Tales of Oppression and Escape* (Detroit: Wayne State University Press, 1998).

lieu of a response, this indicates a probably divine judgment of the supercilious wife who dared taunt the divinely chosen king. It can also be construed as an indication of the chilly relationship between the husband and wife. David emerges victorious from his last sarcastic exchange with Michal, silencing the proud princess's criticism of his demeanor by reminding her ever so subtly of her subordinate status as the daughter of a demoted king (2 Sam. 6.21). Michal disappears from the narrative after this dialogue, having fulfilled her role as David's political tool on the represented level of the story, and as his foil on the representational level.

Michal's characterization does not differ in essence from the characterization of all biblical wives. Their appearances and disappearances, the dramatizations of their inner lives and the omissions of their motivations are controlled by the function they perform within the context of their husband's characterization. From this point of view, the presentation of the biblical wife conforms to the literary presentation of most secondary and peripheral characters in the biblical narrative. Yet whereas the biblical narrative allows the husband to be both a primary and a secondary character, it frames the wife exclusively within the latter category. The gaps in the presentation of Michal are surely tantalizing from the (male?) modern reader's point of view. The modern appreciation for ambiguity and textual indeterminacies may even find her characterization especially appealing from an aesthetic point of view. Nevertheless, the ideological determinants of biblical characterization must not be overlooked. In this context, the gaps in Michal's presentation are indicative of what the narrative finds worthy of narrating. In the case of Michal in particular and the biblical wife in general what is worthy of narration is determined by the extent to which she affects the husband's life, or the extent to which she facilitates his literary characterization. The biblical wife is relevant as a means to an end, the end being the husband-hero.

We have seen that the secondary status and auxiliary function of the biblical wife-figure are not unique to the adultery type-scene but rather typical of the biblical conjugal narrative in general. The adultery type-scene is paradigmatic of other conjugal narratives in yet another important aspect, in its presentation of the husband-hero as morally superior to his wife. Rather than beginning with a discussion of the adultery type-scene I shall first draw on other biblical texts in order to clarify the principle under consideration. The morally inferior wife is prefigured by Eve. The Genesis story establishes a causal link between Eve's moral inferiority and her political subordination to her husband. Because Eve has sinned and caused her husband to sin she is subjugated and controlled by him (Gen. 3.16).[34] The moral inferiority of the wife is presented in the biblical narrative as the justification for her political inferiority. It is therefore essential for the biblical narrative to adhere to the portrait of the morally inferior wife, so as not to challenge one of the fundamental principles of patriarchal ideology.

Abram is shown to concede to Sarai's will concerning Hagar (Gen. 16.5-6), but her political victory is morally questionable as indicated by the description of Hagar's desperate escape to the desert and the angel's compassionate consolation (Gen. 15.7-14). Even when acting as mothers, wife-figures are not allowed to eclipse their husband-heroes morally. Rebekah, who manipulates Isaac into conferring a blessing on Jacob (Gen. 27.5-17), emerges from the scene as a powerful wife-mother, as perhaps more resourceful than Isaac, but not as morally superior to him.[35] Bathsheba, prodded by and in collaboration with Nathan the prophet, succeeds in securing her son's succession to the throne (1 Kgs 1.16-31). She too emerges as more powerful than the old and impotent David, yet she is not morally superior to him. The only biblical husbands who are morally superseded by their wives are villains, whose moral inferiority relative to their wives serves as a means of literary judgment. Thus, for example, Nabal, whose very name ('scoundrel')

34. Judith Ochshorn points out that whereas the punishments of the serpent and Adam are preceded with explicit references to their moral transgressions, in the case of Eve, God 'does not directly link her punishment to her moral transgression'. Ochshorn concludes that this indicates the general biblical attitude to woman as a morally unaccountable beings. See *The Female Experience, and the Nature of the Divine*, p. 149.

35. Christine Garside Allen argues that Rebekah's character has been misinterpreted as the paradigm of female deceptiveness and uxorious disloyalty. She claims that Rebekah successfully passes a divine test when she determines to deceive her husband in order to answer a higher injunction, a 'call out of the law', which is in essence identical to God's call to Abraham. Yet, she does not explain why, in the case of Abraham this call is explicitly recorded whereas in Rebekah's case it is not. She also does not explain why the narrative has found it necessary to focus on Rebekah's deceptiveness rather than on her moral drive, if the latter is indeed what the biblical narrative intends to extol. See her article, 'Who Was Rebekah? "On Me Be the Curse, My Son" ', in Rita M. Gross (ed.), *Beyond Androcentrism: New Essays on Women and Religion* (Missoula, MT: Scholars Press, 1977), pp. 183-216.

epitomizes his villainy, is eclipsed by Abigail his wife in the moral and literary sense (1 Sam. 25). Yet, she is not allowed to surpass or even equal the moral or literary stature of David, her future husband, and one of the Bible's major heroes. Abigail's shrewd actions and perspicacious dialogue with David are recorded in the context of what preceded their marriage. As soon as their marriage is consummated, Abigail disappears from the biblical text, excepting a few perfunctory references to her as one of David's wives (1 Sam. 27.3; 2 Sam. 2.2). Abigail's positive characterization emphasizes Nabal's villainy and presents her as a desirable and prized object. Her transference from Nabal to David signals God's support for David, as He enables his chosen king to win his enemy's beautiful and intelligent wife (1 Sam. 25.3). It is true, then, that Abigail morally supersedes Nabal but she is not shown to be superior in this sense to David.

Since in the Bible what is moral cannot be distinguished from what Yhwh approves, it should not surprise us that hero-husbands are almost without exception shown to be religiously superior to their wives, that is, closer to Yhwh than their wives. Although some wife-figures are shown to act *in accordance with* Yhwh's plans, they are never shown to be directly *motivated by* Yhwh's plans but by their own interest. The implication is that Yhwh is orchestrating the events behind the scenes, that Sarah's zealous protection of Isaac (Gen. 21.9-12), Rebekah's preference for Jacob, and Bathsheba's intervention on behalf of Solomon are all results of God's design; yet none of the wife-figures, and none of the wife-mother figures are allowed to act in *direct response* to God's call. The point I am stressing refers to the literary presentation of Yhwh's relationship to wife-figures. Whereas the husband-heroes are often shown to respond directly to God's call, obeying His will despite their personal interest (e.g. Abraham's willingness to sacrifice Isaac), wife-figures are motivated by their own personal drives, which happen to suit the divine will.[36] The moral inferiority of wives in relation to their husband-heroes is essential because the reverse would challenge

36. This holds true for wife-heroines presented in juxtaposition with husbands who are secondary characters, e.g. for Esther and Ruth. Both are shown to act in accordance with the divine plan, but the text refrains in both cases from explicitly linking the wife's conduct with God. God as a character is curiously absent from the stories of Esther and Ruth. See my article, 'The Status and Role of Female Heroines in the Biblical Narrative'.

the divine preference for the husband-heroes as the spiritual progenitors and leaders of the chosen people.

This second digression on the moral status of the wife-figure in the biblical narrative will explain why in the adultery type-scene it is particularly necessary for the wife to perform a secondary auxiliary role, and why it is inevitable for her to be passive, object-like and mute. Had the type-scene allowed the wife-figure to express her own will, to protest against her husband's deceptiveness, or the monarch's aggressiveness, she might have emerged not only as the real victim but also as the moral hero of the scene. In view of the morally questionable conduct of the husband-hero, any sign of opposition or hesitation on the part of the wife-figure would put her in a morally superior position. It is not merely the political vulnerability of the wife-figure vis-à-vis the monarch that motivates her to comply with both her husband and the monarch's will, but the narrative's reluctance to permit the wife a greater measure of moral integrity relative to her husband's. The same applies to the final adultery type-scene, which features David as both monarch and husband. Any objection on the part of Bathsheba would have jeopardized the moral status of David vis-à-vis his future wife.[37]

Whereas the biblical text is willing to expose the moral vulnerability of most of its male heroes—as a part of monotheistic ideology aimed at demonstrating that only God is perfect—it is not willing to do so at the expense of its patriarchal ideology, aimed at demonstrating that however imperfect men may be, women are even more so. Conjugal scenes allow the wife-figure a measure of autonomy and moral consciousness when the husband's moral standing is not in danger of being compromised. Thus, the conjugal scenes featuring David and Michal, and the one confronting him with his future wife Abigail, allow these women a measure of autonomy and moral strength, as David suffers no liability that might undermine his moral status. But in the scene with Bathsheba, which explicitly condemns David's immoral conduct, the wife-figure is not permitted to express her voice—the narrator thus effectively denies the wife moral agency. Bathsheba will be allowed to express her voice in a later scene that presents her as a mother fighting for the political security of both herself and her son (1 Kgs 1). This conjugal scene does not threaten the delicate balance between the husband-hero and his wife, as the former is characterized not as a powerful sinner, but rather

37. On Bathsheba as an object of sexual desire, see Bach, *Women, Seduction, and Betrayal*, pp. 132-50.

as a vulnerable old man. As David's moral status is not in question, Bathsheba is allowed to assume the stature of an autonomous human being with a will of her own.

That the wife-figures in the adultery type-scene obey this literary-ideological principle of moral inferiority becomes clearer when we consider another adultery scene in which the gender roles are reversed. The scene to which I am referring involves Joseph in the role of the desirable object, and Potiphar's wife as the desirous party.[38] Potiphar's wife is not portrayed as a powerful monarch, with limitless political authority, like her counterparts in the 'standard' adultery type-scene, she is still politically superior to Joseph, the overseer of her estate. Yet, morally she is unambiguously inferior not only to her trusting husband, Potiphar, but especially to Joseph, whom she persistently tries to seduce (Gen. 39.7, 10, 12). Unlike her male counterparts in the adultery type-scene, Potiphar's wife is not shown to commit an error as her male counterparts in the adultery scenes are shown to do. Unlike Pharaoh and Abimelech she knows full well who Joseph is and yet 'she cast her eyes upon Joseph and said "Lie with me" ' (Gen. 39.7). Had Potiphar's wife been a man coveting an unmarried woman, would there be a story to tell? Had Potiphar seduced one of his maids, it is doubtful that the biblical narrative would have bothered to refer to the incident let alone condemn it. Potiphar's wife is condemned because as a married woman she must not have sexual access to any man other than her husband. A married woman who seeks sexual escapades with other men must be portrayed as treacherous, dangerous, lethal. The text stresses that she repeats her adulterous advances to Joseph even after Joseph reminds her of her conjugal status and his own indebtedness to Potiphar (vv. 10, 12). Joseph's explicit and articulate refusal to obey his mistress condemns her while exonerating him. His honesty and uncompromising loyalty to this master point up her treacherousness and disloyalty. Unlike the female objects of desire in the adultery type-scene, Joseph in this scene emerges as an autonomous and morally superior subject. He is given a chance to present his point of view which is fully supported by the narrative data. He thus emerges as both the noble hero and moral hero of the scene. His reasoning reflects not only impeccable moral standards, but also a strong religious sense, as he links his refusal to sin against man to his fear of God:

38. For a reading of Potiphar's wife as a sub-type of the seductive woman, see Bach, *Women, Seduction, and Betrayal*, pp. 34-81.

But he refused and said to his master's wife, 'Lo, having me my master has not concern about anything in the house, and he put everything he has in my hands; there is no one greater than me in the house; nor has he kept back anything from me except yourself, because you are his wife. How then can I do this great wickedness and sin against God?' (Gen. 39.8-9).

Were this passionately moralistic speech to be attributed to any of the desirable wives in the adultery type-scene, the reader's sympathy would have shifted from husband to wife. It would become clear that not only is the wife the wronged victim in the scene, but that the wife is morally superior to both her husband and her claimant. This would require a radical restructuring of the scene: with the wife as victim, God would have to compensate her and scold her husband. This scenario, however, is not only out of step with the principle of the wife's moral inferiority, it is also inconsistent with the didactic message of the adultery type-scene, which is concerned with the moral reprehensibility of the husband's victimization by another man *through* his wife. The scene's interest in the husband's moral predicament and victimization proscribes attention to the wife's victimization and to *her* moral predicament. Such attention might transform the status of the wife from adjunct to heroine.

Furthermore, the adultery type-scene cannot afford to deal with the wife's moral predicament or her victimization because this would interfere with her presentation as both the *means* and the *cause* of the husband-hero's victimization. As her husband's adjunct, the wife not only represents the means through which the hero is blessed, but also the means by which he is tested. As a desirable object, she functions as his reward—as she does in the betrothal type-scene—but also as a potential threat to his security.

In the Genesis type-scene, the life of the husband is spared; in the final adultery type-scene the husband, Uriah, loses his life because of his desirable wife. The wife's role as desirable object is also shown to threaten the survival of her illicit claimant. This is not to say that she is morally responsible for the claimant's or husband's suffering. Neither am I arguing that she is necessarily the direct cause of the disaster visited on her husband, claimant or protector. It would be more accurate to see her as a catalyst rather than a direct cause of male death.[39]

39. David Gunn points out the prevalence of the woman and death motif in the

Sarai/Sarah is not only a threat to Abram/Abraham's security, but to Pharaoh's (Gen. 12.17) and to that of Abimelech (Gen. 20.18).[40]

The thematic linkage between the wife's role in the adultery type-scene and the motif of male death exemplifies a larger thematic pattern in the biblical narrative featuring the wife-figure as life-threatening to her actual or potential husband as well as to her illicit claimant. This is especially true of wife-figures who are either childless or who have not yet borne sons.[41] The desirable wife-figure is particularly life-threatening to a passionate husband-figure. Examples include Dinah and Shechem (Gen. 36.25-26), Samson's first wife (Judg. 14.19), Samson's concubine, Delilah (Judg. 16.30), Abigail and Nabal (1 Sam. 25.37), Tamar and Amnon (2 Sam. 13), and Abishag and Adonijah (1 Kgs 2).[42]

David story, and stresses that often two men lose their lives as a result of their involvement with a woman. Both Ishbosheth, the legitimate owner of Rizpah, Saul's concubine, and Abner, her claimant, die. Both Adonijah, Abishag's claimant, and Joab die, and both Amnon, Tamar's claimant, and Absalom, her protector, die. Gunn does not stress however, that in all these cases woman functions as a wife-figure, either as a desirable potential wife or as an actual wife. In her role as mother, woman is rarely featured as a catalyst of death. See Gunn, *The Story of King David*, p. 43. Karen Horney suggests that the frequent representation of the desirable woman as the cause of death in Western literature reflects man's 'dread' of woman. By projecting women in art and literature as deathly creatures, men 'prove', as it were, that it is not their anxiety but woman's innate deathliness that inspires their dread of her. See Karen Horney, *Feminine Psychology* (New York: W.W. Norton, 1967). On the dichotomy of the good mother and the bad wife in Hebrew literature, including the Hebrew Bible, see Nehama Aschkenasy, *Eve's Journey: Feminine Images in Hebraic Literary Tradition* (Philadelphia: University of Pennsylvania Press, 1986).

40. In the case of the matriarchs, their role as desirable objects has wider national implications, as this desirability—just like their sterility—constitutes an obstacle on the way to fulfilling Yhwh's promise to the patriarchs. See Norman Habel *Literary Criticism of the Old Testament* (Philadelphia: Fortress Press, 1971), pp. 43-64.

41. This may explain why Rebekah—the wife—does not appear to be as threatening as Sarai/Sarah, the infertile wife who has not yet borne sons to her husband. Rebekah, it will be remembered, is not taken into the monarch's house, and the threat she poses for Isaac is more hypothetical than that posed by her counterpart in the previous adultery type-scenes.

42. The lethal female love object, in her role as wife-figure is discussed in Bal, *Lethal Love*. It should be noted that Jezebel is described as a seductress and as a wife-figure. See Bach, *Women, Seduction and Betrayal*, pp. 166-209. The book in general discusses the evolution of the motif of the lethal seductress in the Bible and in Western culture in general.

The circumstances vary widely from one narrative to another, as does the moral judgment of the characters involved; nevertheless, the thematic linkage between the desirable wife-figure and the motif of death, particularly the death of men, is unmistakable. This linkage casts the wife-figure in a threatening role. Her desirability implies disaster and destruction, and the didactic message implied by this thematic configuration does not need to be spelled out.

But the wife does not constitute a threat only to her husband's physical survival. Perhaps more significantly, she threatens his moral integrity. She is the direct cause of his immoral behavior. The wife is the reason for Abram/Abraham's cowardly deceptiveness in the Genesis adultery type-scene, and she is the cause of David's adulterous and murderous act in the final adultery type-scene. It must be stressed that the hero we are dealing with in these scenes is favored by God because of his exemplary upright conduct and fear of God. Abram/Abraham's immoral conduct as well as that of Isaac and David is out of step with their general behavioral pattern. The adultery type-scene is the only one to present the patriarchs as sinners, and it is by far the most objectionable act ever committed by David. Although the patriarchs are not penalized or castigated by God as David is, they give here their poorest performance as God's appointed heroes. The implication is that it is the desirable wife-figure who catalyzes the moral error of husband-hero. The wife-figure in the adultery type-scene is not shown to initiate the sin, or to actively drive her husband to commit a sin, but passive and object-like as she may be, she is the primary reason behind his faux pas. In this sense the wife-figures in the adultery type-scene fit the prototypic mold of Eve who has brought about Adam's downfall, and through it death on the rest of the human race.

Not all biblical wife-figures are cast in as shady a role as the wife-figure in the adultery type-scene. Although the characterization of the wife in the adultery type-scene is paradigmatic of many other biblical conjugal scenes, especially in terms of the wife's moral inferiority to her husband, it is nevertheless only one of the paradigms of conjugal narratives. The other one can be seen in the contest type-scene to which I will turn next.[43] What will be considered first is the structure of this type-scene and its ideological function. I will then examine the charac-

---

43. The term 'contest type-scene' is taken from Williams, *Women Recounted*, pp. 48-49.

terization of the wife-figure in the contest type-scene and juxtapose it with its counterpart in the adultery type-scene.

In some ways the contest type-scene featuring two co-wives and one husband-figure can be seen as the mirror image of the adultery type-scene whose major agents are two husband-figures and one wife-figure. The husband-figures vying for access to and exclusive control over the wife-figure in the adultery type-scene are analogous to the two wife-figures vying for supremacy in their husband's household. But the analogies between these type-scenes highlight all the more dramatically the significant differences between them. The adultery type-scene makes it clear that only one of the male contestants is a legitimate husband, the other husband-figure is discarded as an illicit claimant. By contrast, the contest type-scene, as we shall see, endorses both wife-figures as legitimate. This explains the disparate plot developments and denouements in each type-scene. Whereas in the adultery type-scene only one husband wins exclusive access to the wife, while the other is whisked off the stage, in the contest type-scene both wives remain with their shared husband. The happy ending in the adultery type-scene consists in the successful elimination of a potential or actual polyandrous arrangement (adultery). The happy ending in the contest type-scene consists in the successful perpetuation of the polygynous arrangement, usually through the miraculous fertilization of the barren co-wife. I would like to suggest that these differences reflect the ideological functions of each type-scene. The adultery type-scene serves among other things to de-legitimate a situation where one wife can be shared by two husbands; the contest type-scene on the other hand legitimates a situation where one husband has two wives. The role played by the female and male conjugal partner in each scene also fits the ideological functions of each scene. In the adultery type-scene, the legitimate husband is the victim, the illicit claimant is the victimizer, while the wife plays a rather sinister role as a desirable object. In the contest type-scene the barren wife is the victim, the fertile wife is the victimizer, while the husband plays the role of a rather ineffective peacekeeper. In neither type-scene does the legitimate husband emerge as the victimizer of his wife.

The Contest Type-Scene

The contest type-scene presents one husband and two co-wives, one of whom is barren. The fertile co-wife humiliates the barren wife, intentionally or unintentionally, until the latter is redeemed through divine intervention, becoming fertile and giving birth to one or more sons.[44] In the first contest scene (Gen. 16.1-16) the husband is Abram and the barren wife is Sarai. Realizing that she is incapable of giving sons to her husband, Sarai proposes that Abram take Hagar, her maid, as co-wife. When Hagar becomes pregnant she loses respect for her mistress. In retaliation, Sarai mistreats Hagar, in the wake of which the latter escapes to the desert. God's angel, however, encourages Hagar to return to Abram and Sarai, and Hagar gives birth to Ishmael. The second contest scene (Gen. 21.1-21) features the same protagonists but a somewhat different plot structure. Having given birth to Isaac, Sarah is disturbed by Ishmael's conduct towards her own son and consequently demands that Hagar and Ishmael be expelled from the household. In this version of the story, God, who reveals Himself to Hagar in the desert of Paran, does not encourage her to return to her master, but rather protects her and her son until the latter grows up and marries his own wife. It appears rather obvious that the reason for the difference in the story's two versions is related to the absence of sons in the first scene and the presence of two sons in the second. Hagar has to be returned to the household in the first scene because she has not yet fulfilled her uxorial duty— Ishmael is not yet born. Furthermore, Sarai in the first scene is still barren, and therefore Hagar is not yet expendable. Only after the birth of both sons does the story permit the second wife to depart from the household for good. Most contest type-scenes, however, develop in a different direction, ending with the miraculous fertilization of the barren wife. The elimination of one of the wife-figures is an aberrant rather than normative pattern in the contest type-scene, and even in this exceptional case, the second co-wife is eliminated only after she has fulfilled her primary role by giving birth to a son.

The third contest scene (Gen. 30.1-24) features Jacob as the husband, and Leah and Rachel as co-wives. Here Leah is the fertile wife and Rachel the favored but barren wife. Rachel envies Leah her fertility and tries to match her by offering her maids to Jacob as concubines. Leah for her part competes for Jacob's company and attention. Finally, God remembers Rachel and she gives birth to a son. The fourth contest scene (1 Sam. 1–28) presents Elkanah as the husband, Hannah as the favored barren wife and Peninnah as the fertile wife. Peninnah humili-

44. For a different classification of the contest type-scene as a sub-type of the hero birth story, see Brenner, 'Female Social Behavior', *A Feminist Companion to Genesis*, pp. 206-13.

ates Hannah for her barrenness, and Hannah is exasperated and desperate despite her husband's preference for her. Finally, God responds to
Hannah's anguish and prayer and she gives birth to a son.

In contrast to the adultery type-scene, which presents the desirable
wife, the bone of contention between the two husband-figures, as a
threat to her husband's life, the contest type-scene presents the husband-figure for whom both wives compete as a helpless outsider. No
contest scene as much as alludes to the husband's role in his wives'
antagonistic relationship or suffering. Rather, the husband is frequently
shown to side with the less fortunate of his wives, his barren wife. The
husband is never presented as a potential or actual threat to any of his
wives' well-being or as the cause of his wives' questionable conduct. In
contrast to the adultery type-scene, which alludes to the fundamental
arrangement of one wife and two male contestants as the source of the
problem presented, the contest type-scene carefully precludes any reference to the polygynous set up as the possible source of the conflict
between the female contestants. The contest type-scene minimizes to
the point of denying the husband's role and the polygynous marriage
itself as major catalysts of the contest between the two wives.

None of the contest scenes presents the polygynous arrangement
as the product of the husband's choice or initiative. The polygynous
arrangement is either a given that the narrative does not explain (1 Sam.
1), or the result of other circumstances. The first contest type-scene, for
example, introduces the first wife as the initiator of the polygynous
arrangement: 'And Sarai said unto Abram: "Behold now, Yhwh has
kept me from bearing children, please go in to my maid; perhaps I shall
obtain children through her." And Abram hearkened to the voice of
Sarai' (Gen. 16.2).

In the second type-scene, it is once again not the husband, Jacob, who
takes on an additional wife, but rather his wily father-in-law Laban,
who exchanges Leah for Rachel, thus manipulating Jacob into marrying
two wives (Gen. 29.18-28). It must be stressed, however, that while the
first wife's barrenness justifies polygyny in the first two type-scenes, it
is the husband's preference for another woman that justifies polygyny
in the third type-scene. Yet the scene is careful not to present Jacob as
spurning Leah and opting for Rachel out of his own choice. This would
cast Jacob in the role of his wife's victimizer. Rather, it points out that
the favored wife was Jacob's first choice and that he ends up with two
wives due to Laban's machinations. In this fashion the scene manages

to legitimate the husband's personal preference as an acceptable cause for polygyny without at the same time making this too obvious.

The third contest type-scene presents the polygynous arrangement as a given: 'And he [Elkanah] had two wives: the name of the one was Hannah and the name of the other Peninnah; and Peninnah had children, but Hannah had no children' (1 Sam. 1.2). It is not clear whether Elkanah takes his favored wife Hannah after marrying the fertile Peninnah (as Jacob does), or whether he takes Peninnah having realized that Hannah is barren (as Abram does). What is clear is that Elkanah is not responsible for the conflict between his co-wives and that it is not the polygynous arrangement as such that disrupts the order and renders the wives unhappy. The minimization of the husband's role as the possible cause for the co-wives' rivalry and misery remains a constant element throughout the contest type-scenes. There is no single scene in which the favored wife, for example, taunts and humiliates the less-favored wife. This would point up the husband's role in the conflict, as it would make clear that it is he who determines who is the favored wife. The favored wife's barrenness—the cause that catalyzes the conflict between the co-wives seems to be completely beyond the sphere of the husband's control. What exacerbates the problem is the co-wife's inconsiderate and to some extent immoral conduct vis-à-vis the barren wife. In other words, the conflict is not caused by the husband, but by one wife's physical handicap and the other's undignified conduct.

The first type-scene presents Hagar's condescending attitude toward Sarai as the primary cause of the conflict (Gen. 16.4). Having borne a son to Abram, Hagar begin to despise her mistress. In response to Sarai's protest, Abram concedes all authority to his wife: 'Behold your maid is in your hand, do to her as you please' (Gen. 16.6). But Abram's concession brings about a further complication. Sarai 'deals harshly' with Hagar, causing her to escape to the desert (Gen. 16.7-8). Thus Abram is shown to be innocent both with regard to Sarai's anguish and in relation to Hagar's suffering. This is made even clearer in the second type-scene, according to which Sarah is angered not by Hagar, but by Ishmael, Hagar's son (Gen. 21.9-10). Here Abraham is shown to disapprove of his wife's demand to cast out his concubine and firstborn son (Gen. 21.11). Nevertheless he does not criticize his wife openly. Ordered by God to obey his wife, he sends Hagar and Ishmael away, yet the text stresses that Abraham rises early in the morning, and gives his concubine bread and water, 'putting it on her shoulder' (Gen. 21.14). Abraham is thus forced to send away his concubine; he clearly does it against his will and better judgment. It is noteworthy that although the husband is shown to be understanding toward both his co-wives, he is presented as siding a bit more emphatically with the wife who emerges as the more victimized of the two. In the first type-scene it appears that Sarai is the true victim: barren, helpless and taunted by her maid, her anger at her husband appears to be fully justifiable. By allowing her to deal with Hagar as she pleases, Abram appears to comply with the moral requirements of the situation. In the second type-scene, however, Hagar appears to be innocent, as it is not she but her son who is directly responsible for Sarah's wrath. Whereas the first type-scene reports that Abram complies with his wife's wishes, the second type-scene stresses Abraham's disapproval of his wife's demand to cast out Hagar and Ishmael. Abram/Abraham's conduct is morally impeccable, even-handed and compassionate in both type-scenes. He is a model husband to both his wife and his concubine and completely innocent of their misery. The misery of both wives is a product of their own actions; they are both victims and victimizers in what seems to be an unavoidable and unresolvable rivalry. By minimizing the role of the husband in the conflict, the type-scene incriminates the victims of the contest, rather than the husband, who is in the final analysis the cause of their mutual rivalry.

The third type-scene is more explicit about the benefit accruing to the husband from the contest between the co-wives. The bitter competition between the fertile Leah and the barren Rachel is, it turns out, the necessary instrumental mechanism that presents Jacob with 12 sons who will constitute the foundation of the Israelite nation. Furthermore, the text is slightly more explicit about the role of the husband in the contest. As the names of her first three sons indicate, Leah considers her reproductive capacity not as an end in itself, but as a means by which to win her husband's love (Gen. 29.32-34). While Leah struggles to win what Rachel has—Jacob's love—Rachel struggles to win what Leah has—fertility. Each sister tries to outdo the other in order to secure her position as Jacob's favored wife. Unlike Hagar, who taunts Sarah for her barrenness, Leah does not humiliate Rachel in words or through her attitude. What seems to exasperate Rachel is Leah's ability to give Jacob children: 'And Rachel saw that she bore Jacob no children, and she envied her sister; and she said unto Jacob: "Give me children, or else I die" ' (Gen. 30.1). The favored wife's protest is construed as an expression of despair, not as a valid complaint, for after all Jacob is not responsible for Rachel's barrenness. As Jacob points out in his response, and as the text makes clear several times, it is not the husband but God who made her barren (Gen. 39.31; 30.2, 22). Once again, the husband emerges as innocent and morally superior to both his co-wives. It is not he who causes their misfortune. It is noteworthy that the text does not allow Leah to reprimand Jacob for his love of Rachel and his inattention to herself. This would have highlighted the husband's role in the tragedy of at least one of his wives. What the text does quote is the irrational and morally invalid complaint of the barren wife, which gives Jacob an additional opportunity to reaffirm his status as a God-fearing hero: 'Am I in the place of God who has withheld from you the fruit of the womb?' (Gen. 30.2).

Although the scene admits that Jacob prefers Rachel to Leah, it does not *dramatize* this detail in terms of its effects on Leah. It omits reference to those cases in which Jacob spurns Leah, to 'go in' to his favored wife, Rachel. It never describes Jacob as making a choice between his wives, rather it stresses Jacob's lack of choice in the matter. It dramatizes Jacob's helplessness and the co-wives' manipulative power over their husband. Just as the scene shows Laban foisting Leah on Jacob (Gen. 29.23), it also shows the sisters bartering over their husband. Thus, Rachel allows Leah to sleep with Jacob in exchange for Reuben's mandrakes (Gen. 30.15-16). Jacob emerges from this mini-scene as little more than an object, whereas the co-wives appear to be the ones who determine his moves. His passivity in this contest type-scene is just as essential as the co-wives' cunning bartering, as the configuration establishes the husband not only as the innocent, but as morally superior to both his co-wives.

The first three contest type-scenes establish a delicate balance between the co-wives in terms of moral evaluation. None of the wives is completely innocent, and no one is morally superior to the other, as each is shown to err in her own way. The first contest scene counterbalances Hagar's insensitive taunting of Sarai, her mistress, with the latter's cruel treatment of Hagar, which finally makes her flee to the desert. In the second scene, Sarah is victimized first by her barrenness and later by her jealousy of Hagar, whose son is shown to taunt Isaac. In the case of Leah and Rachel, the latter is shown to be jealous of the former, but there is no explicit and clear judgment on either one of the sisters. As in the previous scenes, there is a balance of culpability between the co-wives, neither one is thoroughly evil or wrong.

The fourth contest abandons this balance for a less ambiguous moral evaluation, positing the barren wife, Hannah, as the innocent victim, and the less-favored wife, Peninnah, as her evil victimizer: 'And her rival used to provoke her sorely in order to irritate her, for Yhwh had closed her womb' (1 Sam. 1.6). What the scene does not abandon is the presentation of the husband as an innocent and somewhat helpless party in this entanglement. Elkanah is not only innocent, he is also especially sympathetic and understanding toward his victimized wife, trying to compensate for her misery: 'But to Hannah he gave a double portion: for he loved Hannah, but Yhwh had shut up her womb' (1 Sam. 1.5). Like Abraham, Elkanah is shown to side with the wife that the narrative considers less fortunate: the one who is not only barren, but also belittled and harassed by her rival. Hannah has nothing but her husband's love. The scene dramatizes Elkanah's concern for Hannah not only through action but also through dialogue: 'Hannah, why do you weep? And why don't you eat? And why are you grieving? Am I not better for you than ten sons?' (1 Sam. 1.8). While the scene goes out of its way to represent the husband's sympathy for his barren wife, it avoids dealing with the impact his conduct may have produced on Peninnah. It is possible that by placing the description of Peninnah's meanness after the description of Elkanah's treatment of Hannah (1 Sam. 1.5-6), the narrator alludes to a causal link between these actions, implying that Peninnah humiliates Hannah *because* of Elkanah's obvious preference for Hannah. Yet there is no explicit reference to Peninnah's feelings: her jealousy, her shame, her own anguish at being the less-favored. Such references would not serve the purposes of the contest type-scene. For one thing, they may call attention to the plight of the unfavored wife, thus requiring some form of reparation, possibly in the form of divine intervention on her behalf. This would cast the husband in the role of his wife's victimizer, which would complicate the plot and divert attention from the primary issue, namely the final miraculous redemption of the barren wife by an omnipotent and just God attending exclusively to the unfortunate and miserable.[45] This may also allude to a conflict of interest between husband and wife, or worse yet, to the fact that the wife's misery is the product of the polygynous arrangement itself.

Yet such conflict of interest does exist. Although the contest type-scene implicitly legitimates polygyny as a divinely sanctioned arrange-

---

45. For a different reading see Meyers, 'Hannah and Her Sacrifice', pp. 93-105.

ment (God is never shown to punish or rebuke a co-wife as he does a would-be co-husband), the polygynous arrangement has little to do with the Bible's monotheistic and national ideology and more to do with the patriarchal structure of ancient Israel. Polygynous marriage in a patriarchal society benefits the husband-father and is politically oppressive for the co-wives involved. In patriarchal and polygynous societies, the major means by which a woman can control her husband's dominance is by withdrawing food and sexual services.[46] The fact that the husband can obtain these services from another wife decreases her chances of gaining compliance from her husband.[47] The husband's access to another wife decreases her power, and may even threaten her and her children's position in the family. But the husband's recourse to another wife's services does not necessarily result in increasing the latter's power or influence, because if her interests happen to be objectionable to him, he will always have the option of resorting to the first wife, or of seeking a third wife. The polygynous arrangement in a patrilocal society increases the husband's control over his wives because it permits him to play them off against each other. Because the wife's only source of power is her influence on her husband, she must compete

---

46. On the patrilocal structure of ancient Israelite marriage, see de Vaux, *Ancient Israel*, I, pp. 26-29. It should be noted that the biblical narrative sanctions patrilocal marriages by linking them to God's will or to the chosen land. Thus, Abraham stipulates that Isaac's chosen bride must consent to leave her country and family and relocate to Canaan (Gen. 24.8). Jacob stays with his father-in-law Laban only temporarily, and so does Moses. On the other hand, Samson's marriage to his first Philistine wife—a non-patrilocal marriage—is a failure. Gideon's concubine who stays in Shechem and the concubine from Judah who returns to her father's home end up bringing disaster on Israel. The matrilocal marriages of Mahlon and Chilon to Moabite women end in death and destruction, whereas Ruth's patrilocal marriage to Boaz is divinely sanctioned. Patrilocal marriage, however, has little to do with morality or religion. As a social institution its causes are varied, but among them is the power distribution between the sexes. As Kathleen Gough points out: 'This [patrilocal marriage] gives a man advantages over his wife in terms of familiarity and loyalties, for the wife is often a stranger'. See her article, 'The Origin of the Family', in Jo Freeman (ed.), *Women: A Feminist Perspective* (Palo Alto: Mayfield, 1979), pp. 83-105 (101).

47. Louise Lamphere, 'Strategies, Cooperation, and Conflict Among Women in Domestic Groups', in Michelle Zimbalist Rosaldo and Louise Lamphere (eds.), *Women, Culture and Society* (Stanford: Stanford University Press, 1974), pp. 97-112 (107).

against his co-wife, which ends up increasing the husband's control even further through the simple strategic principle of control through divisiveness. The contest type-scene may reflect to some extent a social reality in which co-wives fought each other for supremacy in the domestic group. What the type-scene fails to disclose is that female strife is the product of male dominance. As the anthropologist Louise Lamphere points out, competition between women of the same domestic group is directly related to the domestic power structure: women are competitive the more restricted they are by male authority; by contrast they are more cooperative when less dependent on the male head of the family for survival and status.[48]

Instead of referring to the husband's role in generating the bitter competition between the co-wives, the contest type-scene omits any reference to the husband as a possible factor in the rivalry, and neither does it allude to the advantage the husband derives both from the polygynous setup and from the mutual hostility of his wives. Instead it focuses on the co-wives' rivalry and points to their innate jealousy (Rachel and Leah), vengefulness (Hagar and Sarah), or simple meanness (Peninnah) as the primary causes of the dispute. If polygyny and co-wife rivalry are effective patriarchal strategies in society, the literary depiction of polygyny as an acceptable arrangement and the dramatization of wife rivalry constitute narrative strategies in the service of a patriarchal ideology whose purpose is to justify male control over women and legitimate women's subordination to their husbands in the domestic sphere. By making it clear that the husband is supportive of his victimized wife, that he never harasses his barren wife and never oppresses his unfavored wife, the contest type-scene implies that whatever the malaise of the co-wife, it is not the product of the husband's misconduct but of her own inadequacy or her rival's meanness. As we have seen, it is always the fertile wife who oppresses the barren wife, rather than the husband, who has a vested interest in having more sons. It is never the husband who shows inattention toward or impatience with an unfavored wife. This scenario justifies the husband's role as a kind of overseer in the domestic sphere. It creates the impression that, left to their own devices, women would probably destroy each other as

48. Lamphere, 'Strategies', pp. 97-112. Lamphere enumerates other factors that determine the extent of women's competitiveness or cooperation, among them, patterns of inheritance and the extent to which public and domestic spheres are integrated.

well as the entire household. The repeated scene of contending co-wives serves the interests of a patriarchal ideology whose purpose is to justify the existing domestic power structure.

In this sense, the contest type-scene is paradigmatic of biblical conjugal narratives. There is no scene in the entire Hebrew Bible dramatizing the abuse by the husband of his wife, either through unjustified divorce, false accusation of adultery, or even simple neglect. The only exception that comes to mind is the story of King David and Michal. Their last conjugal scene constitutes a sarcastic dialogue between husband and wife, in which the husband has the final word, and at the end of which the text informs us that Michal died childless (2 Sam. 6.23). Yet David's sarcastic words to his wife are not construed as an arbitrary insult but as a justified response to her offensive remarks about his undignified worship of God. David's response presents him as an uncompromising servant of Yhwh and as a husband who knows how to put his wife in her place. Michal's childlessness serves as an implied divine judgment on her attitude toward both Yhwh and her husband.

The contest type-scene is also paradigmatic in its depiction of female rivalry. There is no conjugal narrative in the Hebrew Bible that records a story of co-wives' cooperation and friendship.[49] Neither is there a story depicting a reconciliation of female rivals. Whereas some of the adultery scenes dramatize a reconciliation between monarch and husband, where the latter not only restores the wife but also compensates the husband for his loss, and apologizes for his error (e.g. Pharaoh and Abimelech) the contest type-scenes never end with the reconciliation of the female rivals. Rather, what the contest type-scene ends with is the divinely ordained birth of a son to the barren wife, an outcome which is in the best interests of her husband.[50]

---

49. The motif of women's rivalry crops up in additional narratives in the Bible, e.g. the story of the prostitutes in Solomon's trial (1 Kgs 3.16-27) and the story of the cannibalistic women under Yehoram's rule (2 Kgs 6.26-30). The only biblical narrative to record women's friendship is the story of Ruth, whose happy resolution promotes the patriarchal cause. The friendship of Naomi and Ruth leads to the restoration of the patrilineal genealogy from Elimelch, Naomi's husband, to Obed, Ruth's son and David's ancestor. It is not, as Phyllis Trible suggests, 'a woman's story' about female friendship, but a patriarchal story about the only valid uses of female friendship from a man's point of view. See Trible's *God and the Rhetoric of Sexuality*, pp. 166-99.

50. The motif of female rivalry abounds in Western literature and culture. On the patriarchal uses of this motif see Andrea Dworkin, *Woman Hating* (New York: E.P.

If divisiveness between women is one literary strategy serving patriarchal ideology, assigning the female characters mutually exclusive
roles and capabilities is another. The contest type-scene presents us on
the one hand with a favored-but-barren wife, and on the other with an
unfavored-but-fertile wife. None of the contest scenes introduces a wife
who is both favored and fertile. The reason is clear: without some draw-
back in one of the wives there would be no story. The husband would
not marry a second wife, no conflict would ensue, and no divine intervention would be necessary. More importantly, the wife's inability to
perform her uxorial role, either as a sexual partner or as a reproductive
means is crucial for the legitimation of polygyny.[51] Had the contest
type-scene presented us with a wife who is both fertile and favored how
would it justify polygyny? It would have to admit that polygyny is not a
solution for the wife's inadequacy but rather, as Phyllis Bird suggests,

Dutton, 1974), pp. 29-50. For reflections on female relations in male-authored fiction, see also Louise Bernikow, *Among Women* (New York: Harper & Row, 1980).

51. Pedersen notes: 'Polygamy is one of the ethical demands of old Israel,
because the maintenance of the family is the greatest of all. Under the old simple
conditions there was nothing in polygamy to violate the idea of marriage'. See
Israel: Its Life and Culture, pp. 70-71. Pedersen's justification of polygyny as an
'ethical demand' rests on several unexamined premises. First, he assumes that the
accessibility of several women to one man necessarily produces more children. This
would be true were all men potent and were they all fertile. The fact that sterility
and impotence are never mentioned in the biblical text does not justify such
sweeping generalizations about the historical reality that is not referred to in the
text. Secondly, even if the accessibility of several wives does result in more children per family unit, this does not mean that the family unit must be controlled by
the man who fertilizes his wives. It is equally ethical and logical to let the wives
control the family, while using their husband as a fertilizing agent. In other words,
Pedersen justifies polygyny on the basis of 'the old simple conditions', but fails to
explain the connection between the 'maintenance of the family' and the particular
organization of power-structured relations within the patriarchal family. Thirdly,
Pedersen does not deal with the extension and modification of the polygynous
license, namely the institutions of concubinage and prostitution. If polygyny had
nothing to do with (male) 'licentiousness' as he claims (p. 70), prostitution would
be prohibited and concubinage would be restricted only to fertile concubines.
Fourthly, even if we were to accept that polygyny was required under 'the old
simple conditions', this does not mean that the institution is *ethical* but rather
pragmatic.

'a concession to the man's desire for more than one sexual partner'.[52] By presenting us with a first wife who is either barren (Sarah) or unfavored (Leah), the contest type-scene justifies this deviation from the monogamous arrangement implied by the creation story (Gen. 2.24). The justification is that one wife cannot adequately perform the sexual and procreative duties of a wife. Since these duties are determined by the husband's interest, the wife's inability to satisfy her husband is perceived as *her* failure, and because of this failure the husband is justified in resorting to additional wives in order to satisfy his interests.[53]

A closer look at the contest type-scene reveals two additional techniques serving as legitimating strategies of polygyny: justification and naturalization. While the former validates the custom by presenting reasons for its existence, the latter validates it by omitting reasons that would present the custom as 'natural'. The scenes involving Abraham and Jacob use justification, whereas the scene describing Elkanah and his polygynous household uses the technique of naturalization. For lack of a better term, I shall designate the justification in Abraham's case as 'procreative' in contradistinction to the 'romantic' justification in Jacob's case.

In both cases, however, the justification is based on the failure of the *wife* to perform her role either as procreative or as sexual: Sarai is barren and Leah, Jacob's first wife, is not as beautiful as Rachel, and consequently not as desirable from Jacob's point of view. In the first scene it is the wife who encourages her husband to have intercourse with another woman, her concubine, for procreative purposes: 'And Sarai said to Abram, "Behold now, Yhwh has kept me from bearing children; please go in to my maid; perhaps I shall obtain children through her." And Abram hearkened to the voice of Sarai' (Gen. 16.2). Not only is Sarai shown to take the initiative, but the text emphasizes that Abram obeys his wife's will in taking Hagar for a concubine.

In Jacob's case, polygyny is not justified on procreative grounds, and the identity of the first wife is confused, as Rachel is the first Jacob sees

---

52. Bird, 'Images of Women', p. 52.

53. Attempting to explain the custom of polygyny in ancient Israel, Roland de Vaux enumerates the husband's economic interest (by acquiring a second wife he acquires another servant), the desire for many children, and 'the fact that the Eastern woman, being married very young, ages quickly' (p. 25), namely the husband's sexual interest. De Vaux shows no awareness of the fact that all these 'reasons' serve the husband's interests. See *Ancient Israel*, pp. 24-26.

and likes, whereas Leah is in fact the first wife Jacob marries. What is made clear in the scene is that Jacob prefers Rachel to Leah; it does not clarify Rachel's or Leah's point of view. Unlike Sarai/Sarah neither Rachel nor Leah initiate the polygynous set-up. Also, the polygynous setup in the first case does not compromise Sarai/Sarah's status. When Hagar does challenge the supremacy of her mistress, the latter demands that she be expelled, an element which is repeated in both versions of this contest type-scene (Gen. 16.6; 21.10-14). In the second case the power relations between Rachel and Leah are more balanced, which exacerbates the rivalry between them. The co-wives are sisters of equal social status. Leah has precedence over Rachel as the בכרה (the first-born daughter), as Jacob's first wife, and as his fertile wife. Rachel, however, is the one Jacob meets first, and she is the one he desires. What Leah wins through reproductive performance, Rachel nearly out-weighs through sexual appeal.[54] What tips the scales in favor of Rachel is not her inherent uprightness or God's interest in her, but her husband's preference for her, as will be the case in the story of Elkanah and his favored wife, Hannah. What determines the status of the wife is directly related to the husband's attitude toward her.

What we are noticing, then, is a subtle shift from the justification of polygyny as a more effective procreative means to an implicit justification of polygyny as a means of accommodating the husband's preferences. What we notice in addition is the fact that the decision to create a polygynous arrangement shifts imperceptibly from wife to husband. Finally, the contest scenes move steadily from a situation where only one woman is recognized as a legitimate wife (Sarai/Sarah), to situations

54. On the power balance between Rachel and Leah, see J.P. Fokkelman, *Narrative Art in Genesis* (Assen: Van Gorcum, 1975), pp. 130-39. Although I agree with Fokkelman's description of the power balance between Rachel and Leah, I am not sure it strictly parallels the Jacob–Esau conflict, as Fokkelman argues. For one thing, the conflict between the brothers is not generated by their common interest in the same woman or by their will to achieve higher status through a closer association with her. For what determines the superior status in the case of the brothers is, in the final analysis, God, whereas in the case of the sisters, it is their shared husband. More importantly, in the case of the brothers there is little doubt as to the ultimate winner, whereas in the case of the sisters the balance is kept with only subtle shifts in power, which makes for a more convenient set-up for the principle of 'divide and rule'. This is not to deny the validity of Fokkelman's analysis of the important analogies between the major parts of the Jacob cycle. For a similar analysis, see Fishbane, *Text and Texture*, pp. 40-62.

that blur the status distinctions between the co-wives. The progressive equalizing of the co-wives' status makes it impossible to resolve the rivalry between the co-wives by expelling one of them, namely by establishing a monogamous arrangement. The text, however, is not over-anxious to make these subtle transitions too clear. Thus, in the case of Jacob the narrative presents the polygynous arrangement not as a result of Jacob's search for a second wife he prefers to his first one (Leah); rather the polygynous arrangement appears to be the outcome of unforeseen circumstances and of deceptive machinations on the part of the father-in-law. Although Jacob and Leah are said to be married for seven years before they are joined by Rachel, and although Leah is fertile, the text makes no reference to the sons born to Leah and Jacob during this time period. Rather it goes on to describe the process leading to Jacob's second marriage to Rachel (Gen. 29.26-29). The acceleration of the narrated time in this scene, I would like to suggest, not only conveys Jacob's subjective perception of the events ('and they seemed to him but a few days because of the love he had for her' [v. 20]), it also helps avoid a moral and ideological problem.[55] Had the text allowed more narrating time to the period that elapsed since Jacob's marriage to Leah, it would have had to mention Leah's successful procreative activities. This would necessitate an explanation for Jacob's second marriage: if Leah, Jacob's first wife, is capable of bearing children, why is it necessary to create a polygynous arrangement? The answer would make it perhaps all too obvious that polygyny is not only a solution for the wife's barrenness but the result of the husband's sexual preferences as well. By moving on to Jacob's second marriage as the prelude for the procreative contest between the sisters, the text avoids a problem that bears directly on biblical sexual politics.

The justification technique in the case of Abram and Jacob makes it clear that the polygynous setup was imposed on—rather than freely chosen by—both husbands. In the case of Abram it is the result of his wife's barrenness; in the case of Jacob, the result of Laban's machina-

55. J.P. Fokkelman notes this compression of seven years into one verse, and points out that the usage of the words אחדים ימים serves as an allusion to Gen. 27.44 in which Rebekah instructs Jacob to stay away—ימים אחדים—until Esau's anger subsides. See *Narrative Art in Genesis*, p. 128. For a discussion of narrating and narrated time in the biblical story, see Jacob Licht, *Storytelling in the Bible* (Jerusalem: Magnes Press, 1978), pp. 96-120. See also Bar-Efrat, *The Art of the Biblical Story*, pp. 154-88.

tions.[56] Polygyny here appears as the result of an accident, not as a solution to a vexing predicament. Nevertheless, in both cases polygyny appears to be necessary and unavoidable. In this sense both scenes differ markedly from the final scene involving Elkanah, Peninnah and Hannah. Unlike the previous scenes, here the polygynous arrangement is presented without any explanations: 'He had two wives: the name of the one was Hannah and the name of the other Peninnah. And Peninnah had sons, but Hannah had no sons.' (1 Sam. 1.2). No causal link is established here between Hannah's barrenness and Elkanah's marital relations with Peninnah. The text does not indicate whether Elkanah marries Hannah, his favored wife, after his marriage to Peninnah (as Jacob does), or whether, conversely, he marries Peninnah realizing that his wife is barren. The omission of these details implies that the narrator sees no need to explain or justify it. This is how the naturalization technique operates. By omitting explanations, it implies that nothing needs to be explained, that there is nothing outstanding or questionable in the presented events.

The order in which the contest scenes are presented reveals an increasingly dismissive attitude towards polygyny as a problem to be reckoned with or accounted for.[57] A husband flanked by two or more

---

56. Nevertheless, Jacob appropriates to himself concubines as well. Jacob's concubines, Bilhah and Zilpah, are shown to be given to him by his wives, much as in the case of Hagar and Abram. Yet, whereas Sarai gives Hagar to Abram hoping to be 'built through her', to procure at least one son, Rachel and Leah allow their husband access to their maids as part of their competition for higher status in the polygynous household. Sarai presents as the direct cause for her action the fact that 'Yhwh has prevented me from bearing children' (Gen. 16.2). In the case of Rachel, the cause, as presented by the narrator, is not so much her barrenness as her jealousy of Leah (Gen. 30.1-3).

57. An examination of related episodes reveals that a similar dismissiveness characterizes related episodes dealing with the polygynous marriages of Israel's leaders. While, in the book of Exodus, for example, Moses' marriage to the Cushite woman after his marriage to Zipporah generates some protest on the part of Aaron and Miriam (Num. 12.1), later references to the practice of polygyny by Israel's leaders, like Gideon (Judg. 8.30-31), David (2 Sam. 5.13) and Solomon (1 Kgs 11.3) are mentioned as a natural piece of evidence requiring no explanation. It is true that, in Moses' cases, the text does not explain whether the protest against his second marriage is related to the foreign provenance of the Cushite woman, or to the polygynous aspect of the marriage. Nevertheless, I think we can conclude that it is not treated in the same tolerant way that characterizes the reports on the polygy-

wives increasingly emerges as an acceptable arrangement. The opposite is true of the gender-reversed situation, presenting a wife flanked by more than one husband, namely a polyandrous situation. The adultery type-scene illustrates this development clearly. In the first scene, Sarai is shown to participate in actuality in a polyandrous arrangement (Gen. 12.19). In the second scene Abimelech takes Sarah from Abraham (Gen. 20.2), but the narrator explains that 'Abimelech had not come near her' (Gen. 20.4). In the third scene the wife, Rebekah, remains with her husband, and is not even taken into the king's palace (Gen. 26.8-9) yet she could potentially become accessible to two men. In the fourth adultery scene, the idea of a woman sharing two husbands is not even remotely entertained as a possibility. The lawful husband is removed from the scene through death; the wife passes from the custody of one husband to another. She is not *returned* to her original master. This scene avoids the representation of woman as accessible to two men simultaneously. Polyandrous arrangements are not only heavily censured, they are also progressively deleted from the biblical narrative even as representations of unacceptable behavior.

Although all the participants involved in the Genesis adultery type-scene—notably, Yhwh, the monarch and the husband—seem to be in agreement about the objectionability of polyandry there is no explicit explanation as to why it is sinful or immoral. Only in the final episode involving David and Bathsheba is adultery decried as an act of embezzlement, displeasing to God (2 Sam. 12.9) and morally unforgivable. In order to bring out the immoral aspect of David's adultery, Nathan the prophet stresses that the poor man in his parable had only one ewe lamb whereas the rich man had many flocks and herds (2 Sam. 12.2-3). The moral pathos of Nathan's denunciation is to a large extent determined by the fact that Uriah was monogamous, that he had only one wife, one possession. It is instructive to note that all adultery scenes are implicitly using the same logic in their denunciation of the adulterous act. All of them present the husband as monogamous, although in other scenes the same husband may have more than one wife. Abram/Abraham has a

nous marriages of Israel's later leaders. The critique on Solomon is not directed against his practice of polygyny per se but against the foreign provenance of Solomon's wives, who induced him, as the story suggests, to follow other gods (1 Kgs 11.5-6). It should also be noted that like in the contest type-scenes, it is the co-wives and concubines—rather than the husband—who are blamed for whatever results the polygynous set-up is said to bring about.

concubine Hagar in addition to his wife, yet he is presented as monogamous in both adultery scenes. The reason for this configuration is
clear. A bigamous or polygamous husband would not be as convincing
a victim figure in the adultery type-scene. Since this type-scene validates the husband's exclusive access to his wife's sexuality by resorting
to moral rationalizations based on the husband's relative vulnerability,
it would not serve its didactic purposes to introduce the husband as the
owner of several wives.

The only acceptable solution to a polyandrous—or adulterous—situation is the removal of one of the claimants, and the wife's final
appropriation by a single lawful husband. In the Genesis adultery
scenes, the second claimant is punished and the wife is restored to her
original husband; in the final adultery scene, the first husband is
removed from the scene (through death) and the wife is transferred to
the second claimant. The resolution implies that the restoration of order
to the family is contingent upon the appropriation of a wife by her one
and only husband. In the contest type-scene, conversely, order is not
equated with the wife's exclusive status as the husband's mate but with
fertility. The problem in the contest type-scene is not the conflict
between competing co-wives, but the wife's barrenness. Concomitantly, the removal of one wife (or concubine) is not acceptable. When
Hagar runs away from her oppressive household she is told by Yhwh's
angel to return to her mistress: 'And Yhwh's angel said to her: "Return
to your mistress and suffer under her hands" ' (Gen. 16.9). The reward
for Hagar's suffering will be a 'wild' son and much progeny (Gen.
16.10-12). Although Hagar is shown to be more oppressed by Sarai
than Abram is by Pharaoh, she is not delivered by Yhwh but instead
told to embrace her agony, as this will entitle her to a large number of
descendants. The moral problem of human oppression, and the cause
that might have brought it about (namely the polygynous arrangement),
are not so much as addressed in this context. Similarly, when Hagar and
Ishmael are expelled by Sarah in the second version of the story, Yhwh
justifies the act, not on the basis of Sarah's suffering or the violation of
her rights as a 'lawful' wife, but because Sarah is the mother of Isaac,
'because through Isaac shall your descendants be named' (Gen. 21.12).
Since the contest type-scene defines the underlying problem in terms of
barrenness rather than in terms of the women's rivalry, the resolution of
type-scenes is always related to fertility and the increase of progeny.
This resolution is clearly consonant with the husband's interests, as it

foregrounds the need for progeny as the central problem, and at the same time legitimates the possession of two or more wives.

The patriarchal ideology of the type-scenes under consideration determines to a large extent the manifestations of the national and monotheistic aspects of biblical ideology. In harmony with the national ideology of the biblical narrative the type-scenes under consideration demonstrate that the historical continuity and survival of Israel was supervised and secured by God: God took a personal interest in the lives of Israel's patriarchs (Abraham, Jacob), protecting them and providing them with sons; God supervised the birth of Israel's leaders (Samuel, Solomon); and He is, in the final analysis, responsible for the survival of the nation. In harmony with the monotheistic ideology of the Bible, the type-scenes under consideration demonstrate that God is just and merciful, that He redeems the innocent victim and punishes the evil oppressor. But what determines the identity and gender of the national leader and the innocent victim is often the Bible's implicit patriarchal ideology, which gives man supremacy over woman.

The victim in the adultery type-scene is always the husband who loses his wife to a more powerful rival. The wife in this type-scene is a desirable object, evaluated in terms of the threat she poses her husband. The wife is never portrayed as victimized either by her husband or by her claimant. No biblical narrative dramatizes the ordeal of an innocent wife falsely charged with adultery by a jealous and possessive husband. No biblical narrative portrays a wife's victimization by a husband who turns his attention and affection to another wife or concubine. No biblical narrative considers the tribulations of a woman who is forced to marry and stay united with her rapist, or the deprivations of a divorced woman who is not allowed to share her husband's inheritance. Since in biblical narrative the victimization of a wife by her husband constitutes an impossible contingency, it is unlikely that God would be shown to hearken to and redeem such innocent victims. By contrast God is shown to redeem barren wives. Although the contest type-scene presents the wife's fertilization as *her* redemption, it is obvious that the husband too benefits from this propitious turn of events. After all, the wife's sons will become *his* property, they will inherit from *him* and perpetuate *his* name. In harmony with the husband's interests, it is always the barren wife who is perceived by the biblical narrative as the victim, not the unfavored wife. Consequently, God will be shown to help the former not the latter. Divine redemption is not independent of the Bible's patriarchal underpinnings. It is the biblical perception of the wife as her husband's exclusive property that undergirds the husband's role as victim in the adultery type-scene, just as it is the perception of the wife as a means of reproduction that undergirds her role as victim. The Bible's monotheistic ideology, namely the belief that God is just, and that He takes a personal interest in innocent victims, is closely intertwined with the Bible's androcentric perspective and patriarchal ideology.

Conjugal Narratives: Notes Toward a Comparison

We must finally consider the different characterizations of the wife-figure in the adultery type-scene and in the contest type-scene. We noted earlier that the former is paradigmatic only of one aspect of the biblical wife-figure. This aspect refers to the wife's conjugal role. In this role the wife-figure plays the passive and rather shady role of a desirable object, who poses a threat to both her husband and her claimant. The aspect revealed in the contest type-scene, on the other hand, corresponds to the wife's reproductive role. Here the wife is active and often aggressive, she takes the initiative and is noticed by God. Although the biblical wife often performs both a conjugal and a reproductive role it is nevertheless remarkable that these roles are separated by literary means. Sarai/Sarah, for example, performs both a conjugal and a reproductive role; nevertheless, the narrative contexts in which she fulfills these roles are carefully separated, and her literary characterization is rather different in both contexts. In the adultery type-scene, Sarah plays the conjugal role: she appears as a passive adjunct, her husband's extension, with no distinct point of view. In the contest type-scene she appears as an independent agent, with a will of her own, and a point of view that is largely supported by God. Another example is Bathsheba. We have seen her perform the conjugal role as Uriah's coveted wife and David's obedient servant in the adultery scene of 2 Samuel 11. But Bathsheba performs a reproductive-maternal role as well. In this role she appears in 1 Kgs 1.11-31. Her main function here is to fight for the interests of Solomon, her son. Encouraged by Nathan the prophet to take Solomon's case to King David, she proves herself as an eloquent and shrewd politician, as well as a dedicated mother.[58]

58. Other examples include Rebekah, Zipporah and Rizpah the daughter of Ayah. Rebekah, who is a passive and peripheral agent playing the desirable wife,

The literary separation between the conjugal and reproductive-maternal roles of the biblical wife is clearly not restricted to the type-scenes and characters I have focused on throughout this chapter. It appears to typify the characterization of all biblical wives, although the specific strategy of separation may vary from one case to another. A diachronic consideration of wife-figures, namely their examination by the order in which they are presented in the Bible, reveals a development toward a greater polarization of the uxorial roles. Whereas earlier narratives allow the same wife-figure to function effectively as both conjugal partner and maternal agent—albeit in separate literary contexts—later narratives are increasingly reluctant to let the same wife-figure function both as a 'good' conjugal partner and as a maternal agent.

Rebekah, one of the early wife-figures, is allowed to function as an impressive potential wife, namely as a beautiful bride as well as resourceful and morally principled virgin (Gen. 24.16-67).[59] In a later narrative she is allowed to function as a dedicated mother, although her deception of Isaac leaves much to be desired in terms of her role as actual wife (Gen. 27.5-17). It would seem that Rebekah's dedication to both her husband and her son are mutually exclusive. To be a good mother, Rebekah must be a bad wife. In order to vouchsafe Isaac's blessing for Jacob, she has to encourage the latter to deceive the blind and helpless Isaac. When the biblical wife appears in the capacity of both conjugal partner as well as maternal agent, one of these roles must be either marginalized or compromised. Nevertheless, Rebekah is one of the rare examples of a biblical wife whose conjugal *and* maternal roles are treated with some detail and with a limited measure of respect.

Hannah, a later wife-figure, is impressive as a potential mother but treated rather marginally when characterized as a wife. All we know

---

appears as a shrewd and independent mother (Gen. 24.16-26; 27.5-13). Zipporah, who appears as an indistinct object when fulfilling a conjugal role (Exod. 2.21), emerges as an autonomous agent in her role as mother (Exod. 4.25-26). Rizpah, Saul's concubine, is a passive object of contention between Ishbosheth and Abner (2 Sam. 2.7-12), but in her maternal role she appears to have a mind and will of her own as well as courage and unusual dedication to her dead sons (2 Sam. 21.10-11). In all these cases the female characters do not transcend their restrictive roles as agents, namely as secondary, and often peripheral in relation to the male characters involved. Nevertheless, in their maternal role the same female characters are given a larger measure of autonomy and literary stature.

59. On the characterization of Rebekah in the betrothal type-scene, see my previous chapter on the biblical bride.

about her conjugal role is refracted from her husband's point of view. It is his attitude, actions and speech that give us a glimpse into Hannah's conjugal role (1 Sam. 1.5, 8). For the most part, however, Hannah functions as a potential mother-figure.[60]

David's wives dramatize the uxorial role separation even more clearly. We have already noted the contextual separation in Bathsheba's characterization as wife and mother. We have seen her as an impressive character only in her maternal role. In her conjugal role as Uriah's wife, and as David's future wife, she is both marginal as a literary character and ambiguous from a moral, evaluative point of view. As we have seen in our discussion of the adultery type-scene, Bathsheba is not only an opaque object of desire, but the cause of Uriah's death and of David's moral downfall. Still, Bathsheba is permitted to function as both a conjugal and as a maternal agent. This is not permitted to David's other wives, notably Michal and Abigail. Whereas both wives show resourcefulness and intelligence as conjugal agents, neither of them functions as a maternal agent. Abigail is perhaps one of the most impressive wife-figures. She forestalls David's vindictive retaliation against her husband with diplomatic skill and feminine charm, winning David's heart in the process and becoming his wife (1 Sam. 25.14-43). Although, as we have seen earlier, Abigail is only allowed to morally supersede her villainous husband, Nabal, but not David, the husband-hero. She nevertheless emerges as one of the most positive wife-figures in the biblical narrative. In addition to being intelligent and beautiful, she is also obedient, complying with David's political ambitions as well as with his marriage proposition. One wonders, then, why Abigail, the perfect wife, was not chosen as the mother of the successor to the throne. Why is it Bathsheba, the passive and dubious conjugal agent, who is selected for the ultimate honor of being the king's mother? Not only does Abigail fail to become the king's mother, she is never characterized as a mother at all. We learn from another source that Abigail bore a son (1 Chron. 3.1), but no further detail is offered in the Bible that might have illuminated Abigail's maternal role. I would like to suggest that there is a causal relationship between the emphasis on Abigail's conjugal role and the omission of her maternal role. Abigail does not function as a maternal agent *because* she is the perfect wife-figure. In the capacity of both wife and mother, Abigail might have constituted

---

60. On Hannah's characterization in the annunciation type-scene, see Chapter 3, 'The Biblical Mother: The Annunciation and Temptation Type-Scenes'.

too powerful a female image, one that could have perhaps challenged the glamor of her husband, David. Bathsheba is a safer candidate for the role of significant mother, just *because* she cannot boast of any achievements as a conjugal agent.

Michal too is a powerful conjugal agent. Michal proves herself a resourceful and intelligent wife as she lets David escape Saul's murderous messengers (1 Sam. 19.11-18). She does not hesitate to confront Saul's henchmen and destroy their plot with ruse and cunning. Michal does not stoop to her father's authority and sides with her husband, the man she loves (1 Sam. 18.20). Michal will show the same pride and independence when in a later scene she confronts her husband and derides him for the unbecoming spectacle he has made of himself in front of the crowds (2 Sam. 6.16-23). Unlike Abigail, Michal is neither beautiful nor obedient to her husband, but like the former, she emerges as one of the most interesting and forceful wife-figures in the biblical narrative, and like Abigail she is confined to a conjugal role. If in Abigail's case the narrative avoids dealing with her reproductive-maternal role, in Michal's case it is explicit about her. The text explicitly states that 'Michal the daughter of Saul had no child till her dying day' (2 Sam. 6.23). As we noted earlier, Michal's childlessness may not only reflect the strained marital relationship she has with David, but also divine punishment for her impudence toward her husband-hero, David. In addition to this, the obliteration of her maternal role follows a biblical strategy of dividing and ruling, namely of splitting the wife-figure into disparate roles so as to keep her in her place.

By splitting the wife-figure into conjugal and maternal aspects, either by assigning each aspect a different literary context or by assigning each role to different wife-figures, the conjugal narrative manages to keep the wife-figure in her proper place. Like the strategy of moral subordination discussed earlier, the strategy of role separation ensures that the wife-figure remains secondary and subordinate to her male counterpart. By consistently eschewing the representation of wives who are morally superior to their husband-heroes, the conjugal narrative endorses the idea that wives *deserve* to be politically subordinated to their husbands. By splitting the wife-figure into different roles, the conjugal narrative makes sure that no wife-figure emerges as more significant than her male partner. By displaying wife-figures who are less significant than their male counterparts the conjugal narrative justifies the political subordination of wives to their husbands.

But biblical sexual politics do not work only through the agency of the represented characters and situations. The Bible also manipulates the representational media, namely the literary status, function and relations of the characters involved in order to convey its message.

As we have seen in our discussion of the adultery type-scene the significance of the wife-figure derives from her relationship with her husband. As an object of desire she threatens his life and moral integrity. As his adjunct, she offers an extension of his point of view, rather than an independent perspective on the represented situation. In the contest type-scene, on the other hand, the wife—in her role as potential or actual mother—is allowed to possess a point of view of her own. Yet, as we have seen, what determines the plot development is the husband's interest, for it is the wife *he* prefers who is the focus of the contest type-scene. It is *her* transition from barrenness to fertility that commands our attention. Furthermore, it is her transition to fertility not her characterization that commands our attention. Even in her reproductive-maternal role, the wife-figure is, in the final analysis, what Cheryl Exum calls 'an enabler'.[61] As soon as her reproductive or protective function vis-à-vis the male hero is fulfilled, she disappears from the literary scene.

Soon after Hannah gives birth to Samuel, she is whisked off the stage; just as soon after Michal enables David's escape, and soon after Abigail's protective mission is completed, *they* are whisked off the stage. In addition to serving as enablers for and protectors of the male heroes, the wife-figures often serve as objective correlatives of different phases in their husbands' lives and careers. As Adele Berlin demonstrates, David's wives, specifically his attitude toward them, reflect different stages in his ascension to political power.[62] David's marriage of convenience with Michal reveals him as a calculating politician, as he uses the king's daughter to gain and consolidate his political power. David's relationship with Abigail reveals him as an eager but fair-minded popular leader. His marriage to the beautiful, wise and rich

---

61. The role of enabler and protector is not restricted to the biblical wife. Cheryl Exum discusses the role of women as those who enabled Moses to rise to leadership in her article, ' "You Shall Let Every Daughter Live" ', pp. 63-82. Exum stresses the central role of the female characters in the beginning chapters of Exodus. In my opinion, their significance lies in paving the way to Moses' survival and political leadership.

62. Berlin, 'Characterization in Biblical Narrative', pp. 69-85.

Abigail signals his ability to win people's respect and submission even prior to his nationwide recognition as king. David's sexual relationship with Bathsheba presents the king at the peak of his power, while signaling the beginning of his descent. His forbidden lust for the married woman parallels his desire to expand his empire, as well as the manner and extent to which he oversteps his authority. Abishag, the young and beautiful concubine who is rounded up to keep King David warm, personifies David's waning days as a senescent and impotent ruler (1 Kgs 1.1-4).

Berlin argues that no easy generalization can be made concerning David's wives, as each of them reveals not only different psychological, moral and temperamental traits, but also different categories of literary characterization.[63] Abishag, for example, can be seen as an agent, who is a function of the plot or the setting. Abigail is in some ways the incarnation of the ideal wife. By contrast, Michal and Bathsheba in 1 Kings 1–2 can be seen as full-fledged characters. Although I agree with Berlin that David's wives reveal different characteristics and different modes of characterization, I do not think that this heterogeneity defies categorization. It seems to me that David's wives exemplify rather than challenge the restrictive representation of the wife-figure in the conjugal narratives. For despite the considerable differences between them they are all secondary in significance and function relative to David, their husband-hero. Even in the few and limited scenes in which Michal or Abigail appear to dominate the narrative, it is David, not his wives, who motivates the plot development. He is the story's *raison d'être*.

1 Samuel 19 is not interested in Michal as an autonomous character but rather in dramatizing for the reader David's narrow escape from Saul. The implication is that God is in fact working behind the scenes to safeguard David's survival against all odds. Similarly, the attention given to Abigail is motivated by the need to explain David's political achievements even while confronting stronger enemies, of the like of Nabal. Abigail's collaboration with David is intended to dramatize the subtle ways in which God is transferring power and status from David's enemies to David. Abigail's actions not only explain how David gains power and authority but as a beautiful, intelligent and obedient woman she also embodies the prize David wins along with his political victory

63. Berlin, 'Characterization in Biblical Narrative', p. 78.

over Nabal. In like fashion, Bathsheba in 1 Kings 1–2 does not figure as a full-fledged character, but rather as an agent in a plot describing the shift in political power from David to Solomon. Her major function in this scene is to protect the interest of her son, and to pave the way to the throne just as Michal paves David's way to the throne. This does not mean that Michal, Abigail and Bathsheba in 1 Kings 1–2 are peripheral and insignificant characters. The fact is that they exemplify some of the most complex and well-developed wife-figures in conjugal narratives. Nevertheless, the form and function of their characterization is determined by their husband-hero. The significance of Michal, Abigail, Bathsheba and Abishag, as well as the evaluation of their characters, is contingent upon their hero-husband's attitude towards them.[64] In this sense, despite their heterogeneity, the restrictive framework subordinates them both in terms of their represented characteristics and their literary status to the husband-hero, who is inevitably the major human subject of the biblical conjugal narrative.

Thus, both the structure of biblical conjugal narratives and the characterization of their male and female protagonists reflect the androcentric thinking and the patriarchal ideology that inspire biblical marriage laws. The double standard allowing the husband to do what is forbidden the wife and assigning him the status of her master and possessor is codified into the literary patterns that make up the conjugal narrative. The patriarchal ideology implicitly justifies this double stan-

---

64. What frequently determines the evaluation of wife-figures in conjugal narratives is not so much their attitude toward God, but their attitude toward their husband-heros. The good wife is the wife who acts in the interest of her husband-hero; the bad wife undermines his interests. This evaluative principle dominates the acrostic poem in Prov. 31.10-31, which describes the ideal wife. The 'woman of valor' is the wife whose *husband* 'trusts in her'. 'She does him good and not evil all the days of her life' (vv. 10-12). The 'good' that the perfect wife does her husband is described in the poem through the wife's indefatigable effort to manage her husband's property, increase his financial gain and give him a good reputation. The wife's incessant work allows her husband to be 'known in the gates, as he sits among the elders of the land' (v. 23). This industrious, charitable (v. 20) and wise (v. 26), upper-middle-class woman is rewarded not through God's recognition but through the satisfaction and praise of her husband and sons: 'Her sons rise up and call her blessed, her husband also, and he praises her' (v. 28). In the entire poem there is only one reference to God: 'Grace is deceitful and beauty is vain, a woman who fears Yhwh she shall be praised' (v. 30). Compare Ochshorn, *The Female Experience*, pp. 191-93.

dard by subordinating the wife-figure to the husband-hero on a moral-religious, national and artistic level. By presenting the wife as morally inferior to her husband-hero, by presenting God as taking a special interest in the husband (and only tangentially in the wife), by presenting the husband as a national hero (patriarch or king), and by using the wife-figure as an adjunct or foil to the character of the husband, the conjugal narrative implies that wives *deserve* to be politically subordinate to their husbands because of their *innate* inferiority relative to their husbands. The political discrimination against wives is thus elevated into a logical, natural, moral and divinely sanctioned principle.

The patriarchal strategies that prevail in the conjugal narratives we have considered here dominate what can be seen as the archetypal conjugal narrative, involving the first husband and wife, the story of Adam and Eve. Eve is portrayed as morally inferior to Adam, because it is she who causes him to sin against God, by offering him the fruit of the forbidden tree (Gen. 3.6).[65] The text shows no awareness of the fact that Eve is punished a priori, even before her alleged sin by the mere fact that she is created second to Adam, that the purpose of her creation is to alleviate his loneliness (Gen. 2.18). It is also not recognized that Eve's a priori secondariness may in some way be related to her alleged sin: the possibility that Eve was more susceptible to temptation because she was not there when God ordered Adam not to eat of the forbidden fruit is not mentioned in the text. Like the wife-figures who follow her, Eve too is shown to be the cause of her husband's moral-religious sin. Yet, whereas in the conjugal narratives we have examined the justification of the wife's inferior status is rather implicit and subtle, in the creation story, it is more explicit. It is patently presented as morally correct and divinely sanctioned punishment: 'And to the woman He said: "I will greatly multiply your pain and your travail; in pain you shall give birth to children, and your desire shall be for your husband and he shall rule over you" ' (Gen. 3.16). The principles couched in God's address to Eve offer a mythic paraphrase of the legal, political principles underlying the wife's role: her conjugal duty is to bear children to her husband, to belong exclusively to him ('your desire shall be for your husband') and to accept his authority. The circular reasoning of patriarchal ideol-

---

65. Phyllis Trible romanticizes Gen. 2–3 as 'a love story gone awry' and argues that the story is inspired by an egalitarian view of the sexes. See *God and the Rhetoric of Sexuality*, pp. 72-143. For a rebuttal of her interpretation, see Ochshorn, *The Female Experience*, pp. 210-17.

ogy is dramatized in this story more blatantly than in any other conjugal narrative; woman is politically oppressed because she is inferior to man. To 'prove' that she is inferior the conjugal narrative presents her as secondary to her husband—only he is shown to have a relationship with God, whereas her significance lies in her relationship with her husband. In addition, the narrative describes her as morally inferior to her husband, by ascribing to her a sin greater than his own. The allegedly moral inferiority of the wife-figure validates the legal discrimination against women, as described in the beginning of the chapter. In this fashion, the biblical narrative complements biblical law. By constructing the wife-figure as inferior to her husband, it sets up an image that in many ways is far more effective a strategy of biblical sexual politics than explicit legal injunctions.

Chapter 6

THE IDEAL DAUGHTER: USEFUL GAPS
AND SOME DIDACTIC IMPLICATIONS

Much in the same way that biblical mothers are characterized in relation to their sons, the few narratives dealing with daughter-figures rarely make reference to their mothers. Biblical daughters are the children of fathers, and unlike their male counterparts who are allowed to experience an array of conflicting allegiances to their fathers—one thinks of such examples as Jacob's sons and David's sons—the repertoire of the biblical daughter is limited. Biblical daughters are liminal creatures living in an uncertain space, at risk both in their father's house and outside it.[1] Yet, the father's responsibility for his daughter's demise is often obscured, as is the patriarchal system that robs daughters of power and status. The biblical narrative is more likely to foreground the exceptional case that permits daughters to inherit their father's possessions (Zelophehad's daughters in Num. 27.3-4 and Achsah in Judg. 1.15).[2] It also presents daughters as instigators of father–daughter incest, thus reversing the more likely scenario that has been suppressed by patriarchal civilization (Lot's daughters in Gen. 19).[3]

---

1. See the discussion of Achsah, Jephthah's daughter, the concubine in Judg. 19 and other daughter figures in Bal, *Death and Dissymmetry*, especially pp. 95-127. See also Karla G. Shargent, 'Living on the Edge: The Liminality of Daughters in Genesis to 2 Samuel', in Brenner (ed.), *A Feminist Companion to Samuel and Kings*, pp. 26-42.

2. For a discussion of Zelophehad's daughters, see Ankie Sterring, 'The Will of the Daughters', in Brenner (ed.), *A Feminist Companion to Exodus to Deuteronomy*, pp. 88-101.

3. See Ilona Rashkow, 'Daughters and Fathers in Genesis... Or, What is Wrong With This Picture?', in Brenner (ed.), *A Feminist Companion to Exodus to Deuteronomy*, pp. 22-36. On the suppression of father–daughter rape in Western culture and literature, see Christine Froula, 'The Daughter's Seduction: Sexual Violence and Literary History', in Lynda Boose and Betty S. Flowers (eds.), *Daughters*

One of the more detailed narratives about father–daughter relationships is the story of Jephthah's daughter in Judg. 11.34-40. This narrative offers us a rare instance in which a father and a daughter exchange
words. This rare exchange is a prelude to the nameless daughter's death.
She unwittingly condemns herself as she goes out to greet her father,
who had vowed to sacrifice to Yhwh the first to leave his house.[4] Phyllis
Trible praises the daughter as the courageous victim of a faithless father's foolish vow.[5] By indicting Jephthah, Trible absolves the text and
reaffirms its moral authority. By idealizing the nameless daughter, she
ignores the patriarchal investments in the positive portrayal of a per-
fectly obedient daughter. For, as I will argue here, there is a didactic
reasoning behind the idealization of female self-abnegation. Lamentation and mourning—the responses Trible accepts as adequate interpretations of the women's fate—forestall questioning. They make it
impossible to ask about the patriarchal investments of a story about a
self-abnegating daughter, who is willing to sacrifice her life for a father
who has egregiously erred.

The second question that will occupy us in what follows is the manner in which the daughter's story is both told and erased. It is as if the
narrator does not wish us to dwell too much on this disturbing story.
Though the brief narrative somewhat disrupts the flow of events, the
daughter's loss is bracketed within the broader description of the
father's military exploits. The elliptical description, the gaps in information, the embedding of the story in the context of Jephthah's other
adventures, the ambiguity that marks the narration subdue the tragic
edge of the story.[6] While the general features of the daughter are approvingly sketched out, she remains an enigma, a suppressed voice that is
not quite heard out. What will preoccupy us in this chapter then are the

and Fathers (Baltimore: The Johns Hopkins University Press, 1989), pp. 111-35.
For useful discussions of the father–daughter relationship in Western culture and
literature see Lynda Boose, 'The Father's House and the Daughter in It: Structures
of Western Culture's Daughter-Father Relationship', in Boose and Flowers (eds.),
Daughters and Fathers, pp. 19-74.

    4.   On violence in the father's speech and the danger of going out, see J. Cheryl
Exum's analysis of the story of Jephthah's daughter in *Fragmented Women*, pp. 16-
41. On the boundaries of the father's home as a trope in Western literature and culture, see Boose, 'The Father's House and the Daughter in It'.

    5.   See *Texts of Terror*, pp. 93-116.

    6.   On the ambiguity of the narrative, see David Marcus, *Jephthah and His Vow*
(Lubbock: Texas Tech Press, 1986), especially pp. 52-55.

literary strategies that on the one hand express and on the other repress the story and voice of the biblical daughter.

The Uses of Ambiguity

The narrative about Jephthah's sacrifice of his one and only daughter is embedded in the larger narrative about Jephthah, taking up six compact verses (Judg. 11.34-40) within the larger story that comprises 40 verses (Judg. 11.1-3; 12.1-7). It is constructed as a sad interlude disrupting the flow of two success stories: Jephthah's victory over the Ammonites (Judg. 11.12-33) and his successful conquest in his battle with the Ephraimites (Judg. 12.1-6).[7] Considered synchronically, Jephthah's encounter with his nameless daughter forms a contrastive analogy with the public success story that frames it, and a complementary analogy with the introduction of Jephthah as a private man (Judg. 11.1-5). Read diachronically, Jephthah's encounter with his daughter creates an emotional 'slope', as it follows the description of Jephthah's political and moral-religious ascent. The emotional effect produced by Jephthah's encounter with his daughter parallels the emotional nadir with which Jephthah's personal description begins. Although our interest will lead us to focus on this narrative in the next few pages, it should be kept in mind that this story is by no means an independent narrative unit; neither does it constitute the central episode in the story of Jephthah. The structural and thematic relations between this unit and the frame story will be discussed in detail later. Jephthah's daughter first appears in Judg. 11.34 without ever being introduced to the reader: 'And Jephthah came to Mizpah, to his home, and here [הנה] his daughter is coming out towards him with timbrels and dances and she is the only one; beside her he does not have a son or a daughter.'[8] The

---

7. Although the story of Jephthah per se begins in Judges 11.1, with the introduction of his familial roots and his early biography, one should consider Judg. 10.6-18 as the general exposition to Jephthah's story, as it describes the political chaos and oppression of the Israelites by their enemies—notably the Ammonites—a situation which explains and catalyzes Jephthah's ascent to the position of judge. On the problems of narrative delimitation in the Hebrew Bible, see Perry and Sternberg, 'Caution: A Literary Text!', pp. 608-63, but especially pp. 631-42 (Hebrew).

8. The RSV translates: 'and behold his daughter came out to meet him'. By rendering יצאת in the past tense, the translation misses the narrative break which the original text effects by the transition from the consecutive verbs in the past to the

reason for the omission of even the most rudimentary information about Jephthah's daughter is indicative of her literary status in the story: she is a secondary character in the unfolding drama. Her significance to the story derives from her relationship with her father and the impact she will have on him. Had she not made the fatal mistake of coming out of the house to greet her father, she might have been consigned to oblivion, as is her mother, who is never mentioned in the course of the story. Likewise had Jephthah not made his fatal vow to sacrifice the first creature coming out of his house (Judg. 11.31), one wonders if his daughter would be mentioned at all. The existence of Jephthah's daughter as a literary character is predicated on the intersection of her actions with the major plot line of the narrative, which consists of her father's actions. What brings Jephthah's daughter into existence is an accident: her unpredictable (from Jephthah's and the reader's point of view) emergence from her father's house. Verse 34 establishes the fundamental rules that will undergird the daughter's presentation henceforth: she is nameless, she is identified and defined by her filial relationship with Jephthah, and it is this relationship that underlies her characterization and determines her significance in the story.

Jephthah's daughter is not introduced by name because her name— her own character and identity, independent of her relationship to Jephthah—is of little relevance to the story.[9] The narrator stops the narrative flow to introduce the daughter as Jephthah's 'only one' (יחידה), repeating for emphasis and clarification that 'beside her he does not have a son or a daughter'. More than this presentation characterizes the daughter, it clarifies what the daughter represents for the father, and what consequently her loss will mean to him. It is also inserted as an explanation for Jephthah's desperate outcry and mourning gesture which follow in v. 35. The daughter's appearance is framed with the parameters of Jephthah's sight. The adverb והנה (usually rendered as

daughter's action which is rendered in the present tense. It also weakens the impression that the daughter's action is not an independent event, but rather, it is reported as part of what Jephthah sees. On the literary significance of transitions in verb tenses, see Maya Fruchtman, 'A Few Notes on the Study of Biblical Narrative', *Hasifrut* 6, pp. 63-66.

9.   In the biblical context a name signifies more than a mere appellation whose purpose is to distinguish one person from the others. The process of naming, as demonstrated in the creation stories (Gen. 1–2), for example, is a process of calling something into being and investing it with both existence and distinctive essence.

'behold') switches the narrative point of view from that of the omniscient, authoritative narrator to the subjective point of view of Jephthah, yet it does not necessarily detract from the validity of the statement.[10] Rather than question the validity of Jephthah's point of view, the switch effectuated by והנה reflects the horrifying twist of events, the sudden and unexpected switch from Jephthah's public victory to personal defeat. The omission of the transformator 'and he saw' intensifies the abrupt transition in Jephthah's consciousness and the horrifying surprise he is experiencing. The only one who is unaware of the ironic incongruity between appearance and 'reality' is the daughter. Greeting her father with timbrels and dance the daughter is presented as a victim of dramatic irony, as she is the only one who is not aware of the gruesome meaning of her joyful actions. The incompatibility of her joy and Jephthah's grief further intensifies the incongruity between her limited knowledge and 'reality'. For it is not only Jephthah, but the narrator and the reader as well who become aware of the perfect congruity between the daughter's actions and Jephthah's wording of his vow. The daughter's coming out to greet her father echoes the words Jephthah uses in his vow. He vowed that 'the one who will come out to meet me' (היוצא אשר יצא, lit. 'the comer forth who will come forth to meet me'), will be sacrificed. The verse describing his daughter's actions echoes these words by ascribing יצאת לקראתו (lit. 'coming forth toward him') to his daughter. The root יצא appears for the fourth time in the chapter in the daughter's submissive response to her father: 'do to me according to what came out [יצא] of your mouth' (v. 36).[11] While the first two uses of the root are hypothetical, presenting the act of 'coming out' as a possibility, the third use is predicative, it presents the verb as an actuality.

---

10. The words ורק היא יחידה mean literally, 'and only she alone'. As such, they can be construed as a retroactive adverbial clause, referring to the previous verb יצאת, namely, she alone came out to greet him. They can also be construed (as they usually are) as anticipatory adjectival clause, paralleled and complemented by the following phrase, 'beside her (ממנו, lit. "from him") he does not have a son or a daughter.'

11. On the use of הנה as a transformator from objective omniscient narration to a character's subjective point of view, see Bar-Efrat, *The Art of Biblical Story*, pp. 61-64 (Hebrew). Although there is no explicit factive verb to denote that the narrator uses Jephthah's point of view to describe the events 'as they are', the use of והנה implies here a 'perspectival subordination', namely an agreement between the character's and the narrator's point of view. See Meir Sternberg, 'The Truth vs. All the Truth'.

Yet, even as the daughter is said to come out, it is still unclear whether the daughter's coming out of her house to greet her father will in fact seal her fate as the burnt offering her father vowed to offer Yhwh. It is only the fourth use of the root, this time applied not to 'whatever came out of Jephthah's house', but to 'whatever came out of Jephthah's mouth' that clinches the fate of Jephthah's daughter. It is the father's word that determines the daughter's verdict. Furthermore, it is the daughter's consent to accept 'whatever came out' of her father's mouth that seals her fate.

The daughter's actions are not only syntactically framed within the father's point of view, psychologically and experientially too they echo what she assumes to be her father's expectation. Her joyous greeting follows her father's victory just as later on her mourning will follow both temporally and aetiologically her father's grievous outburst. Thus the verse introducing the daughter depicts her most important characteristic—her complete obedience to her father—a quality that in the final analysis has elevated her into an institutionalized heroine (Judg. 39–40). At the same time, however, the verse is careful to point out that the daughter's fateful action—although a result of the father's victory—is not a direct performance of his will. The daughter dooms herself—unknowingly. She is responsible for her death just as much as her father is, if not more, for after all Jephthah is not shown to instruct her to come out of the house to greet him. To the extent that the daughter's greetings are the effect of her independent initiative she too is responsible for her death. Later in the chapter the daughter will be shown to have a measure of independence and a will of her own as she asks for two months in which to mourn her virginity with her female friends (v. 37), a request which the father is shown to grant. To some extent, the daughter actively participates in the process leading to her own demise. Her death is the product of a collaborative effort on the part of herself and her father. This point is of extreme importance in the framework of the patriarchal narrative. For although the narrative seeks to demonstrate the fatal mistake of Jephthah as judge and leader and his tragedy as father, it stops short of depicting him as a brutal sacrificer of his daughter. From this point of view, our narrative agrees with the compositional principles of all father–daughter narratives in the Hebrew Bible: a father is never shown to be the direct perpetrator of his daughter's demise. Rather he is shown as a helpless victim of unforeseen circumstances, caught in the web of conflicting allegiances, and insurmountable constraints.[12] By portraying the daughter as coming out to meet her father of her own accord, the introductory verse (introducing the daughter) establishes that she too is responsible—however innocently and tragically—for her end.

In so far as the daughter's actions themselves are concerned, there is nothing obtrusively peculiar about them. Women greeting victorious warriors and celebrating the defeat of national enemies with 'timbrels and dances' (תפים ובמחלת) appears to have been a custom in ancient Israel (Exod. 15.20; 1 Sam. 18.6; Ps. 68.26).[13] The conventional element in the daughter's actions contributes to the credibility of the story. Yet, the daughter's recourse to this convention differs in certain respects from the way in which the biblical narrative normally presents it. For one thing, Jephthah's daughter appears to come out alone rather than as a part of a throng of women, although the plural of תפים and מחלת suggests music making and dancing by several women. In addition, whereas in the case of Miriam who is said to lead the Israelite women with תפים ובמחלת after the victory over the Egyptians, the words of her song are actually quoted (Exod. 15.21), as they also are in the case of the women who celebrate David's victory over the Philistines (1 Sam. 18.7), here the words of the song are not quoted. While these deviations from the conventional representation of the custom are not sufficient to undermine the verisimilitude that the narrative successfully achieves by invoking a conventional custom, they nevertheless reflect the pragmatic considerations that may have inspired them. For one thing, had Jephthah's daughter been shown to come out to greet her father with a group of women, this may have caused some doubt concerning the identity of 'the comer forth to meet' Jephthah. Jephthah could have opted for another female greeter perhaps a maid, a neighbor or one of his (unmentioned) concubines, all of which would be more easily dispensable. But this would have dramatically altered the story, as a dispensable woman

12. A *leitwort*, or a leading word, is a verbal form—an actual word, an idiomatic expression, a root or a sound pattern—which appears with some frequency in a certain context, thus calling attention to its semantic meaning and emphasizing the concept or idea it signifies. The verbal form does not have to recur in identical form; often it is the variations on the form that most effectively generate meaning. See Martin Buber, *The Way of the Bible* (Jerusalem: 1964), pp. 284-309 (Hebrew).

13. See Carol Meyers, 'Miriam the Musician', in Brenner (ed.), *A Feminist Companion to Exodus to Deuteronomy*, pp. 207-30.

would not have elicited from Jephthah as much grief and anguish as his one and only daughter. And Jephthah's grief is not an ancillary element in the story but one of its underlying, motivating principles, without which the lesson the story teaches concerning a rash vow would be lost.[14] Since the story seeks to dramatize the reprehensible results of a rash vow, it would be rather ineffective to depict a less than utterly objectionable and shocking result; hence the text's emphatic description of the victim not only as Jephthah's daughter, but also as his one and only child. Anything less than that would not have served the didactic purpose of the narrative. On the other hand, anything more, that is, a sacrifice of a son, might have caused too many problems in a literary context in which sons figure as the central symbol of familial, national and religious continuity.

Having introduced the daughter from the father's point of view, her actions forming an object clause of what her father sees and understands, the narrative goes on to unfold the events from the father's point of view: 'And then when he saw her, he rent [קרע] and you have become my troubler [עכר], and I have opened my mouth to Yhwh and I cannot go back' (Judg. 11.35). The quick succession of the verbs 'saw' [ראה] 'rent' [קרע] and 'said' [אמר] conveys the spontaneity of Jephthah's reaction to the unexpected appearance of his daughter and his shock at seeing her. While rending of his clothes functions as a symbolic index of his grief and mourning, his words indicate both by their content and their structure the despair he experiences. The expletive אהה that opens Jephthah's exclamation is a howl of grief, preceding the cause for this howl—'my daughter' בתי.

Apparently, 'you have brought me to my knees [כרע] and you have been among my enemies [כרע]' is a selfish accusation. Instead of considering his daughter's fate, Jephthah accuses her of collaborating with his ill-wishers. On another level, however, this exclamation is a pointed expression of grief and helplessness. Verse 34 emphatically reiterates the fact that Jephthah's daughter is his only child in order to explain what motivates Jephthah's emotional outburst. After all, Jephthah is described as 'a mighty man of valor' (Judg. 11.1), a tough outcast and a courageous warrior who is not likely to break down easily. Jephthah

14. The motif of a rash vow resulting in the sacrifice of a beloved child is common in other literatures as well. The most famous example is the story of Agamemnon who has vowed to a sacrifice to the Goddess Artemis the most beautiful creature in his entire kingdom: his own daughter, Iphigenia.

endears himself to the reader in admitting that it is he who has 'opened his mouth to Yhwh'—the use of the pronoun אנכי ('I myself') stresses his own culpability—and he also admits that because he has 'opened his mouth to Yhwh' he cannot 'go back', namely, revoke his vow. Had Jephthah rebuked his daughter for coming out of the house without consulting him, it would have been easier to construe his outburst as an unfeeling accusation. But instead what the exclamation dramatizes is Jephthah's bitterness, despair and anger. The words 'you have brought me low' and 'you have become my troubler' are words that befit a description of military or political defeat. The words the narrator puts in Jephthah's mouth thus continue the chilling contrast between the military victory Jephthah has just reaped and his private tragedy, between his expectation to be raised and elevated through his victory, and his unexpected demotion; it plays up the reversal of circumstance that turned his faithful daughter into one of his enemies. The repeated root כרע in the form of an infinitive absolute, and the fourfold repetition of the consonants כר and גר in Judg. 11.35 intensify phonetically the semantic meaning of 'rend', 'bring low' and 'troubler', the words in which they occur.

What adds to the expressive force of Jephthah's exclamation are its incoherence and syntactic rupture. Rather than increase the cohesion of the four clauses making up Jephthah's sentence, the copulative waw which repeats three times underscores the flawed logical and causal sequence through the use of a formal conjunctive that fails to operate on a semantic level. In essence the nominal 'and you have become my troubler' (lit. 'you are among my troublers') adds little—from an informational point of view—to the verbal clause with which it is conjoined by a copulative waw. One can argue that the nominal clause that normally denotes a state is syntatically more emphatic than the verbal clause that refers to an action.[15] Thus, by telling his daughter that she has become one of his enemies, Jephthah asserts that her bringing him low is an irreversible action resulting in a permanent condition of enmity between father and daughter. The parallelism between these clauses is then synonymous or complementary, in that the second clause repeats as well as intensifies the semantic meaning of the first.[16] The third and fourth

15. GKC, pp. 450-51.

16. On biblical parallelism, see James L. Kugel, *The Idea of Biblical Poetry: Parallelism and Its History* (New Haven: Yale University Press, 1981); Berlin, *The Dynamics of Biblical Parallelism* (Bloomington: Indiana University Press, 1985).

verbal clauses further emphasize that what has been done is irreversible. The perfect tense of פצה ('open'), is semantically reinforced by the assertion that what came out of Jephthah's mouth is irrevocable: 'I cannot go back'. While the relationship between the final two clauses is complementary more than synonymous, it still fails to explain what it is that came out of Jephthah's mouth and why it is irrevocable, just as the previous two clauses fail to explain why the daughter has become her father's troubler and why he thinks she has undermined him. The basic message of this combined sentence is that the daughter has inflicted on her father a dreadful disaster which cannot be undone, but despite its verbosity it fails to communicate why this is so. Yet, the description of Jephthah's vow makes it possible for the reader to understand the father. But what does the daughter know?

At this point, the text does not explain what the daughter knows. The reader is left to surmise that Jephthah tells his daughter about his vow, but the narrator refrains from being explicit. The text is ambiguous both about how much the daughter knows and about the precise consequence of the vow, namely whether or how she was sacrificed. One possible explanation is that the narrator avoids explicitness and repetition that might indict the male protagonist and generate too much sympathy for the female character.[17]

Although the daughter is portrayed as unaware of the implications of her own actions and of her father's vow, the text refrains from pointing up excessively the fact that her father is directly responsible for her demise. Rather, what it gives expression to is the sense that the daughter has become the cause for her father's demise. Jephthah's outcry does not necessarily reflect the authorial point of view, but it is nevertheless the only explicit evaluation of the daughter's actions, the expressive effectiveness of which was made clear above. There is no alternative judgment of the situation, either from the daughter's point of view, from the narrator's point of view, or from Yhwh's point of view. Rather than exposing Jephthah as a selfish coward, the text depicts him as a victim: a victim through his own wrongheaded actions, but a victim

17. The absence of a clear reference to the daughter's prospective sacrifice or to the vow, cannot be explained merely by the fact that the text has already referred to it previously (vv. 30-31). Repetition is a hallmark of biblical prose, just as much as informational omissions; it is valid to question both phenomena whenever they occur. On the strategies of repetition and its function in the biblical narrative, see Sternberg 'The Structure of Repetition in the Biblical Story', pp. 109-50.

nonetheless. The text is not bringing out Jephthah's unfair and immoral treatment of his daughter, but his confounded reaction to a devastating turn of events, one which he clearly has not anticipated.

An explicit reference to the vow at this point might also render less credible the daughter's calm and collected response that immediately follows her father's outcry: 'And she said to him, "My father, you opened your mouth [פה] to Yhwh, do to me according to what came out of your mouth, as Yhwh has done for your revenge upon your enemies, upon the Ammonites"' (v. 36). This is the first time in which the daughter is shown to open her mouth. Just as her deeds in v. 34 are an extension and a reflection of her father's actions—as she is rejoicing in his military victory—so her words here present her as an extension and reflection of her father's words. Not only does her speech denote accep-tance and submission, it also echoes the very words used by her father. Instead of asking for clarification, instead of questioning the value and validity of her father's words, she echoes her father's 'I opened [פצה] my mouth to Yhwh' with 'you opened [פצה] your mouth to Yhwh'. She also retains the obliqueness we noted in Jephthah's speech, contending herself with the rather general and vague 'do to me' rather than specifically referring to the actual deed in question. Furthermore, the daughter justifies her submission by reminding her father that fulfilling his vow to Yhwh is a just and venerable deed as Yhwh has defeated the Ammonites, Jephthah's enemies. The daughter describes Yhwh's defeat of the Ammonites as a service rendered to Jephthah personally; rather than say 'as Yhwh has avenged the Ammonites on our behalf', or 'on the behalf of Israel', she uses the second person singular personal pro-noun 'you' and possessive pronoun 'your', saying: 'as Yhwh has done revenge for *you* upon *your* enemies, the Ammonites'. The parallel between 'do to me' (עשה) framing the father–daughter relationship and 'did to you' (עשה) ascribed to Jephthah's relationship with God, alludes to the idea that the daughter owes as much obedience to her father, as her father does to Yhwh. This parallel reflects the hierarchical structure placing father above daughter, and Yhwh above the human father. The verb עשה repeats for the third time in v. 37, and here too it is presented as part of the daughter's speech. Only in its fourth appearances is the verb עשה ascribed to the father: 'and her father did [עשה] to her his vow which he had vowed' (v. 39). The repetition of the verb 'to do' is not only an oblique substitute for that which the narrative tries not to express explicitly, it also conveys the cooperation of the daughter with her father's scheme. Jephthah's final 'deed' (sacrifice of his daughter) would not have been possible without the consent of his daughter implied in the repeated use of the vague yet weighty עשׂה. The daughter's speech mirrors her father's speech, by creating a chiastic structure paralleling in reverse order the verbal expressions and fundamental ideas contained in the father's speech. Whereas the former begins with the idea that his daughter has defeated him and turned into one of his enemies, the daughter's response ends with the reminder that Jephthah has defeated—through Yhwh's help—his real troublers—his enemies the Ammonites. And whereas Jephthah's speech ends with his fatal opening of his mouth to Yhwh, the daughter's speech begins with this idea, using the very same idiom (opening one's mouth to Yhwh).

Although the daughter might know that her life is at stake, she appears not only to be willing to obey her father, but also to justify him. The narrator could not be more effective in constructing the perfect filial role model. Jephthah's daughter is the supreme image of the perfect daughter, whose loyalty and submissiveness to her father know no limits. She understands his predicament and the irrevocability of a vow once uttered to Yhwh. The text does not present her as the tragic obedient servant of Yhwh, but as the obedient daughter of her father. Jephthah does not hesitate to fulfil his vow to Yhwh, just as his daughter does not hesitate to obey him. Had she challenged her father, Jephthah's daughter would be implicitly challenging Yhwh's authority as well, for the vow was made to Him, and she is the means of realizing it. A protest or a howl of despair on the part of Jephthah's daughter would have unduly highlighted her tragedy. The daughter's calm response and subsequent silence permit the reader to remain focused on the father's grief. Had Jephthah's daughter been shown to ask for pity, had she asked to be spared, had she turned to Yhwh with a plea for mercy, the narrative would have tipped the scales too much in her favor, so much so that Jephthah's refusal to grant her life would have cast both him and Yhwh in a rather questionable role. The daughter's outcry or protest would have necessitated the father's recourse to force. This scenario, however, would cast Jephthah in the role of a heartless villain and shift too much sympathy to the daughter—an unwelcome result.

Instead of a desperate plea, a protest or a howl of despair comparable in its effect to that of Jephthah's verbal expression of dismay and helplessness, the narrative shows the daughter to ask for a two-month respite in which to mourn for her 'virginity': 'And she said to her father,

"Let this be done to me, let me alone two months that I may depart and go down upon the mountains, and bewail my virginity, I and my female friends" ' (v. 37). Whereas Jephthah's expression of grief is spontaneous and emotional, his daughter's request is just as calm as her response, and the arrangement for which she is asking has a formulaic and ritualized quality. Whereas in Jephthah's case, the text dramatizes the gestures and the words of the grief-stricken father, in the daughter's case it contents itself with a summary description: 'and she departed, she and her female friends, and bewailed her virginity upon the mountains' (v. 38). How Jephthah's daughter mourns and laments is not specified.[18] It is not specified mainly because the narrative as a whole is only marginally interested in the daughter's point of view, and mainly interested in the impact she has on her father (in the first part of the narrative) and on putative institutional developments. Her lament is not personal but public, not specific but general. It is enacted in a certain time and in a specific time frame. And indeed the daughter's request is shown to generate an annual custom in which 'the daughters of Israel went yearly to lament the daughter of Jephthah the Gileadite four days a year' (v. 40). The request of Jephthah's daughter and its granting

---

18. The literary gap in our narrative that ignores or denies the daughter's grief and horror at the situation has been noticed as early as the first century CE. Pseudo-Philo has composed a lamentation sung by Jephthah's daughter prior to her death. This inspired Peter Abelard's *planctus* on Jephthah's daughter written in the twelfth century. Both imaginative reconstructions of the daughter's feelings prior to her death present her as courageous, decisive, pious and heroic, and censure her father for his thoughtlessness and carelessness. For a detailed analysis of these poems and the literary traditions on which they draw, see Margaret Alexiou and Peter Dronke, 'The Lament of Jephthah's daughter [*sic*]: Themes, Tradition, Originality', *Studi Medievali* 12 (1971), pp. 819-63.

There is a striking similarity between Trible's approach to the narrative—her near-glorification of the daughter, condemnation of the father and those of the pseudo-Philo and of Peter Abelard. This suggests, among other things, that the approach 'which retells sympathetically stories of terror about women' need not necessarily be defined as feminist or even modern, as Trible presents it. See her article, 'A Daughter's Death: Feminine Literary Criticism and the Bible', *MQR* 22 (1983), pp. 176-89 (176). It should be noted that Jewish midrash also takes a sympathetic approach to Jephthah's daughter (variously called Sheila, Achsa, Adulah). According to one legend Jephthah was punished for his sacrifice. See Louis Ginsberg, *The Legends of the Jews*, IV (Philadelphia: Jewish Publication Society of America, 1968), pp. 43-47.

demonstrates some form of redress, a measure of grace and an emotional outlet for the reader to exorcize her own horror at the unfolding narrative. It gives Jephthah a chance to demonstrate magnanimity and reinforces the impression that the father is the victim rather than initiator of the unfortunate circumstance. Thirdly, it underscores the fact that the daughter has freely collaborated with her father in that by the end of two months she 'returned to her father and he did to her his vow that he had vowed' (v. 39). The daughter is shown to have returned out of her own free will; she was not forced unto the altar, but rather cooperated with her father in what the narrative presents as an unavoidable and irrevocable act.

Jephthah's willingness to let his daughter roam the mountains to mourn her virginity also tells us more about him than about her.[19] That he allowed her a period of grace before her death demonstrates that he did not wish to harm her, that he did love her, and that there was nothing at all he could do to revoke his vow. The fact that the daughter goes off to the mountains with her female friends does not help us understand her as much as it helps us appreciate the tragedy of the father.

If in the first part of the narrative the daughter acts as an extension of her father, accepting his judgment and justifying it, in the second part her words and actions seem to be subjected to the aetiological interest of the narrator. This is dramatized by the daughter's only two speech acts, which are framed by Jephthah's speech acts.[20]

The narrator uses the daughter's first speech act as an endorsement of the father's point of view (v. 36), while using the second speech act denotes a daughter's submission to her father in a particular personal context—the second speech act extends the meaning of the personal act into the public and national sphere. Both speech acts present the daughter as the passive object of another's actions. In v. 36, the predicate of the main clause is 'do to me'. In the following verse, the main clause uses the same idiomatic expression, this time in the passive form: 'let this be done to me'. Both speech acts are in the desiderative mode, the

---

19. For an interpretation of בתולי ('my virginity') as a reference to youthful age, see Peggy L. Day, ' "From the Child is Born the Woman": The Story of Jephthah's Daughter', in Peggy L. Day (ed.), *Gender and Difference in Ancient Israel* (Minneapolis: Fortress Press, 1989), pp. 58-74.

20. On speech acts in the biblical narrative see, Gloria Sheintuch and Uziel Mali, 'Towards an Illocutionary Analysis of Dialogue in the Bible', *Hasifrut* 30-31 (1981), pp. 70-75 (Hebrew).

first being a jussive and the second being a cohortative. The daughter thus appears to *choose* to obey her father. She *chooses* to be the culprit.

Then what *do* we know about this nameless daughter? We know that she is Jephthah's only daughter—how hard it must have been for him to part with her—and that she is a virgin. Her virginity is mentioned three times in the course of the narrative. The first time it is implied by the daughter's own words: 'that I may depart and bewail my virginity' (v. 37). The second time it is implied by the narrator's third person report: 'and [she] bewailed her virginity upon the mountains' (v. 38). The third time the narrator confirms explicitly her intact sexuality: 'and she had not known a man' (v. 39). It is possible to understand the repeated emphasis on the daughter's virginity as a valorizing statement. Like beauty, virginity in women seems to be a mark of high distinction.[21]

A similar technique of selective disclosure is at work in the narrator's report about what was supposed to actually 'be done' to the daughter. 'And then [ויהי] at the end of two months she returned to her father and he did to her the vow that he had vowed and she had not known a man and it became a custom in Israel' (v. 39). But what precisely is it that Jephthah 'did' to his daughter?

The adverb ויהי can be taken as a possible clue. It introduces the father's return from war, and the daughter's return home. But while the first ויהי introduces specific actions expressive of intense emotion, the second ויהי suppresses rather than expresses; both details and emotions are hidden rather than disclosed. The ויהי in v. 35 introduces Jephthah's intense confusion and despair, whereas the second ויהי introduces a series of verbs with no emotive value. Jephthah's daughter is said to 'return' (שב) to her father and he is reported to have done (עשׂה) to her what he had vowed (נדר) to do. The verb 'return', (שב) which is applied to the daughter in v. 39 in a literal sense, echoes the figurative return which is negatively ascribed to Jephthah—reported as saying that he cannot 'return' (שב), namely, retract his vow. The use of the same root in both contexts highlights the interdependence between the father's inability to 'return' and the daughter's obligation to 'return'. Because the father cannot return, namely undo his vow, his daughter is com-

---

21. Examples are Rebekah (Gen. 24.16), Tamar (2 Sam. 13) and Esther (2.17). Biblical poeticians interpret good looks as a sign of distinction in both male and female characters. It must not be forgotten, however, that only female characters are implicitly praised for their virginity.

pelled to return, namely give up her life according to his vow. But the
juxtaposition of the verbs also highlights the contrast in the emotional
charge attached to both verbs. The father's inability to 'return' constitutes the emotional and dramatic climax of the scene, the daughter's
return to her father—although much more horrifying in its implications—is presented objectively and dispassionately. The text does not
disclose her feelings upon her return nor her father's feelings as he
'did' to her according to his vow. Instead of explaining what it is that
Jephthah did to his daughter, the text repeats once again what we
already know about her: 'and she did not know a man' (v. 39). The dry
report on the custom purportedly inspired by Jephthah's daughter also
fails to give us the information we need. That it became a custom for
Israelite women to mourn (חנת) 'four days a year' (v. 40) merely shifts
our focus from the daughter to the annual custom.

The ambiguity of the text has generated much debate among sacrifi-
cialist and non-sacrificialist exegetes, the latter's arguing that the narrator's reticence indicates that Jephthah did not sacrifice his daughter
after all.[22]

But why the ambiguity? What purpose does it serve in our context? I
would like to suggest that the ambiguity mitigates the horror of the
story. By refraining from specifying what happened to the daughter, the
narrator forgoes the necessity to explain or justify Jephthah's behavior.

A zigzagging movement can be discerned in the narrative, reflecting
the narrator's constant fluctuation between an attempt to criticize Jephthah and to defend him, the narrator's reluctance to give us the basic
details about what 'really' happened. Jephthah's howl of pain is antiph-
onally counterbalanced by the daughter's calm response. The horror of
having to commit violence on an innocent victim is mitigated by allowing the victim to delay the verdict, the act of the sacrifice itself is only
hazily evoked and immediately followed by the reference to the annual
custom as if to note that this episode was not (should not be?) taken
lightly. Yet, the report on the annual mourning fails to reproduce the
manner in which the women bewail Jephthah's daughter. The narrator
does not bother to detail the words of the lamentations for Jephthah's
daughter, whereas in other contexts, the biblical narrator does not spare
narrative space to record (or invent) the (appropriate) lamentation. Thus
the biblical text details David's lamentation for the fallen Saul and his

22. For a succinct survey, see Marcus, *Jephthah and his Vow*, pp. 28-54.

son Jonathan in battle (2 Sam. 1.17-27) or David's lamentation for his beloved son, Absalom (2 Sam. 19.1). In the case of Jephthah's daughter, not only is the father not shown to lament his daughter, but the lamentations that were included in the annual ritual of mourning are omitted or suppressed. Although the daughter is said to be the origin of a custom, her name is suppressed throughout the narrative. The narrator thus reports to the reader that the daughter has not been forgotten, while appearing to forget her name, or rather allowing the reader to forget her.

Too many details about the daughter's inner world, as well as about her gruesome end would have shifted attention away from her father and his mistake. This is apparently not the desired impact of the narrative. Detail and clarity might have resulted in a need for a more serious redress than a single verse on some annual custom. Ambiguity has a dampening impact, it understates what might otherwise be highly disturbing and problematic. For one thing it defends the father against possible accusations of ruthlessness and callousness. In some ways the avoidance of too much information about the daughter's end also prevents a radical questioning of Yhwh's peculiar silence.

Shifts, Omissions and Conciseness as Patriarchal Strategies

The abrupt shift from the daughter's story to the story of the Ephraimites' rebellion against Jephthah signals the return of the Jephthah narrative to its central theme: the military exploits of the judge. The story about the Ephraimites' insurrection (Judg. 12.1-6) parallels and complements in many ways the story of the Ammonites' provocation, preceding the daughter's sacrifice (Judg. 11.1-33). In both stories Jephthah's enemies—the Ammonites and the Ephraimites—are portrayed as the 'bad guys', responsible for the outburst of the war (Judg. 11.4; 12.1). In both cases Jephthah tries to prevent war through diplomatic negotiations. The text quotes in detail the protracted conciliatory message Jephthah addresses to the Ammonites (Judg. 11.12-27), and his equally conciliatory though less elaborate address to the Ephraimites (Judg. 12.2-3). In both stories, Jephthah not only emerges as a peace-seeking politician, but also as a devout follower of Yhwh, as he repeatedly invokes His name (Judg. 11.9, 21, 23, 24, 27; 12.3). Yhwh's support for Jephthah also appears as a factual statement offered by the omniscient and reliable biblical narrator (Judg. 11.11, 29, 32). In both cases the enemy refuses to hearken to Jephthah's pacifying address, and in both cases Jephthah succeeds in defeating his enemies, with the implicit or explicit support of God (Judg. 11.32-33; 12.4-6). The thematic and structural analogies between these stories highlight the strangeness of the interlude about Jephthah's daughter. The military stories are stories of success, they begin with a note of threat and anxiety and end with victory. The daughter's story is one of failure. While the public Jephthah scores success the private Jephthah is defeated.

As a story of despair and defeat, the daughter's story parallels the exposition to the Jephthah narrative (Judg. 11.1-4). Here we meet Jephthah as a private person, a son of a harlot, who is expelled from his father's house by his brothers who refuse to share Gilead's inheritance with Jephthah, for he is the son of 'another woman' (Judg. 11.2). Jephthah flees to Tob, where he is joined by pariahs like him, whom the text characterizes as 'worthless' (ריקים) (Judg. 11.3). The shift in Jephthah's fate occurs when the war with the Ammonites breaks out, for then the elders of Gilead ask Jephthah to become their leader (Judg. 11.5-11). If we were to divide the narrative into four segments, the introduction (vv. 1-5), the battle with the Ammonites (vv. 6-33), the sacrifice of the daughter (vv. 34-40), and the battle with the Ephraimites (Judg. 12.1-6), then the first and the third segments—presenting Jephthah as a private man—are also stories of defeat, whereas the second and fourth segments presenting Jephthah as a public figure are stories of victory and success. In the first and third segments Jephthah appears as a passive and impotent subject, one who is caught in the throes of external circumstances, in the second and fourth segments he emerges as active and resilient, a subject who takes charge of the situation and changes historical events. Moreover, the cause for Jephthah's demise in the first and third segments is a woman who is closely related to him. In the first segment it is Jephthah's mother, whose social status as a harlot (*zonâ*) brings about Jephthah's expulsion from his father's house. In the third segment it is his daughter, whose unpredictable emergence from his house forces him to offer her as a burnt offering to Yhwh in accordance with his vow. Considered diachronically, the four segments constitute an antiphonal movement, with the women signaling the descending motion and the all-male, military, public environment signaling Jephthah's ascent. The fourth and final segment describing Jephthah's victory delineates an ascending movement, as if to block out the memory of the dooming and damning women. And like the fourth movement, which does not even vaguely mention the daughter's death or its impact on Jephthah, so the final postscript makes no reference to the women in Jephthah's life: as it summarizes the judge's career with the usual solemn formula: 'And Jephthah judged Israel six years, and Jephthah the Gileadite died and was buried in one of Gilead's cities' (lit. 'in the cities of Gilead') (Judg. 12.7).

The six verses that constitute the daughter's story present then a single episode in the broader narrative about Jephthah. It is a sad interlude in Jephthah's career. But soon afterwards, the text goes on to report on Jephthah's military victory over the Ephraimites: his daughter's death has, it would seem, little impact on Jephthah's military exploits.

Jephthah's daughter is not mentioned prior to her appearance in Judg. 11.34, and her life as a character barely spans six verses. Just as the daughter leaps out from the void so is she consigned to oblivion after her appearance. The narrative postscript constitutes in fact a harsher death sentence than the one unwittingly proclaimed by Jephthah, as it neutralizes the impact of the unjust sacrifice and draws the curtain on the character of the daughter forever.

Phyllis Trible construes the ending of the narrative as a kind of solace:

> The narrative postscript, then, shifts the focus of the story from vow to victim, from death to life, from oblivion to remembrance. Remarkably, this saga of faithlessness and sacrifice mitigates, though it does not dispel, its own tragedy through the mourning of women.[23]

While I agree that the ambiguous ending mitigates the horror of the story, I think the shift of focus from the father's deed to the women's custom results in eclipsing the daughter's story. To be satisfied with the ambiguous and evasive ending is to silence the question about the relationship between gender and the story. Would this story still be possible had the daughter been a son? Or the same had Jephthah's daughter been a son? Could the narrator afford the same extent of reticence and ambiguity in telling us about the sacrifice of a male child?

Had Jephthah's Daughter Been a Son: A Speculative Digression

The structural analogies between our story and Genesis 22 have been noted by several critics.[24] Both stories are about fathers who find them-

---

23. *Texts of Terror*, p. 107.

24. See, e.g., Edmund Leach, *Genesis as Myth and Other Essays* (London: Jonathan Cape, 1969), pp. 37-38. For a critical analysis of Gen. 22, see Carol Delaney, 'The Legacy of Abraham', in Gross (ed.), *Beyond Androcentrism*, pp.

selves compelled to sacrifice to God an only child. In Genesis 22, the child, Isaac, is spared. In the other, the child is in all probability sacrificed. To what extent is the happy ending of Genesis 22 related to the fact that Isaac is a son? To what extent is the expendability of Jephthah's daughter related to her femaleness?

While Yhwh is peculiarly silent in our story, He intervenes energetically on behalf of Isaac. Just as Abraham is getting ready to sacrifice his one and only (יחיד) son, Yhwh makes a dramatic appearance through a special messenger: 'And the angel of Yhwh called out to him from heaven and said: "Lay not your hand upon the lad, and do not do anything to him, for now I know that you are a God-fearing man and you have not spared your son, your only one, from me" ' (Gen. 22.12). The common tendency is to use Abraham's faithfulness as an explanation for Yhwh's vigorous intervention on behalf of Isaac. But Jephthah's story does not show him to be in any way faithless. Like Abraham, Jephthah refrains from dissuading Yhwh. Jephthah has two months in which to find a way to revoke his vow, but he does not do it. Does this show faithlessness to Yhwh?

In our story, God is only mentioned in the participants' dialogues (vv. 35-36), as one to whom vows are made. In Genesis however, God is shown to be an active and independent character, the subject of actions, not merely an indirect object, to whom certain vows are made. This is dramatized not only through Yhwh's propitious intervention just before Isaac's sacrifice, but in the introductory verse of the entire narrative: 'And then after these things, God tested Abraham' (Gen. 22.1). This verse makes it clear that the events that are to follow have been engineered and orchestrated by Yhwh, that Yhwh is not only capable of intervening and changing the course of human actions at will, but also that he is the primary and unquestionable controller of human actions and historical events. Above all, this verse clarifies to the reader that what is about to happen is 'merely' a trial: that Yhwh is not *really* interested in Abraham's sacrifice. The text reassures the reader right from the beginning that Yhwh is in control of the situation, and that He will not let events get out of hand. A similar reference to Yhwh in our

217-36. See also Bal, *Death and Dissymmetry*, pp. 109-13. Bal suggests that both narratives are concerned with a rite of passage—the male rite is successful; the female, aborted.

chapter would indicate that the daughter's unhappy ending is the result of Yhwh's design—an awkward conclusion. By suppressing Yhwh, our narrator forestalls uncomfortable questions.

As noted earlier, the common tendency is to blame the unhappy ending of our story on Jephthah's alleged faithlessness.[25] However Jephthah's vow may simply indicate that he is uncertain of his military victory over the Ammonites, and that he seeks to ensure victory by making a vow to Yhwh—but why should it be taken as an attempt to test God, or as an expression of faithlessness? To condemn Jephthah as unfaithful on the grounds that he has tested Yhwh would require a similar evaluation of Gideon, who is shown to 'test' God. Not only does Gideon ask Yhwh's angel for a 'sign' (אות) (Judg. 6.17), but when satisfied that it is indeed God's angel who revealed himself to him, Gideon goes on to ask Yhwh Himself for a sign, before setting out to battle the Midianites (Judg. 6.36-37), and not content with this sign, he continues to 'test' Yhwh by asking for yet another sign (Judg. 6.39-40). Nevertheless, Yhwh is not angry at Gideon for having tested Him again and again. Gideon's hesitation and doubt do not result in God's punishment; on the contrary, He continues to give Gideon explicit instructions during the battle (Judg. 7.4-9) and helps him win the war. It is not possible to single out Jephthah as faithless and foolish without indicting Gideon as well as Samson.

Furthermore, if Jephthah's vow is condemned as an expression of faithlessness, we must also condemn Jacob for making a vow to Yhwh (Gen. 28.20-22). In Jacob's case the vow would appear to be even a more blatant expression of faithlessness as it follows Yhwh's explicit assurance: 'And behold, I am with you, and will guard you wherever you go, and will bring you back to this land, for I will not leave you until I have done that which I have promised you' (Gen. 28.15). Despite this solemn promise, Jacob 'vows a vow' that echoes Yhwh's promise. But whereas Yhwh's words are presented in the affirmative and indicative voice, Jacob repeats the words as a protasis in a conditional sentence, thus questioning God's affirmation: 'If God will be with me, and will guard me on this way on which I go and will give me bread to eat and clothes to wear so that I return to my father's house in peace, then Yhwh shall be my God' (Gen. 20–21).[26] It can be said that Jacob's

---

25. See, e.g., Phyllis Trible's evaluation of Jephthah's vow as foolish and faithless in *Texts of Terror*, pp. 93-102.

26. It should be noted that Jacob and Jephthah use an almost identical terminol-

vow is more dramatically expressive of doubt and hesitation than is Jephthah's, for the latter never questions his loyalty to Yhwh, and never makes his allegiance contingent upon God's favors and compensations. Yet, Jacob is not punished for apparent lack of faith. The opposite is the case; Yhwh indeed fulfills his promise to Jacob, and gives him numerous descendants—an expression of divine providence and blessing. A vow in itself is not necessarily then an expression of faithlessness. Yet Jephthah's daughter is not spared.

As a female descendant, Jephthah's daughter is what René Girard calls 'a sacrificeable victim'. As an only child she resembles the unsacrificeable victim—Isaac. As a female, she appears to be more expendable. Girard explains that in ritual sacrifice, a society seeks 'to deflect upon a relatively indifferent victim, a "sacrificeable" victim, the violence that would otherwise by vented on its own members, the people it most desires to protect'.[27]

As an only child, a son would be an extension of Jephthah, as a female she is different. That difference destroys her. In narrative terms, the daughter is dispensed with after a brief description. This would not be possible in the case of Isaac, as much for his being Abraham's son, as for his being male. As a virgin, who is unattached to a man, Jephthah's daughter's death would not incur vengeance. As a female character, her elimination from the text would not entail serious disruption.

The Genesis narrative links the potential sacrifice of Isaac to one of the major organizing themes in the Hebrew Bible, the theme of the covenant. Yhwh is quoted as telling Abraham at the end of the momentous trial:

> because you have done this thing, and have not withheld your son, your only one, I will indeed bless you, and I will indeed multiply your seed as the stars in heaven and as the sand that is upon the shore, and your seed will inherit the gate of his enemies (Gen. 22.16-17).[28]

ogy in regard to their 'return in peace' to their homes. It should also be added that like Jephthah, Jacob too offers something in return for God's help. In addition to his loyalty, he promises God that he will dedicate the place where he slept as God's house, and that he will dedicate for Yhwh one tenth of everything the latter will give to him (Gen. 28.22).

27. See *Violence and the Sacred* (trans. Patrick Gregory; Baltimore: The Johns Hopkins University Press, 1977), p. 4.

28. The repeated use of the absolute infinitive, (lit.) 'blessing I will bless you' and 'multiplying I will multiply you', increases the emphatic tone of this promise.

The causal link between the potential sacrifice of Isaac—interpreted as Abraham's faithfulness to Yhwh—is repeatedly established in the course of the narrative (Gen. 22.12, 16, 18). The daughter's sacrifice on the other hand is not linked to any enduring biblical motif. The reference to the annual custom of the daughters of Israel may express an indirect critique on the part of the narrator of the entire episode, but the sacrifice remains precisely that—an episode. It is never again mentioned in the course of the Hebrew Bible.

In Genesis 22, the narrative not only reports that Abraham builds an altar, piles up the wood, places his son on top of the wood and stretches his hand to the knife (vv. 9-10), it also reports Yhwh's response to these actions: first ordering Abraham to desist from the act, and later explaining why it is not necessary to carry out the sacrifice: 'for now I know that you are a God-fearing man, for you did not spare me your son, your only one' (Gen. 22.12). The angel of Yhwh calls out to Abraham once again to bless him and repeat His promise regarding innumerable descendants (זרה lit. 'seed') in compensation for Abraham's willingness to give up his one and only son (vv. 15-19). Thus the narrative is not only clear and detailed about the father's actions, but also about Yhwh's response, two of the most blatant gaps in the story of the daughter's sacrifice.

Could the narrative be as opaque and ambiguous were Jephthah's child a son? Could the narrative maintain its credibility and authority had it used the same evasive techniques in describing the sacrifice of an only son? One may also ask, what would have happened had the daughter opted for life, had she run off during her two-month respite on the mountains, had she rebelled? To what extent did Jephthah's daughter gain access to the biblical text thanks to her willingness to submit to victimization, thanks to her obedience? A better understanding of biblical sexual politics may throw new light on the characterization of daughters in general and on the particular aspects of the Jephthah story that have been debated for a very long time.

Chapter 7

THE BIBLICAL SISTER: REDEEMED BY HER BROTHER?

The biblical narrative does not deny the existence of relationships
between sisters, but it often deprives this moment of the same complexity and depth. Scholars who have correctly identified parallels in
the Jacob–Esau and Rachel–Leah stories have failed to note that while
Jacob and Esau settle their dispute, the sisters' conflicts remain unresolved.[1] More importantly, both conflictual and collaborative relationships between sisters are shown to be inspired by an overriding interest
in giving birth to sons, securing the love of a husband, or ensuring the
genealogical continuity of a father. The interaction between Lot's
daughters, for example, is determined by their desire to realize their
procreative mission through their father (Gen. 19.31-38), much as
Zelophehad's daughters are preoccupied with securing the name of
their deceased father (Num. 27.1-11). Lot's elder daughter asks her
sister to sleep with Lot to 'make alive seed from our father' (Gen.
19.34), while in one of the rare occasions in which they are shown to
communicate with each other, Rachel asks Leah for Reuben's mandrakes in exchange for a night with Jacob (Gen. 30.14-15). No biblical
sister is shown to help or protect another sister. The young Miriam is
shown to watch out for her little brother Moses, only to be later rebuked
by Yhwh for criticizing his conduct.[2] The most detailed narratives
about sister-figures present them as victims who depend for deliverance
on their respective brothers. In the following discussion of the stories of
Dinah (Gen. 34) and Tamar (2 Sam. 13), the characterization of the

---

1. See, e.g., Fokkelman, *Narrative Art in Genesis*, pp. 139-44, and especially
Fishbane, *Text and Texture*, pp. 55-62.

2. Carol Meyers finds evidence for a theory that sees Miriam as a founder or
representative of a historical institution of female musicians. See 'Miriam the
Musician', pp. 207-30. On Miriam's prophetic status and pro-Miriamic traditions,
see Phyllis Trible, 'Bringing Miriam out of the Shadows', in Brenner (ed.), *A Feminist Companion to Exodus and Deuteronomy*, pp. 166-86.

victimized sister and the redeeming brother will be examined with a view to questioning the patriarchal investments in this scenario.

Most of the discussions of Genesis 34 and 2 Samuel 13 tend to take at face value the stories of sisters' rape and their subsequent avenging by their respective brothers. For the most part, the focus of the discussions has been the motivations of the 'good' brother and his transaction with the rapist.[3] But even exceptional analyses focusing primarily on the relationship between brother and sister, notably in 2 Samuel 13, interpret the brother's interference on behalf of his sister as an act of compassion and devotion.[4] A question that deserves to be asked, however, is why is the sister in both narratives a victim of rape, and why does she not avenge her own rape? The historicist answer would be: because this was impossible in ancient Israel. This sort of answer posits the biblical narrative as a 'reflection' of 'historical reality' rather than as a story whose goal is to teach a lesson. What are the lessons taught by the stories of Dinah and Tamar? Beyond the functions of Tamar's story as a political justification of Solomon's accession to the throne, what are the sexual-political investments of this story and the parallel story in Genesis 34?[5]

Plot, Narration and Ideology in the Stories of Dinah and Tamar

The major characters in both stories are a villain, a hero and a victim. The victim-sister functions mostly as a catalyst for the conflict between villain and hero. She is the factor who determines the culpability of the

3.   For discussions of Gen. 34 see, e.g., Meir Sternberg, 'A Delicate Balance in the Rape of Dinah', *Hasifrut* 4 (1973), pp. 195-231 (Hebrew); Nisan Ararat, 'Reading According to the "Seder" in the Biblical Narrative', *Hasifrut* 27 (1978), pp. 15-34 (Hebrew); Haviva Nissim, 'On Analyzing a Biblical Story', *Hasifrut* 24 (1977), pp. 136-43 (Hebrew). For literary analyses of 2 Sam. 13, see, e.g., George Ridout, 'The Rape of Tamar', in Jared J. Jackson and Martin Kessler (eds.), *Rhetorical Criticism* (Pittsburgh: Pickwick Press, 1974), pp. 75-84; Charles Conroy, *Absalom Absalom!* (Rome: The Biblical Institute Press, 1978), pp. 17-40; Bar-Efrat, *The Art of the Biblical Story,* pp. 199-235 (Hebrew); J.P. Fokkelman, *Narrative Art and Poetry in the Books of Samuel,* I (Assen: Van Gorcum, 1981), pp. 99-125.

4.   See Phyllis Trible's reading of the story of Tamar in *Texts of Terror*, pp. 37-64.

5.   To the extent that the story of Tamar has been considered as a political one, it was court politics and the ideological justification of the Solomonic monarchy that dominated most discussions. For a succinct survey, see Gunn, *The Story of King David*, pp. 21-26.

villain and heroism of the brother. The actions of both villain and hero
are directed at her, the villain abusing her and her brother avenging her
abuse. She herself, however, does not participate actively in the plot.
She is passive both as an object of the villain's desire and aggressions,
and as an abused victim of rape. Although she is clearly the direct victim of the villain's abuse, the sister in both stories is not *aided* by her
brother in her attempt to punish the aggressor, but rather *replaced* by
him. She is not even consulted by her brother, who determines himself
how to punish the rapist. Having fulfilled her role as a rape victim, the
sister clears the way for her brother-hero to step in and restore 'moral'
order.

This brief survey of the major structural parallels between the stories
is not meant to detract from the differences between the texts of Genesis 34 and 2 Samuel 13. Thus, for example, Shechem, Dinah's rapist,
falls in love (אהב) with her and tries to marry her (Gen. 34.3-4), whereas
Amnon loves (אהב) Tamar before the rape and hates (שׂנא) and rejects
her afterwards (2 Sam. 13.1, 15, 17). Dinah's brothers, notably Simeon
and Levi, are shown to wreak havoc on the entire city of Shechem
in response to their sister's rape (Gen. 34.25-29), whereas Absalom,
Tamar's 'real' brother (in contrast to Amnon who is related to her only
though David), arranges only for Amnon's murder (2 Sam. 13.28-29),
sparing David's other sons (vv. 30-33). The stories also differ in the
ways they characterize the sister. Whereas Dinah is shown inadvertently to bring about her rape by coming out (יצא) 'to see the daughters
of the land' (Gen. 34.1), Tamar goes out to Amnon's house because
David instructs her to do so (2 Sam. 13.7). Tamar is furthermore shown
to resist her rape (vv. 11-13). She resists Amnon's decision to chase her
out (v. 16), and is shown to be deeply distressed by her rape (vv. 19-
20). The text in Genesis 34, by contrast, gives no details about Dinah's
reaction to her rape and does not explain whether or not she chose to
stay in Shechem's house after her rape (Gen. 34.26).

2 Samuel 13 is unambiguous in its indictment of the rapist and vindi-
cation of the avenger. Genesis 34 offers a more ambivalent evaluation
of the characters involved. Amnon in 2 Samuel is unambiguously characterized as a sly, corrupt and ruthless character. Not only does Amnon
pretend to be sick in order to lure his sister to his bedside (vv. 6-10), not
only does he rape an innocent virgin who is his half-sister (vv. 11-14),
but when his desire is satiated he humiliates her further by chasing her
out of his house (vv. 15-18). Amnon's conduct is inexcusable. Charac-

terization of the villain in Genesis 34, on the other hand, is far less clearcut. Shechem's most important redeeming feature is his attempt to reverse the harm done to Dinah by seeking to marry her. His love for Dinah, however, is compromised by the deceptiveness he and his father exhibit in their negotiations with Dinah's brothers and with their own compatriots (Gen. 34.11-12, 20-23).[6] Thus, Shechem is not incriminated to the extent that Amnon is, but neither is he fully exonerated.

The same difference in evaluative strategy applies to the characterization of the brother-hero in both chapters. While 2 Samuel 13 offers an unambiguously sympathetic portrait of Absalom, Genesis 34 is more ambiguous in its evaluation of the brother's revenge. As pointed out, Absalom is shown to punish only Amnon; he does not seek out Jonadab, Amnon's best friend and others who might have been implicated in the rape (vv. 30-33). Dinah's brothers, on the other hand, murder and pillage the entire city of Shechem, destroying many innocent and helpless Canaanites who have undergone circumcision in accordance with the brothers' manipulative demands (vv. 13-14). While the brothers show no restraint in their ruthless revenge on the Shechemites, Absalom waits two years before he finally takes revenge on Amnon (v. 23). Jacob's rebuke of Simeon and Levi (Gen. 34.30) gives expression to the narrator's reservations vis-à-vis the brothers' actions, whereas David's mourning (אבל) and longing (כלה) for Absalom (2 Sam. 13.37-39) speak for this text's positive evaluation of Absalom's conduct.

Neither narrative questions the brothers' right to act on their sisters' behalf. Jacob rebukes Simeon and Levi for endangering the family's survival in Canaan, not for their decision to take the law into their own hands. Similarly, 2 Samuel 13—much more insistent on the brother-hero's positive evaluation—does not question Absalom's decision to do the same thing. Since it precedes a well-planned revenge, Absalom's bidding his clamoring (זעק)[7] sister to 'be quiet', is construed as an expression of loving care, not as a brutal act of suppressing a raped woman's bitter plea for justice: 'And Absalom her brother said unto her, "Was Amnon your brother with you? And now my sister be quiet, he is your brother, do not take this thing to heart." And Tamar sat deso-

---

6.　Compare Sternberg, 'A Delicate Balance', pp. 206-11.

7.　The verb זעק (v. 19) refers not only to crying out aloud or clamoring, it also has a forensic meaning. Fokkelman is right in observing that in bidding her to be quiet, Absalom 'does not want Tamar to take legal action', for he wishes to 'take the law into his own hands'. See *Narrative Art and Poetry*, p. 111.

late at the house of Absalom her brother' (v. 20). Whether it is considered as a concerned attempt on Absalom's part to console Tamar or as a brilliant strategic maneuver meant to allay Amnon's suspicions, most critics endorse the implicitly positive evaluation of Absalom's response.[8] But the consolation of the 'good' brother paves the way to edging Tamar out of the story. The brothers' willingness to take up cudgels on behalf of their sisters justifies the elimination of the victim from the story of the rape's revenge. The brothers' response to the victimized sister in both narratives is just as problematic as the law ensuring that the rape victim's *father* ought to be monetarily compensated by the rapist (Exod. 22.15-16; Deut. 22.28-29). For both the rape laws and the narratives are based on the assumption that the real victim is the raped woman's father or brother.[9] What has not been questioned by critics is the imperceptible shift from rape victim to male relative and the implicit premise that the latter has a right to represent the former.

By depicting the brothers' revenge on behalf of the sister as natural, both Genesis 34 and 2 Samuel 13 ratify the brother's right to represent his sister. By presenting Absalom's representation of Tamar as unambiguously positive, the latter text valorizes it. The brother's right to avenge his sister's rape does not, however, compel him to do so. He is free to decide whether or not he ought to take action on his sister's behalf; he has no obligation to do so nor has his sister the right to ask for his intervention. The brother's freedom to choose, however, restricts

---

8.	Bar-Efrat explains that Absalom silences Tamar in order to hide his plans to take revenge on Amnon. See *The Art of the Biblical Story*, p. 226. Fokkelman suggests that Absalom silences Tamar because he wishes to spare Tamar 'the misery and humiliation involved' in his plan to prosecute Amnon. See *Narrative Art and Poetry*, p. 111. Trible also construes Absalom's response to Tamar's anguish as a gentle and considerate gesture: 'Although Amnon seduced and polluted Tamar, Absalom support and protects her.' See *Texts of Terror*, p. 52.

9.	The law in Exodus allows the father to determine whether his raped daughter be given to her rapist as wife. The Deuteronomic law, on the other hand, leaves the father no such option, compelling the rapist to pay the father fifty shekels of silver and marry the raped daughter for good, that is, without the option of divorce. Calum Carmichael considers the Deuteronomic law to be more considerate of the woman involved. Surely compelling a raped woman to become the permanent wife of her rapist amounts to a more severe penalty for the raped woman than for her husband-rapist, who remains free to procure additional spouses for himself while the victim must remain permanently and exclusively dependent upon the man who raped her. See Carmichael, *Women, Law, and the Genesis Tradition*, pp. 46-48.

the sister's freedom and right to act in her own behalf. The mere possibility that her brother *may* avenge her renders her own action superfluous. Thus, although Tamar does not know whether or not Absalom will punish her rapist, she obeys his instructions and keeps quiet in his house. The brother has the right to protect/replace his sister, while she —by accepting his protection—is obliged to obey him.

Tamar is shown to obey both her brothers and her father, yet neither her father's various requests and orders (vv. 5, 7, 10-11, 15, 20) nor Tamar's obedient responses (vv. 8-10, 20) are what the text perceives as problematic.[10] It could be argued, however, that were it not for the patriarchal order compelling the unmarried daughter and sister to obey her father and brothers, Tamar may never have gone to Amnon's house in the first place. The real victimization of Tamar does not begin with her rape by Amnon but with David's ordering her to go to Amnon's house and prepare food for her would-be sick brother. Her victimization does not end with Absalom's apparently benevolent instructions for her to 'be quiet'. For if Amnon robs Tamar of her virginity, Absalom robs her of her own voice. In many subtle ways the protection of the sister by her 'good' brother is just as harmful as her abuse by her 'bad' brother. As indicated, Absalom is not shown to share his plans with Tamar. She sits 'desolate' at her brother's house for two years not knowing whether her rape will be avenged and her rapist punished. While Absalom's secrecy may have been beneficial from his point of view, it can be construed as a source of additional stress for Tamar. The redeeming effects of Tamar's two-year-long incarceration at Absalom's house are rather dubious, and in some ways this ordeal can be compared with the one she has suffered at the hands of her 'bad' brother. Yet, the text does not pursue the implications of this possibility. From this narrative, Absalom emerges as a 'good' brother.

Despite its ambiguous characterization of Dinah's brothers, like 2 Samuel 13, Genesis 34 refrains from questioning the brothers' authority. As already noted, the text may question the extent and ferocity of their revenge, but not their fundamental right to take action on behalf of their sister. The chapter may be ambivalent about the brothers' deceptive and ruthless treatment of the villain(s) involved, it may criticize the brothers' failure to consult with their father and inform him about their intentions to destroy the entire city (Gen. 34.30), but there is no indica-

10. On the prevalence of the command–execution pattern in the Tamar narrative, see Conroy, *Absalom Absalom!*, pp. 18-19.

tion from the text that their failure to consult Dinah about their actions is perceived in any way as wrong-headed. It can be argued that the brothers could not have consulted with their sister because at Shechem's house (v. 26) she was out of reach. But there is no indication that Dinah's absence interferes in any way with the brothers' decisions and actions. What is even more remarkable is that when the brothers finally reach their destination, and take (לקח) Dinah out of Shechem's house (v. 28), they are not shown to exchange words with Dinah, although, apparently, their entire operation was motivated by their concern for her well-being. As noted, Absalom also does not consult Tamar, but rather asks her to be quiet. Yet the reader is encouraged to believe that the sisters' silence infers consent, and that in both cases the brothers' interests are identical with their sisters'. Both chapters, their differing evaluative strategies notwithstanding, endorse the brothers' revenge as the proper response to their sisters' rape. The brothers' dismissive and patronizing attitude toward their sister implies, however, that this endorsement is inspired less by a concern for the interests and needs of the abused sisters themselves than by a patriarchal ideology whose goal is to safeguard a brother's authority over his female sibling.

The different evaluative strategies employed by Genesis 34 and 2 Samuel 13 regarding the villain and the hero apply to the stories' respective characterization of the victims involved. The generally ambivalent descriptive mode of Genesis 34 manifests itself in the ambiguous characterization of Dinah, whereas the insistence on Tamar's unblemished innocence and overwhelming grief presents her as a *bona fide* victim.

Rape and the Father's Home

The ambiguity of Genesis 34 is expressed in the many information gaps surrounding Dinah's motivations and behavior. While in the case of Tamar the text offers detailed information that leaves no doubt about her innocence, in Dinah's case it is difficult to reconstruct the events preceding the rape, as well as her motivations. While Genesis 34 begins with Dinah's venturing out of her father's house—which leads to her rape (vv. 1-2)—2 Samuel 13 begins with an elaborate description of Amnon's and Jonadab's plot to lure Tamar into Amnon's house (vv. 1-7). The temporal ordering of events in the beginning of Genesis 34 suggests a causal link between Dinah's leaving her home and her rape:

And Dinah the daughter of Leah, whom she had borne to Jacob, went out [יצא] to see the daughters of the land. And Shechem the son of Hamor the Hivite, the leader of the land, saw her; and he took her [לקח] and lay [שכב] with her, and raped [ענה] her' (Gen. 34.1-2).

The verb 'to see' (ראה) and the noun 'the land' are applied to Dinah and Shechem respectively, which reinforce the causal linkage between Dinah's actions and Shechem's reactions. Yet, I do not see any reason to argue that Dinah went out of her father's home specifically to seduce or be seduced by Shechem.

On the basis of intricate calculations of Dinah's age some argue that the girl went out of the house for sexual reasons, and interpret v. 2 as a seduction rather than a rape.[11] The sexist premise of such arguments is that mature women are unrapable. Though, as we shall see later, the text does not justify Dinah's action, nowhere does it suggest that Dinah wished to be raped or sought to seduce or be seduced by Shechem. It is Shechem who is said to 'take' (לקח), 'lie' (שכב), and 'rape' (ענה) Dinah, while Dinah is a direct object of all three actions.[12]

Where Genesis 34 is suggestive and ambivalent, 2 Samuel 13 is rather emphatic in its implicit indictment of Amnon. The chapter's detailed description of Amnon's plot to ensnare Tamar by pretending to be ill leaves little doubt as to his full responsibility for the rape. Although Jonadab, his friend, is shown to mastermind the details of the plot to lure Tamar to Amnon's bedside, the text indicates that he does not share Amnon's culpability for the rape itself.[13] Unlike Dinah, who leaves her home voluntarily, Tamar 'goes to the house [בית] of Amnon

---

11. Inspired by traditional commentators like Rashi, Nisan Ararat argues that the verb ראה indicates than Dinah wished to be seen (in the sexual sense) as well as to see. See 'Reading According to the "Seder" ', pp. 18-19. For a survey of rabbinic readings of Dinah's story, see Naomi Graetz, 'Dinah the Daughter', in Brenner (ed.), *A Feminist Companion to Genesis*, pp. 306-17.

12. Ararat interprets literally the Hebrew לקח, which—in contexts involving male–female interaction—usually refers to a woman's appropriation by a man through sex or marriage. See 'Reading According to the "Seder" '. According to Ararat, Shechem 'took' Dinah to his home (p. 18). He interprets the verb *'nh* not as referring to rape but to 'sleeping with a virgin'. (p. 19.) Calum Carmichael also prefers to interpret Dinah's rape as a mere seduction. See *Women, Law, and the Genesis Traditions*, pp. 44-48. For the opposite view, see Sternberg, 'A Delicate Balance', p. 197.

13. See Bar-Efrat, *The Art of the Biblical Story*, pp. 204-208.

her brother' (v. 8) on David's orders: 'And David sent home to Tamar, saying: "Go now to your brother Amnon's house [בית] and prepare for him food [ברה]" ' (2 Sam. 13.7). She ends up at Amnon's house having obeyed her father's orders, just as she later finds herself in Amnon's bedroom having obeyed Amnon's whims: 'And Amnon said to Tamar: "Bring the food [ברה] into the room ברה, so I eat כדר out of your hand." And Tamar took the cakes [לבב] that she had made, and brought them to Amnon her brother, into the room [חדר]' (v. 10). The detailed description of Tamar's movements from her home to Amnon's house and to his room, and the repetition of the terms 'house' or 'home' (בית) and 'room' (חדר) clarify beyond any doubt that, unlike Dinah, Tamar did not leave her proper place voluntarily, but rather was ordered by her father and manipulated by her half-brother to come so dangerously close to the latter's bedside. Whereas the text in Genesis 34 gives us no details about what transpires between Shechem and Dinah at the former's house, the text in 2 Samuel 13 makes it clear that Amnon 'took hold of her' (חזק) and that she did her best to resist the rape (vv. 11-13): 'But he would not listen to her, and he was stronger than her (חזק) and raped her and lay with her' (v. 14). Having been abused at the house of her villainous brother, Tamar finds refuge at the house (בית) of her good brother: 'And Tamar sat desolate at the house (בית) of Absalom her brother' (v. 20).

The references to 'house' (בית) signify the beginning and end of Tamar's ordeal. Her tragedy begins when she leaves her protected environment and ends with her arrival at Absalom's house. Implicit and explicit references to 'home' (בית) also signify the beginning and the end of Dinah's ordeal. It begins with her 'going out' (יצא)—one assumes out of her father's house—and concludes with her and her brothers 'going out' (יצא) of Shechem's house (v. 26). Despite the considerable differences in the presentation of Dinah's and Tamar's rapes, both sisters appear to be raped *outside of their own home*. For both, the danger seems to lurk *outside* their protected environment, that is, outside the houses of their male custodians. This configuration precludes the possibility that the male custodians themselves—father, brother, husband—may abuse their control and rape their protégée.[14]

---

14. Until rather recently scholars have been reluctant to discuss the prevalence of the rape of women by male family members. See Florence Rush, *The Best Kept Secret* (New York: McGraw-Hill, 1987); Judith L. Herman, *Father–Daughter Incest* (Cambridge, MA: Harvard University Press, 1987). On the prevalence of

By contrasting Shechem's house and Jacob's home, or Amnon's house and Absalom's home, the biblical text justifies the restriction of the female dependent to her 'proper place'. This message is especially blatant in Genesis 34, which implies that, at least to some extent, Dinah's venturing outside of her own home has brought about her rape.

While the biblical text admits that some male custodians are will-ing—under duress—to offer up their female dependents for molestation by a corrupt crowd *outside* the house, it never describes a rape of a female dependent—daughter, sister or wife—*by* her male custodian or *inside* his house. Thus, for example, the biblical text admits that Lot offers to 'take out' his virgin daughters in an effort to satisfy the corrupt Sodomites (Gen. 19.8), who are threatening to break down his door (Gen. 19.9) in their attempt to molest Lot's male guests (Gen. 19.5). But when the biblical text describes Lot's own sexual relations with his daughters, it emphatically exonerates Lot, instead presenting his daugh-ters as the initiators and perpetrators of the incestuous 'rape' (Gen. 19.31-38). Similarly, Judges 19 admits that the old Benjaminite host offers to the clamoring crowd outside his house his own virgin daughter and his guest's concubine: 'Here is my daughter the virgin, and his concubine, I will if you please take them out and you may rape [אנה] them, and do with them as you please, but to this man you must not do this outrage [נבל]' (Judg. 19.24). While the host's daughter is spared, however, the concubine is not. A gang rape, apparently resulting in her death, takes place all night long *outside her host's house* (Judg. 19.25-26).[15] Once again, rape is described as taking place in a hostile, outside world. The Judaite concubine is raped by strangers. The male custodian is shown to consent to the molestation of his female dependent only when hard-pressed to do so. Interestingly, in both Genesis 19 and Judges 19, the virgin daughters offered up by their fathers are both spared, staying safely ensconced in their fathers' houses. The only father in the Bible who is actually shown to participate in bringing

rape in marriage, see Diana E.H. Russel, *Rape in Marriage* (New York: Macmillan, 1982). See also, Paula Webster, 'Politics of Rape in Primitive Society', *Heresies* 6 (1978), pp. 16-22.

15. The Hebrew text does not clarify whether the concubine has merely lost consciousness or whether her falling down (נפל) on the threshold and failing to answer her master's orders to 'rise up' (Judg. 19.27-28) imply that she is speechless with exhaustion, has lost consciousness, or is, in fact, dead. Compare Phyllis Trible, *Texts of Terror*, p. 79.

about his own daughter's rape is David, but he is said to do so unwittingly (2 Sam. 13.6-7).

The description of male custodians as bodyguards of sorts and the correlative description of the outside world as a danger zone result in justifying male control over female dependents. This, in turn, means validating the confinement of the female dependent to her custodian's home and restricting her freedom.

It is therefore not surprising that two of the three rape accounts in the Bible are described as the direct consequence of the female victim's voluntary departure from her custodian's home. Like Dinah, said to 'go out' of her protected environment, the Judaite concubine is said to leave (זנה) her husband's home and to go (הלך) to the 'house of her father' (Judg. 19.2).[16] The reason for the concubine's move is not explained, just as Dinah's wish 'to see the daughters of the land' leaves much to the reader's imagination. It is possible that the reticence about these women's motives is related to an implied stricture against a woman's venturing into the outside world on her own. Would not too much explaining ultimately justify such moves? We do not know why the Judaite concubine chooses to leave her husband's home and return to her father's, just as we do not know what it was that Dinah wished to see or find out about the 'daughters of the land' (Gen. 34.1). While their motivations remain unclear, the effects of their actions are spelled out dramatically for the reader. Dinah pays for her exploratory adventurism with her virginity, while the concubine, apparently having no virginity to sacrifice, must pay with her life. Dinah and the Judaite concubine are not the only ones to pay for crossing the threshold of their custodians' homes. This move implicates their male custodians as well as large numbers of other males in a bloody confrontation, confusion and insecurity. Because of Dinah's uncalled-for move, the whole city of Shechem is demolished, which, as Jacob makes clear, may endanger the lives of his entire family (Gen. 34.30). The move of the Judaite concubine results in even greater damage, as it brings about a violent civil war between the Benjaminites and the other tribes in the wake of which the entire tribe of Benjamin risks complete obliteration (Judg. 20). Had the narratives meant to decry the acts of rape alone, they could conceiv-

---

16. The Hebrew original is ambivalent in its description of the concubine's desertion of her husband. The verb זנה is applied to her and may be understood as 'left', 'betrayed' or as 'played the harlot'. Whatever the precise meaning, זנה frequently carries negative connotations.

ably begin with a description of the rapists' actions. Genesis 34 could
have begun with v. 2, with a characterization of Shechem and a description of his assault on Dinah, while Judges 19 could begin in v. 15, with
the arrival of the Levite and his concubine at Gibeah, which is precisely
where the Levite begins his summary account to the Israelites (Judg.
20.4). The linkage of the disastrous events described in these chapters
to the woman's crossing the threshold of her male custodian at her own
initiative is by no means coincidental. It implies that grave consequences may ensue from the male custodian's failure to control his
female dependents.

While Genesis 34 and Judges 19 appear to disapprove of the male
custodian's failure to properly restrain his female dependent, 2 Samuel
13 seems to disapprove of the custodian's failure to 'protect' her
sufficiently. By describing the manipulative machinations of Amnon
and the unsuspecting attitude of David, the text turns David into a victim of dramatic irony. The narrator, the reader and the villain share the
knowledge that is denied the male custodian. This constellation satirizes
the misplaced confidence and innocence of David. It points up the fact
that an unsuspecting and unwatchful father may turn into his own
daughter's victimizer. By presenting the rapist as the victim's half-
brother, and by describing such extenuating circumstances as illness
and a request for food as the causes that ultimately enable Tamar's
rape, the text implies that even the closest relatives must not be trusted
and even the most disarming circumstances must not allay a good
father's suspicions. The frequent repetition of the cognate אח and אחות
are not only meant to highlight the fact that the narrative is dealing with
a family drama, it also calls attention to the fact that even so-called
brothers, let alone other male relatives, are not to be trusted by a watch-
ful male custodian.[17] The ironic tension between the frequent references
to Amnon's formally fraternal relationship with Tamar (vv. 2, 4, 5-8,
10-12) and the reality of his lustful motives indicates that appearances
may be deceiving and, when a virgin daughter is involved, no amount

17. George Ridout suggests that the repetition of the words 'brother' and 'sister'
seeks to impress upon the audience 'the kinship relations of the characters involved
in this appalling story'. This repetition, according to Ridout, communicates to us in
a convincing and poignant manner the 'rendering apart of the royal house'. See
'The Rape of Tamar', pp. 77-78. According to Bar-Efrat, the repetition of these
cognates emphasizes the contrast between Absalom, who treats Tamar as a brother
ought to, and Amnon who does not. See *The Art of the Biblical Story*, pp. 203-204.

of suspicion is sufficient. The repetition of the words 'food' (ברה) and 'cakes' (לבב) (vv. 5-10) reinforces the ironic tension between innocent appearances and hidden motives. The repetition of the noun *byt*, noted earlier, is also not coincidental. By sending 'home' (בית) to his daughter a message ordering her to 'go' (הלך) to Amnon's home (בית) (v. 7), David has begun a chain of events leading inexorably to Tamar's demise. The patriarchal message of 2 Samuel 13 does not differ in essence from that implied by Genesis 34 (or Judges 19). Despite its insistence on Tamar's innocence, this text, too, punishes the rape victim in the final analysis. For its emphatic description of the dangerous world amounts to implicit advice to keep the daughter-sister at home, consequently restricting her freedom and autonomy.

As noted earlier, 2 Samuel 13 is much more emphatic in its presentation of the sister as an innocent victim of rape. While the Genesis 34 text does not clarify to what extent Dinah resists her rape, its counterpart describes with great detail Tamar's attempts to do so. In response to Amnon's invitation to 'come lie with' him (v. 11), she is quoted as saying:

> No, my brother, do not rape [ענה] me, for this must not be done in Israel,
> do not commit this outrage [נבל]. And I, where will I carry my shame?
> And you will be like one of the base men in Israel, and now, please
> speak to the king for he will not withhold me from you (2 Sam. 13.12).

In her attempt to dissuade Amnon from raping her, Tamar appeals to national custom ('this must not be done in Israel') and to Amnon's moral sense ('do not commit this outrage'). She tries to arouse his pity ('...where will I carry my shame?') and speaks to his self-interest ('and you will be like one of the base men in Israel'). Finally, Tamar tries to appeal to Amnon's reason, assuring him that he could have her through lawful marriage. Whether we interpret Tamar's pleas as rhetorical ploys, as 'a kind of panicked catalogue of reasons for Amnon to desist, a desperate attempt at persuasion', as Robert Alter sees it, or whether we consider them, as Phyllis Trible does, as sober and sincere expressions of wisdom, it is clear that Tamar does all she possibly can to prevent the rape.[18] By describing in detail Tamar's effort to resist, the narrator insures the reader's sympathy for her. If Tamar's conduct prior to her rape testifies to her unquestionable innocence, what befalls her after

18. See Alter, *The Art of Biblical Narrative*, p. 73 and Trible, *Texts of Terror*, pp. 45-46.

her rape presents her as the ultimate victim. Unlike Shechem, who seeks to marry Dinah after the rape, Amnon is overcome with intense hatred for Tamar, who tries to dissuade him: 'And she said to him: "No, for this evil is even greater than the other one you have done to me, to send me away", but he did not wish to listen to her' (v. 16). Once again, Tamar's pleas are to no avail. She is shown to be doubly abused, first by the rape, then by Amnon's refusal to marry her, according to what biblical law requires in this case. The description of Tamar's mourning, her rending of her striped garment—one reserved to virgin princesses— her putting ashes on her head, her going (הלך) and crying out loud (זעק) in public (vv. 18-19) underscores the contrast between her initial description as a desirable princess (vv. 1-2), and her present status as a despised, abused and rejected rape victim. Whereas Genesis 34 omits Dinah's reaction to her rape, this text focuses at great length and with considerable sympathy on Tamar's anguished reaction to her humiliation. It would appear that no greater difference could separate the characterizations of these sisters.

Rape as Institution or Experience

This difference creates the impression that while Genesis 34 is concerned with the institutional aspect of Dinah's rape, 2 Samuel 13 in describing Tamar's reactions to her rape in great detail is interested in the experiential aspect of a sister's rape. The subtle differences between the stories suggest that in the case of Dinah the offense is against the father's dignity, whereas in the case of Tamar the offense is against the female victim.[19] Yet a closer reading of 2 Samuel 13 reveals that this narrative too, despite its focus on what it presents as Tamar's point of view is concerned less with the rape victim and more with notions of honor and the nation's morals. In both chapters the offenses against national dignity and the family's honor override the woman's suffering. In Genesis 34, Dinah's brothers are said to be 'grieved' and 'very angry' because 'he [Shechem] has committed an outrage [נבל] in Israel' by sleeping with Jacob's daughter, and 'this thing [כן] must not be done [עשה]' (v. 7). The reference to Dinah here as 'Jacob's daughter' implies that what the brothers find outrageous is not the abuse of Dinah herself, but the humiliating offense to her status as Jacob's daughter. The refer-

---

19. Nissim,'On Analyzing a Biblical Story', p. 140.

ence to 'Jacob's daughter' implies that by offending Dinah, Shechem also offended Dinah's father and her brothers. The dignity of the family and of the Israelite nation are here at stake, not the physical and emotional aggression suffered by the girl herself. One could argue that by condemning rape as an offense against the victim's father and brothers, and even the entire nation, the biblical definition of rape underscores its objectionability. It seems to me, however, that by extending its parameters to include family and nation, the biblical definition of rape diffuses the fundamentally sexual-political core of the crime of rape; it blurs the fact that only men can be rapists, and it denies the fact that women are its primary victims. By broadening its scope to include the institution of the family and the entire nation, the biblical definition turns rape into a crime against the victim's custodians. If the real crime is committed against the family and the nation, or against a code of honor, it would seem logical, for example, that the victim's father be monetarily compensated and that the rapist try to restore the family's honor by marrying the victim. The ideology of the rape narratives complements the logic of the biblical laws on rape that ensure that the victim's father be compensated and that the family's honor be redeemed by encouraging the rapist to marry his victim (Exod. 22.15-16; Deut. 22.28-29).

Though put in Tamar's mouth, the references to rape in 2 Samuel 13 are essentially based on the same terms of opprobrium used in Genesis 34. Here too it is described as 'an outrage' (נבל), which 'must not be done in Israel' (v. 12) and whose perpetrator would be as 'one of the base men [נבל] in Israel' (v. 13). Tamar is not shown to dread her possible physical and emotional injuries; the closest reference addressing her own personal loss is contained in the rhetorical question 'And I, where will I carry my shame [חרף]?' What is implied by this question is that as a rape victim, Tamar expects to be further humiliated and victimized, this time by society. The text does not question Tamar's double punishment. Tamar's sad prognostication is in fact confirmed by the description of her two-year-long 'desolate' (שמם) isolation at the house of Absalom. Yet, one would expect that the social sanctions be applied to the rapist, the one who 'commits an outrage in Israel', not to his victim. Amnon, not Tamar, ought to have been concerned about 'shame', and Tamar rather than Amnon and Absalom ought to have been the focus of the narrative. Instead, the chapter focuses on Amnon's actions and Absalom's reactions while Tamar virtually disappears from the text. What will be redeemed by Absalom's revenge is the family's, or rather his own, honor. How his revenge affects Tamar is unknown. What is clear is that rape according to the Bible is a crime that stigmatizes the victim, not the victimizer, and a crime that is best avenged through a third party.

The stigmatization of the rape victim is invoked even more emphatically in Genesis 34. Here instead of 'shame' (חרף), the text uses the word 'defile' (טמא). The word appears three times in the chapter, once in reference to Jacob's perception of the rape ('And Jacob heard that he defiled Dinah, his daughter' [v. 5]) and twice in reference to the brothers' point of view ('and they spoke because he had defiled Dinah, their sister' [v. 13]; 'and they looted the city because they had defiled their sister' [v. 26]). Although here too rape is presented as 'an outrage in Israel', the perpetrator of the crime, Shechem, does not seem to be stigmatized by 'doing what must not be done'. Rather, it is Dinah who is considered 'defiled'.

What Dinah's brothers set out to rectify is the family's damaged honor. Even as they agree that their sister was molested against her will, the word used to describe her ordeal does not convey her physical or emotional suffering but the symbolic stigma attached to a rape victim. What is outrageous to the brothers is the fact that their sister was made into a זנה, or harlot: 'And they said: "Should he treat our sister like a harlot [זונה]?" ' (v. 31). Instead of questioning the brothers' comparison of a rape victim to a woman who sells sexual favors for monetary gain, most contemporary critics accept and justify it. For example, it has been argued that Shechem indeed treated Dinah as a harlot because he offered to pay her father off.[20] Another critic stigmatizes the rape victim by explaining that the brothers use זנה in the sense of פלגש or concubine.[21] The references to defilement (טמא) in the story of Dinah do not differ much from the references to shame (חרף) in Tamar's story. Tamar is mouthing the patriarchal interpretation of rape as she implores Amnon to marry her. In full accordance with the biblical rape laws, Tamar

20. See Sternberg, 'A Delicate Balance', p. 215.

21. Ararat, 'Reading According to the "Seder" ', p. 31. This interpretation is rather unconvincing, given the significant difference in status and rights between a concubine and a harlot, as demonstrated by Louis Epstein in *Marriage Laws in the Bible and the Talmud* (Cambridge, MA: Harvard University Press, 1942), pp. 49-61. See also David Mace, *Hebrew Marriage: A Sociological Study* (New York: Philosophical Library, 1953), pp. 121-41.

appears to be more outraged by Amnon's rejection than by her rape: 'And she said to him: "No, for this sending me away is a greater evil than the one you have done to me" ' (v. 16).

How is it possible for Tamar to see her expulsion as a greater evil than her rape? Some may be led to believe that Tamar's response lends authority to the biblical rape laws.'[22] The rape laws compel the rapist to marry his victim and to pay her father (Deut. 22.28-29; Exod. 22.15). Until recently it has been assumed that these laws indeed secure the interest of the raped woman. However, it is not the raped woman but her father who receives monetary compensation for the rape. Furthermore, the raped woman must marry her rapist.[23] The law seeks primarily to protect the father's interests and legal authority as the custodian of his daughter's virginity. The patriarchal law also penalizes the daughter by forcing her to marry her assailant, her rapist forever, the law penalizes her as well. The rape laws and the rape narratives refer to rape as an institution based on a male honor code and on male financial and legal interests. The solution they offer does not redeem the woman, but rather her custodians. By presenting the patriarchal interest as the victim's, the text 'proves' that the law is just and valid. In effect, however, the description of Tamar's response is prescriptive. It reflects the way in which a raped woman *ought to react to her rape.* As the perfect daughter and sister who unquestioningly obeys her father's and both her brothers' orders, Tamar also epitomizes the perfect rape victim. In the final analysis, Tamar's protest against Amnon indicates that violating the law is worse than violating a woman. Tamar's outcry decries the threat to the institution of rape, more than the act of rape itself.

Though 2 Samuel 13 is more emphatic in its treatment of the rape victim, its underlying concern is not with the experience of rape and what it means to the victim. Tamar is indeed permitted to speak out, which her counterpart in Genesis 34 does not do. But, as we have seen, the terms of her speech—the fundamental concepts put into her mouth—reveal a concern with the institutional violation perpetrated by the rape. In both texts the institutional aspects of rape take precedence over its experiential aspects. In both texts it is not so much the harm

---

22. See, e.g., Bar-Efrat, *The Art of the Biblical Story*, p. 222.

23. As Judith Ochshorn put it: 'His [the rapist's] good feelings towards her [the raped woman] may be imagined. He was forced to pay her father and marry her; he could not divorce her; and the only one who benefitted from all of this was her father.' See *The Female Experience and the Nature of the Divine*, p. 207.

done to the girl herself, but the threat posed to the patriarchal order. The victim's physical pain is not even mentioned, while her emotional stress is depicted in 2 Samuel 13 as a direct result of the rapist's rejection.

The Shift from Sister to Brother

In both narratives, the sisters disappear as soon as the 'good' brothers step in. Dinah appears for the last time in Genesis 34 in conjunction with her brothers' vengeful reprisal: 'And they [the brothers] killed Hamor and Shechem his son by the sword, and took Dinah from Shechem's house and went out' (Gen. 34.26). What happens to Dinah after her 'rescue' remains unknown. Tamar too virtually disappears from the biblical text upon the appearance of Absalom. As in the case of Dinah, the last reference to Tamar describes her in her brother's custody (2 Sam. 13.20). It is not known whether this highly sympathetic character is doomed to perpetual desolation, or whether her rapist's death has released her from her imposed isolation at Absalom's house.

Neither narrative clarifies whether or how the brothers' revenge affected the lives of the raped sisters. It would seem that the sisters are no longer necessary to the context describing the restoration of patriarchal order. The narrative focus shifts from sister to brother. The disappearance of the sister enables the brother to replace her as the primary victim of the injustice committed by the 'bad' brother. The disappearance of the sister also makes for a 'cleaner' transition to the brother(s)—the real hero(es) of both narratives. In order for the brother to effectively replace his sister as the wronged party, the latter must disappear as unobtrusively as possible. Too much, or even *any* attention to the wrong sister *after* the revenge may shift the focus back to the sister. The sister's disappearance makes it easier for the narrator to create the impression that both have suffered the same injustice, and that the sister's compensation lies in the brother's revenge.

The Suppression of the Sister's Emotional Attitude

What makes the transition from sister to brother easier is the suppression of the sister's emotional attitude towards the rapist. Whereas in both narratives the text offers explicit statements about the rapist's passion for the woman, it does not offer much information about her inner world. While Genesis 34 makes no reference to Dinah's feelings vis-à-vis Shechem, it leaves no doubts about the latter's feelings toward

Dinah: 'And he [Shechem] cleaved [דבק] to Dinah, the daughter of Jacob, and he loved [אהב] the girl, and he spoke on her heart' (v. 3). The intensity of Shechem's feelings is conveyed by the synonymous expressions דבק and אהב, and by his subsequent attempt to marry Dinah. The text is also explicit about Amnon's intense feelings for Tamar:

> And it was afterwards that Absalom the son of David had a beautiful sister and her name was Tamar, and Amnon the son of David loved [אהב] her. And Amnon was so distressed that he fell sick because of his sister Tamar, for she was a virgin, and it seemed impossible to Amnon to do anything to her (vv. 1-2).

It can be said that at this point Amnon's love for Tamar is presented as equally intense as Shechem's love for Dinah. The difference between the two is that after the respective rapes Shechem falls in love with Dinah but Amnon is said to *stop* loving Tamar: 'And Amnon hated [שׂנא] her [with] a very great hatred, for the hatred [with which] he hated her was greater than the love [with which] he had loved [אהב] her, and Amnon said to her: "Get up, go" ' (v. 15). Despite this important difference, both narratives associated rape with intense love on the part of the rapist. The rapist's contempt and hatred for his victim is presented not as *the cause* of the sexual assault but as the *result of it*.[24] It is perhaps more significant that despite the differences in the characterization of the villain, both narratives find it necessary to be explicit about their emotional attitude toward the victim. But while both texts emphasize the intensity of the rapists' attraction for their prospective victims—a common patriarchal myth in the interpretation of rape—there is silence about the sisters' responses to the rape and the rapists. We have no summary statements about the feelings of Dinah or Tamar, either before or after their respective rapes. The words and actions ascribed to the raped Tamar (vv. 16, 18-19) do not reflect her feelings toward Amnon, as much as they indicate her horror at the fate awaiting her as a raped virgin. Tamar's protest against Amnon's order to chase her out (v. 16) as well as her mourning gestures (vv. 18-19) are largely determined by the prospect of being stigmatized and outcast. They do not convey her anger at Amnon. Tamar's refusal to leave Amnon after her rape (v. 16)

---

24. See Sternberg, 'A Delicate Balance', pp. 198-203. See Ararat, 'Reading According to the "Seder" ', and Nissim, 'On Analyzing a Biblical Story', for a rebuttal of Sternberg's interpretation.

certainly cannot be construed as an expression of love: at the same time it does not reflect rage or hatred. Tamar's mourning gestures dramatize her sorrow about her demise, but they do not specify what she feels about Amnon.

The suppression of the sisters' emotional attitudes toward her rapist makes it easier for the shift in focus from sister to brother to take place. Thus, the rage and hatred that one would expect the sisters to experience are displaced in the biblical narrative and ascribed to the brother. While the text remains silent about Dinah's feelings about her rape, it offers us a direct and unequivocal presentation of her brothers' emotional reaction to it: 'and the men were grieved [עצב], and they were very angry [חרה]' (Gen. 34.7). Similarly, while we are not told what Tamar feels about Amnon, we are told what Absalom feels: 'for Absalom hated [שׂנא] Amnon, because he had raped his sister Tamar' (2 Sam. 13.22). There is a notable resemblance between the technical presentation of the brothers' inner world and that of the rapist. In both cases the emotions are very intense. Dinah's brothers are *very* angry as well as 'grieved'. This emphatic rendering of the brothers' feelings is structurally analogous to the rendering of Shechem's emotional reaction, which also uses a synonymous parallelism (דבק/אהב) for emphasis. In both cases, the text uses the top scale of certainties by offering an unequivocal statement about both the rapists' and the brothers' feelings. In the case of Amnon and Absalom, there is even a certain semantic resemblance, in that both are said to experience hatred (שׂנא) in reaction to the rape: Amnon hates (שׂנא) Tamar and Absalom hates (שׂנא) Amnon.

The Justification of the Brother

It is noteworthy that while both narratives dismiss the sister's reaction to her rape, both find it necessary to make some reference to her father's reaction to it. Genesis 34, which altogether omits Dinah's point of view, is reticent and, in accordance with its general technique of characterization, rather ambiguous in its presentation of Jacob's reaction. 2 Samuel 13, which does not report Tamar's actions and words after her rape, gives us a clearer and less equivocal description of the father's point of view. In both narratives, in other words, the father's emotional reaction to the rape is rendered with greater directness and explicitness than his daughter's. This is striking because in both narratives the father-figures appear to be rather peripheral, anyway more ancillary to the development of the plot than their daughters. Thus there is no information about Dinah's reaction to her rape, while Jacob is reported to 'keep quiet' (חרש) until his sons return from the fields (Gen. 34.5) and David is described as 'very angry' (חרה), without proceeding to act on his anger (2 Sam. 13.21). Both fathers are shown to be equally angered by the rape and equally unable to do anything about it. It would be wrong, however, to construe the fathers' reactions as indifferent. In both narratives, the text conveys the impression that the father *fails to act*, not that he doesn't care. Verse 5 in Genesis 34 states explicitly that Jacob 'kept quiet until they [his sons] came in'. The temporal clause indicates that Jacob did not hold his peace indefinitely, and that he did speak with his sons upon their return from the field. It would seem that in both narratives the father's anger is channelled into the brothers' actions. When Jacob rebukes Simeon and Levi for their brutality, he shows concern for the extremity of their actions, not for their having taken action to avenge their sister. David who is said to be 'very angry' and who fails to act is conveniently replaced by Absalom. Minimization of the father's role justifies the brothers' actions. The brothers' reactions would not have been necessary had the fathers been shown to react. By minimizing the fathers' participation, the narrative allows the brothers to emerge as the female victims' true custodians.

A close reading of Genesis 34 reveals that the references to Dinah as a sister (אחות) often serve to justify the brothers' brutal actions. In some ways, the story of Dinah's rape serves as a prelude to the destruction of Shechem. The more outrageous her victimization, the more justified their bloody reactions. Thus, for example, v. 13 explains that the brothers deceive Shechem and Hamor because the former 'defiled Dinah their sister'. Verse 25, which describes the murderous actions of Simeon and Levi, refers to them as 'Dinah's brothers', after having identified them as 'Jacob's sons'. The description of the brothers' pillaging of Shechem also appears to repeat what is already known, namely that this repetition is to remind the reader of Dinah's brothers' motivations. The references to 'Dinah' and 'their sister' implies that what we are witnessing are not wanton acts of violence, but expressions of anger and a keen sense of justice and brotherly commitment.

Similarly, the detailed description of Amnon's corruption clarifies that he deserves Absalom's uncompromising hatred and vindictive treatment. The emphasis on Tamar's innocence and helplessness vindicates Absalom's implicit decision to spare no means in avenging her victimization. The insistence on Tamar's innocence throws into relief Amnon's baseness. The gradual build-up of empathy for Tamar parallels the growing resentment against Amnon. As Yairah Amit observes rightly, all these rhetorical measures serve one purpose: 'to present Amnon as thoroughly guilty, and indirectly to create a positive foundation, or reservoir of sympathy, for the characterization of Absalom'.[25]

Another aspect both narratives refrain from treating is the brothers' personal investment in killing the rapist. It has been suggested that Amnon's real purpose in raping Tamar was to damage Absalom's political prospects.[26] As the full brother of a raped princess, Absalom would be a poor competitor for David's throne. If we continue this line of thinking, it is possible to speculate that Absalom's retaliation was also politically motivated, for Amnon's death paved Absalom's way to David's throne. What is significant is the fact that the text in both narratives refrains from spelling out the brothers' personal motives for retaliation.

The stories of Dinah and Tamar validate the intervention of their respective brothers on their behalf, but they do not do so at the expense of the father's or husband's patriarchal right over the woman. This may explain why brothers are shown to come to the defense of unmarried sisters only. Married sisters in the biblical narrative are either never raped or have no brothers. While the unattached Dinah has 12 avenging brothers, the Levite's concubine who has been raped by strangers and abused by her own husband has no brother at all to avenge her. The biblical narrative presents only unmarried sisters as having brothers. The biblical narrative also refrains from bringing brother-right and father-right into conflict. The brother does not overstep the limits of his sphere of dominance by intruding into the father's authority; rather he is shown to take action where the father fails to do so. One may speculate that had the victim's father reacted on her behalf the brothers' interference would be unjustified.

Another factor that appears to validate the brothers' intervention on behalf of their sisters is God's absence from both narratives. Unlike Joseph, who manages to escape from Potiphar's wife (Gen. 39.7-14), no female prospective rape victim in the Bible is shown to be capable of

25. Yairah Amit, 'The Story of Amnon and Tamar: A Reservoir of Sympathy for Absalom', *Hasifrut* 32 (1983), p. 84 (Hebrew).

26. Ariella Deem, ' "Cupboard Love": The Story of Amnon and Tamar', *Hasifrut* 28 (1979), pp. 100-107 (Hebrew).

defending herself or of being helped out by God. While potential male victims are somehow spared, either through their own ruse or divine intervention, the rape of female victims appears to be unavoidable unless they are virgins offered up as substitutes for a potential male victim. Thus, Lot's virgin daughters who are offered up to the Sodomite crowd as substitutes for Lot's male guests (Gen. 19.5-8) are spared thanks to the miraculous intervention of the three guests who turn out to be Yhwh's messengers (Gen. 19.10-17). Similarly, the virgin daughter who is offered up by her father to the Benjaminite crowd as substitute for his Levite is spared thanks to the latter's intervention (Judg. 19.22-26). Yet, God seems to be absent not only from the rape scenes of Dinah, the Levite's concubine and Tamar, but also from the events that succeed these rapes. The descriptions of the rapes and of the revenge of the male custodians make no reference to Yhwh.

The suppression of any reference to God in the rape and vengeance scenes of Genesis 34 and 2 Samuel 13 is all the more blatant due to Yhwh's presence in the narratives that precede and follow them. Whereas none of the participants in Genesis 34 reveals any awareness of God's presence or authority, His name is invoked several times in the narrative that precedes it (Gen. 33.10-11, 20). While God appears to be unaware of or indifferent to Dinah's rape and its aftermath, He appears as soon as this ordeal is over, ordering Jacob to build for Him an altar in Bethel (Gen. 35.1). While Tamar does not invoke the name of God either before or after her rape as a possible redeemer or avenger, in the narrative immediately following it, the anonymous woman hired by Joab to intercede with King David on behalf of Absalom invokes the name of God several times (2 Sam. 14.11, 13, 14, 16, 17, 20). God makes an even more dramatic appearance in the narrative that immediately precedes Dinah's rape as He sends Nathan the prophet to castigate and punish David for his adulterous affair with Bathsheba (2 Sam. 12). By completely suppressing any references to God in both narratives, the text is able to underplay God's absence from the represented events. Any reference to God in these contexts is likely to elicit the question why God has not intervened on behalf of the raped woman, either as redeemer or as avenger. For while it is true that God does not intervene to protect Uriah, the text shows God to be highly displeased with David's conduct (2 Sam. 11.27) and to intervene as Uriah's avenger (2 Sam. 12.1, 7). The crime of adultery (the sexual appropriation of another man's wife) is shown to be punished by God; the punishment for rape (the sexual assault on a woman) is punished by her male custodian. Rape does not appear to displease God as much as adultery does (see Chapter 5 on the biblical wife). Furthermore, had God been shown to intervene on behalf of the raped sister, and had He prevented the rape or punished the rapist, there would be no need for the brother to protect or avenge her. There is a very close correlation between the sister's vulnerability and the brother's ability to exercise his authority as her custodian.

Yet by validating the brother's right to protect his sister, the patriarchal ideology only perpetuates the sister's political impotence; it reinforces her inability to protect herself or to resort to legal authorities. On a deeper level, this ideology suggests that where a father fails to take control a brother must step in to replace him. For the right to protect is also the right to dominate. If the sisters are to look to their brothers for protection against rapists, they cannot possibly be their equals. One of the lessons taught here is that when one form of male control is defunct, a woman must resort to another form of male control. By suppressing female images, as well as the possibility of Yhwh's assistance, the narratives suggest that an unmarried woman whose father is for some reason unavailable can and should count for help on her brother only.

Conclusion

But why of all the biblical sisters are Dinah and Tamar raped? As in the case of Dinah, Tamar's rape occurs at a crucial moment of genealogical transition. Dinah is raped just as Jacob grows old, and his hegemony passes on to his descendants. As Jacob's only daughter, Dinah could conceivably become a tribal ancestress, along with her brothers. Dinah would, in all probability, become a tribe if not for her rape. The function of the rape become clear in view of the problems a female tribe poses within a patriarchal framework. By stigmatizing Dinah, and disposing of her through the narrative discussed above, the problem is resolved.

Tamar is raped at an equally important juncture in the history of the Davidic line, just as King David's sons begin to compete for access to the throne. If Amnon is eliminated through death, Tamar, a possible candidate as David's heiress, is eliminated through rape. Otherwise, she could conceivably become David's heiress, a queen. But as a legitimate queen, a queen whose status does not depend on her husband, Tamar presents a problem. While Michal, Saul's daughter and David's wife, is denied progeny, arguably a form of elimination, Tamar's candidacy is eliminated through rape. As we have seen, the sister's rape is also a convenient justification of the authority of brothers over their female sibling. For both Absalom and Dinah's brothers intervene too late, their intervention neither prevents nor affects the subsequent humiliation and misery to which the sister is condemned. Though it may seem that the brother's intervention restores justice by punishing the enemy, what is in fact restored is the patriarchal order: the intruder is chased out and the stigmatized sister is eliminated from the narrative. It may not be coincidental then that the most detailed stories about sisters are also stories about rape that ultimately validate the authority of brothers to act as surrogate fathers.

POSTSCRIPT

Narratives are powerful tools that mould our interpretation of people and events and shape our consciousness. Biblical narratives constitute particularly influential and problematic interpretive lenses because of the way in which they construct power relations between women and men. It is not the historical element in these narratives that I question in this book, but rather the idea that biblical narratives carry or convey an absolute truth about the appropriateness and desirability of the subordination of women to men. This book analyses biblical narratives with a view to highlighting the ideological prescription embedded in them. I am interested in women as both narrative characters in the text, as well as readers who have been constructed by the text. In this book I tried to question the Bible's sexual politics and its hold on our interpretation of reality. I am using the possessive pronoun 'our' despite my awareness of the social, religious, racial and political differences among women readers. Despite these differences and the critiques of women as an essentialist category I believe that the theoretical possibility of the concept of woman is a fundamental ingredient in any feminist reading of any text. Only a relentless focus on the woman as reader and the reader as a woman promises to result in a consistent identification of the modus operandi of the Bible's patriarchal ideology.

In this book I have not sought to include all the narratives relating to women. Rather, what I tried to do was to map out general categories that should help us identify the mechanisms underlying biblical representations of women. These categories consider women characters not as specific individuals in isolation from each other, but rather as types or figures, as mothers, brides, wives, daughters and sisters. The characterization of mothers suggests that women are valorized for their ability to protect and care for their sons. At the same time women's natural procreative ability is questioned and undermined. The implicit correlation between fertility and moral superiority suggests that barrenness in women is not merely a tragic accident but a moral flaw. While mothers are permitted to outsmart their male counterparts and surpass them morally, wives are usually constructed as inferior to and more confined than their male counterparts. Brides are not given the prerogative of speech in conjugal settings. Conjugal narratives validate the husband's perspective while the (non-maternal) wife emerges as a passive object, as marginal and largely insignificant. The successive transformations in the betrothal contest annunciation and temptation scenes display a mechanism of ideological naturalization, a mechanism that uses repetition in order to present as natural a rather problematic social reality.

While narratives about mother–daughter relationships are suppressed, narratives about father–daughter relationships are presented as limited episodes that usually lead to the girl's death or destruction. The girl is usually shown to venture out of the confines of her father's house, a move that leads to disaster. The daughter is implicitly blamed for her tragic end. While the father's motives are made clear, the daughter's are obfuscated or suppressed. The suppression of the daughter's point of view results in the representation of her victimization as an unnecessary accident that causes much grief to her father. The daughter is often represented as a sister as well. While sisterhood is shown to offer little comfort to women, brothers are depicted as reliable authority figures. Brothers avenge their sisters' rape by wreaking havoc on the male perpetrators. The sister's own right to take action is a suppressed possibility, as her point of view is more often than not obscured, while that of her brothers is placed at the very center of the narrative.

The subordination of the sister to her brother, the daughter to her father, the wife to her husband and the mother to her son is justified, validated and naturalized through the use of narrative strategies defined here as biblical sexual politics. This term captures as well the various discursive manifestations of the Bible's patriarchal ideology. By reading this sexual politics as a woman—and I would like to emphasize the indefinite article here stressing my perspective as only one of several possibilities—I offer here a feminist, unapologetic resistant re-vision of the Hebrew Bible.

BIBLIOGRAPHY

Adar, Zvi, *The Biblical Narrative* (trans. Misha Louvish; Jerusalem: Department of Education and Culture of the World Zionist Organization, 1959).

Alexiou, Margaret, and Peter Dronke, 'The Lament of Jephthah's Daughter: Themes, Tradition, Originality', *Studi Medievali* 12 (1971), pp. 819-63.

Allen, Christine Garside, 'Who Was Rebekah? "On Me Be the Curse, My Son" ', in Gross (ed.), *Beyond Androcentrism*, pp. 183-216.

Alter, Robert, *The Art of Biblical Narrative* (New York: Basic Books, 1981).

—'How Convention Helps Us Read: The Case of the Bible's Annunciation Type-Scene', *Prooftexts* 3 (1983), pp. 115-30.

Amit, Yairah, ' "Manoah Promptly Followed His Wife" (Judges 13.11): On the Place of Woman in the Birth Narratives', in Brenner (ed.), *A Feminist Companion to Judges*, pp. 146-56.

Ararat, Nisan, 'Reading According to the "Seder" in the Biblical Narrative', *Hasifrut* 27 (1978), pp. 15-34 (Hebrew).

Arpali, Boaz, 'Caution: A Biblical Story! Comments on the Story of David and Bathsheba and on the Problems of Biblical Narrative', *Hasifrut* 2 (1970), pp. 580-97 (Hebrew).

Aschkenazy, Nehama, *Eve's Journey: Feminine Images in Hebraic Literary Tradition* (Philadelphia: University of Pennsylvania Press, 1986).

—*Woman at the Window: Biblical Tales of Oppression and Escape* (Detroit: Wayne State University Press, 1998).

Auerbach, Erich, *Mimesis: The Representation of Reality in Western Literature* (trans. Willard Trask; Garden City, NY: Doubleday, 1953).

Austin, J.L., *How to Do Things with Words* (Cambridge, MA: Harvard University Press, 1962).

Bach, Alice, 'The Pleasure of her Text', in Alice Bach (ed.), *The Pleasure of Her Text: Feminist Readings of Biblical and Historical Texts* (Valley Forge, PA: Trinity Press International, 1990), pp. 25-44.

—'Signs of the Flesh: Observations on Characterization in the Bible', in Alice Bach (ed.), *Women in the Hebrew Bible* (New York, 1999), pp. 315-65.

—*Women, Seduction, and Betrayal in Biblical Narrative* (London: Cambridge University Press, 1997).

Bal, Mieke, 'Introduction', *Poetics* 13 (1984), pp. 3-4.

—*Lethal Love: Feminist Literary Readings of Biblical Love Stories* (Bloomington: Indiana University Press, 1987).

—*Death and Dissymmetry: The Politics of Coherence in the Book of Judges* (Chicago: University of Chicago Press, 1988).

—*Murder and Difference: Gender, Genre, and Scholarship on Sisera's Death* (trans. Matthew Gumpert; Bloomington: Indiana University Press, 1988).

Bar-Efrat, Shimon, *The Art of the Biblical Story* (Tel Aviv: Sifriat Poalim, 1979) (Hebrew).

—'Some Observations on the Analysis of Structure in Biblical Narrative', *VT* 30.2 (1980), pp. 156-57.

Barrett, Michele, *Women's Oppression Today: Problems in Marxist Feminist Analysis* (London: Verso, 1980).

Beattie, D.R.G., 'Ruth III', *JSOT* 5 (1978), pp. 39-48.

Beauvoir, Simone de, *The Second Sex* (trans. H.M. Parshley; New York: Vintage, 1974 [1952]).

Berlin, Adele, 'Characterization in Biblical Narrative: David's Wives', *JSOT* 23 (1982), pp. 69-85.

—*Poetics and Interpretation of Biblical Narrative* (Sheffield: Almond Press, 1983).

—*The Dynamics of Biblical Parallelism* (Bloomington: Indiana University Press, 1985).

Bernikow, Louise, *Among Women* (New York: Harper & Row, 1980).

Bible and Culture Collective, *The Postmodern Bible* (New Haven: Yale University Press, 1995).

Bird, Phyllis, 'Images of Women in the Old Testament', in Rosemary Radford Ruether (ed.), *Religion and Sexism: Images of Women in the Jewish and Christian Traditions* (New York: Simon & Schuster, 1974), pp. 41-88.

Bloom, Harold, and David Rosenberg, *The Book of J* (New York: Grove Weidenfeld, 1990).

Boose, Lynda, 'The Father's House and the Daughter in It: Structures of Western Culture's Daughter-Father Relationship', in Boose and Flowers (eds.), *Daughters and Fathers*, pp. 19-74.

Boose, Lynda, and Betty S. Flowers (eds.), *Daughters and Fathers* (Baltimore: The Johns Hopkins University Press, 1989).

Booth, Wayne C., 'Freedom of Interpretation: Bakhtin and the Challenge of Feminist Criticism', in W.J.T. Mitchell (ed.), *The Politics of Interpretation* (Chicago: University of Chicago Press, 1982), pp. 51-82.

Bream, Howard N., *et al.* (eds.), *A Light Unto My Path: Old Testament Studies in Honor of Jacob M. Myers* (Philadelphia: Temple University Press, 1974).

Brenner, Athalya, *The Israelite Woman: Social Role and Literary Type in Biblical Narrative* (Sheffield: JSOT Press, 1985).

Brenner, Athalya (ed.), *A Feminist Companion to Genesis* (Sheffield: Sheffield Academic Press, 1993).

—*A Feminist Companion to Exodus and Deuteronomy* (Sheffield: Sheffield Academic Press, 1994).

—*A Feminist Companion to the Latter Prophets* (Sheffield: Sheffield Academic Press, 1995).

—*The Intercourse of Knowledge: On Gendering Desire and 'Sexuality' in the Hebrew Bible* (Leiden: E.J. Brill, 1997).

—*A Feminist Companion to Samuel and Kings* (Sheffield: Sheffield Academic Press, 1994).

—*A Feminist Companion to Judges* (Sheffield: Sheffield Academic Press, 1993).

Brenner, Athalya, and Fokkelien van Dijk-Hemmes, *On Gendering Texts: Female and Male Voices in the Hebrew Bible* (Leiden: E.J. Brill, 1993).

Brenner, Athalya, and Carol Fontaine (eds.), *Reading the Bible: Approaches, Methods and Strategies* (Sheffield: Sheffield Academic Press, 1997).

Briffault, Robert, *The Mothers: A Study of the Origins of Sentiments and Institutions* (3 vols.; New York: Macmillan, 1927).

Brooten, Bernadette J., 'Early Christian Women and Their Cultural Context: Issues of Method in Historical Reconstruction', in Collins (ed.), *Feminist Perspectives on Biblical Scholarship*, pp. 73-77.

Buber, Martin, *On the Bible* (ed. Nahum N. Glatzer; New York: Schocken Books, 1968).

—*The Way of the Bible* (Jerusalem, 1964) (Hebrew).

Butler, Judith, *Gender Trouble: Feminism and the Subversion of Identity* (New York: Routledge, 1990).

Campbell, Edward F., *Ruth* (AB; New York: Doubleday, 1981).

Cantaella, Eva, *Pandora's Daughters: The Role and Status of Women in Greek and Roman Antiquity* (Baltimore: The Johns Hopkins University Press, 1987).

Carmichael, Calum M., *Women, Law and the Genesis Tradition* (Edinburgh: Edinburgh University Press, 1979).

Chatman, Seymour, *Story and Discourse: Narrative Structure in Fiction and Film* (Ithaca, NY: Cornell University Press, 1978).

Chodorow, Nancy, *The Reproduction of Mothering: Psychoanalysis and the Sociology of Gender* (Berkeley: University of California Press, 1978).

Chodorow, Nancy, and Susan Contratto, 'The Fantasy of the Perfect Mother', in Barrie Thorne and Marilyn Yalom (eds.), *Rethinking the Family: Some Feminist Questions* (New York: Longman, 1982), pp. 54-75.

Coats, George W., 'Widows Rights: A Crux in the Structure of Genesis 38', *CBQ 34* (1972), p. 464.

Collins, Adela Yarbro (ed.), *Feminist Perspectives on Biblical Scholarship* (Chico, CA: Scholars Press, 1985).

Conroy, Charles, *Absalom Absalom!* (Rome: The Biblical Institute Press, 1978).

Culler, Jonathan, *On Deconstruction: Theory and Criticism After Structuralism* (Ithaca, NY: Cornell University Press, 1982).

Culley, Robert C., *Studies in the Structure of Hebrew Narrative* (Philadelphia: Fortress Press, 1976).

Darr, Katheryn Pfisterer, *Far More Precious than Jewels: Perspectives on Biblical Women* (Louisville, KY: John Knox Press, 1991).

Day, Peggy L., ' "From the Child is Born the Woman": The Story of Jephthah's Daughter', in Peggy L. Day (ed.), *Gender and Difference in Ancient Israel* (Minneapolis: Fortress Press, 1989), pp. 58-74.

Deem, Ariela, 'Cupboard Love: The Story of Amnon and Tamar', *Hasifrut* 28 (1979), pp. 100-107 (Hebrew).

—*Zot ha-pa'am* (This Time) (Tel Aviv: Reuven Mas, 1986). (Hebrew)

Deen, Edith, *All of the Women of the Bible* (New York: Harper & Row, 1955).

Delaney, Carol, 'The Legacy of Abraham', in Gross (ed.), *Beyond Androcentrism*, pp. 217-36.

Diamond, Irene, and Lee Quinby (eds.), *Feminism and Foucault: Reflections on Resistance* (Boston: Northeastern University Press, 1988).

Dijk-Hemmes, Fokkelien van, 'Sarai's Exile: A Gender-Motivated Reading of Genesis 12.10–13.2', in Brenner (ed.), *A Feminist Companion to Genesis*, pp. 222-34.

—'The Great Woman of Shunem and the Man of God', in Brenner (ed.), *A Feminist Companion to Samuel and Kings*, pp. 218-30.

Dinnerstein, Dorothy, *The Mermaid and the Minotaur: Sexual Arrangements and Human Malaise* (New York: Harper Colophon, 1976).

DiStefano, Christine, *Configurations of Masculinity: A Feminist Perspective on Modern Political Theory* (Ithaca, NY: Cornell University Press, 1991).

Dworkin, Andrea, *Woman Hating* (New York: E.P. Dutton, 1974).

Eagleton, Terry, *Literary Theory: An Introduction* (Minneapolis: University of Minnesota Press, 1983).

Eilberg-Schwartz, Howard, *God's Phallus and Other Problems for Men and Monotheism* (Boston: Beacon Press, 1994).

Ellman, Mary, *Thinking about Women* (New York: Harcourt Brace Jovanovich, 1968).

Engels, Frederick, *The Origin of the Family, Private Property and the State* (ed. and Introduction Eleanor Burke Leacock; New York: International Publishers, 1972).

Epstein, Louis, *Marriage Laws in the Bible and Talmud* (Cambridge, MA: Harvard University Press, 1942).

Ermarth, Elizabeth, 'Fictional Consensus and Female Casualties', in Heilbrun and Higonnet (eds.), *The Representation of Women in Fiction*, pp. 1-18.

Exum, J. Cheryl, 'Promise and Fulfillment: Narrative Art in Judges 13', *JBL* 99.1 (1980), pp. 43-59.

—' "You Shall Let Every Daughter Live": A Study of Exodus 1:8–2:10', in Mary Ann Tolbert (ed.), *The Bible and Feminist Hermeneutics* (Chico, CA: Scholars Press, 1983), pp. 63-82.

—' "Mother in Israel": A Familiar Story Reconsidered', in Russell (ed.), *Feminist Interpretation of the Bible*, pp. 73-85.

—*Fragmented Women: Feminist (Sub)versions of Biblical Narratives* (Valley Forge, PA: Trinity Press International, 1993).

—'Second Thoughts about Secondary Characters: Women in Exodus 1.8–2.10', in Brenner (ed.), *A Feminist Companion to Exodus and Deuteronomy*, pp. 75-87.

Exum, J. Cheryl, and D.J.A. Clines (eds.), *The New Literary Criticism and the Hebrew Bible* (Valley Forge, PA: Trinity Press International, 1993).

Felman, Shoshana, *Writing and Madness: Literature/Philosophy/Psychoanalysis* (Ithaca, NY: Cornell University Press, 1985).

Fetterley, Judith, *The Resisting Reader: A Feminist Approach to American Fiction* (Bloomington: Indiana University Press, 1977).

Fewell, Danna Nolan, and David M. Gunn, *Gender, Power, and Promise: The Subject of the Bible's First Story* (Nashville: Abingdon Press, 1993).

Figes, Eva, *Patriarchal Attitudes: Women in Society* (New York: Persea Books, 1970).

Fisch, Harold, 'Ruth and the Structure of Covenant History', *VT* 32 (1982), pp. 425-37.

Fish, Stanley, *Is There a Text in this Class? The Authority of Interpretive Communities* (Cambridge, MA: Harvard University Press, 1980).

Fishbane, Michael, *Text and Texture: Close Readings of Selected Biblical Texts* (New York: Schocken Books, 1979).

Fokkelman, J.P., *Narrative Art in Genesis* (Assen: Van Gorcum, 1975).

—*Narrative Art and Poetry in the Books of Samuel*, I (Assen: Van Gorcum, 1981).

Fontaine, Carole R., 'A Heifer from thy Stable: On Goddesses and the Status of Women in the Ancient Near East', in *The Pleasure of her Text: Feminist Readings of Biblical and Historical Texts* (Valley Forge, PA: Trinity Press International, 1993), pp. 69-96.

—'The Abusive Bible: On the Use of Feminist Method in Pastoral Contexts', in Athalya Brenner and Carole R. Fontaine (eds.), *A Feminist Companion to Reading the Bible* (Sheffield: Sheffield Academic Press, 1997), pp. 84-113.

Foucault, Michel, 'What is an Author?', in Josue V. Harari (ed.), *Textual Strategies: Perspectives in Post-Structuralist Criticism* (Ithaca, NY: Cornell University Press, 1979), pp. 141-60.

—*Power/Knowledge: Selected Interviews and Other Writings 1972–1977* (ed. Colin Gordon; New York: Pantheon, 1980).

Froula, Christine, 'The Daughter's Seduction: Sexual Violence and Literary History', in Boose and Flowers (eds.), *Daughters and Fathers*, pp. 111-35.

Fruchtman, Maya, 'A Few Notes on the Study of Biblical Narrative', *Hasifrut* 6, pp. 65-66.

Frymer-Kensky, Tikva, *In the Wake of the Goddess: Women, Culture and the Biblical Transformation of Pagan Myth* (New York: Free Press, 1992).

Fuchs, Esther, 'Contemporary Biblical Literary Criticism: The Objective Phallacy', in Vincent L. Tollers and John Maier (eds.), *Mappings of the Biblical Terrain* (Lewisburg: Bucknell University Press, 1990), pp. 134-42.

—' "For I Have the Way of Women": Deception, Gender and Ideology in Biblical Narrative', in J. Cheryl Exum and Johanna W.H. Bos (eds.), *Reasoning With the Foxes: Female Wit in a World of Male Power* (Semeia 42; Atlanta: Scholars Press, 1988), pp. 68-83.

—'The Literary Characterization of Mothers and Sexual Politics in the Hebrew Bible', in Collins (ed.), *Feminist Perspectives on Biblical Scholarship*, pp. 117-36.

—'Marginalization, Ambiguity, Silencing: The Story of Jephthah's Daughter', *Journal of Feminist Studies in Religion* 5.1 (1989), pp. 35-46.

—'Status and Role of Female Heroines in the Biblical Narrative', *Mankind Quarterly* 23 (1982), pp. 149-60.

—'Structure, Motifs and Ideological Functions of the Biblical Temptation Scene', *Biblicon* 2 (1997), pp. 51-60.

—'Who is Hiding the Truth? Deceptive Women and Biblical Androcentrism', in Collins (ed.), *Feminist Perspectives on Biblical Scholarship*, pp. 137-44.

Furman, Nelly, 'His Story Versus Her Story: Male Genealogy and Female Strategy in the Jacob Cycle', in Collins (ed.), *Feminist Perspectives on Biblical Scholarship*, pp. 107-16.

Gallop, Jane, *Reading Lacan* (Ithaca, NY: Cornell University Press, 1985).

Ginsberg, Louis, *The Legends of the Jews*, IV (Philadelphia: Jewish Publication Society of America, 1968).

Girard, René, *Violence and the Sacred* (trans. Patrick Gregory; Baltimore: The Johns Hopkins University Press, 1977).

Gordis, Robert, 'Love, Marriage, and Business in the Book of Ruth: A Chapter in Hebrew Customary Law', in Bream *et al.* (eds.), *A Light Unto My Path*, pp. 241-64.

Gough, Kathleen, 'The Origin of the Family' in J. Freeman (ed.), *Women: A Feminist Perspective* (Palo Alto: Mayfield, 1979), pp. 83-105.

Graetz, Naomi, 'Dinah the Daughter', in Brenner (ed.), *A Feminist Companion to Genesis*, pp. 306-17.

Greenberg, Moshe, 'The Vision of Jerusalem in Ezekiel 8–11: A Holistic Interpretation', in James L. Crenshaw and Samuel Sandmel (eds.), *The Divine Helmsman: Studies on God's Control of Human Events, Presented to Lou H. Silverman* (New York: Ktav, 1980), pp. 145-46.

Gross, Rita M. (ed.), *Beyond Androcentrism: New Essay on Women and Religion* (Missoula, MT: Scholars Press, 1977).

Gunn, David, *The Story of King David: Genre and Interpretation* (JSOTSup, 6; Sheffield: JSOT Press, 1978).

Habel, Norman, *Literary Criticism of the Old Testament* (Philadelphia: Fortress Press, 1971).

Heilbrun, Carolyn G., and Margaret R. Higgonnet (eds.), *The Representation of Women in Fiction* (Baltimore: The Johns Hopkins University Press, 1983).

Heilbrun, Carolyn, and Catherine Stimpson, 'Theories of Feminist Criticism: A Dialogue', in Josephine Donovan (ed.), *Feminist Literary Criticism: Explorations in Theory* (Lexington: University Press of Kentucky, 1975), pp. 61-73.

Herman, Judith L., *Father–Daughter Incest* (Cambridge, MA: Harvard University Press, 1981).

Hoffman, Yair, 'Between Conventionality and Strategy: On Repetition in Biblical Narrative', *Hasifrut* 28 (1979), pp. 89-99 (Hebrew).

Horney, Karen, *Feminine Psychology* (New York: W.W. Norton, 1967).

Hyman, Ronald T., 'Questions and Changing Identity in the Book of Ruth', *USQR* 39.3, pp. 189-201.

Irigaray, Luce, *Speculum of the Other Woman* (trans. Gillian C. Gill; Ithaca, NY: Cornell University Press, 1985).

Jameson, Fredric, *The Political Unconscious: Narrative as a Socially Symbolic Act* (Ithaca, NY: Cornell University Press, 1981).

Janeway, Elizabeth, 'Women and the Uses of Power', in Hester Eisenstein and Alice Jardine (eds.), *The Future of Difference* (New Brunswick: Rutgers University Press, 1985).

Johnson, Barbara, *The Critical Difference: Essays in the Contemporary Rhetoric of Reading* (Baltimore: The Johns Hopkins University Press, 1985).

Johnson, Marshal D., *The Purpose of the Biblical Genealogies* (London: Cambridge University Press, 1969).

Kugel, James L., *The Idea of Biblical Poetry: Parallelism and Its History* (New Haven: Yale University Press, 1981).

Lamphere, Louise, 'Strategies, Cooperation, and Conflict Among Women in Domestic Groups', in Michelle Zimbalist Rosaldo and Louise Lamphere (eds.), *Women, Culture and Society* (Stanford, CA: Stanford University Press, 1974), pp. 97-112.

Lauretis, Teresa de, *Alice Doesn't: Feminism, Semiotics, Cinema* (Bloomington: Indiana University Press, 1984).

—*Feminist Studies/Critical Studies* (Bloomington: Indiana University Press, 1984).

Leach, Edmund, *Genesis as Myth and Other Essays* (London: Jonathan Cape, 1969).

Lerner, Gerda, *The Creation of Patriarchy* (New York: Oxford University Press, 1986).

Levenson, Jon D., and Baruch Halpern, 'The Political Import of David's Marriages', *JBL* 99 (1980), pp. 507-18.

Licht, Jacob, *Storytelling in the Bible* (Jerusalem: Magnes Press, 1978).

Mace, David, *Hebrew Marriage: A Sociological Study* (New York: Philosophical Library, 1953).

MacKinnon, Catherine A., *Feminism Unmodified: Discourses on Life and Law* (Cambridge, MA: Harvard University Press, 1987).

—'Feminism, Marxism, Method, and the State: An Agenda for Theory', in O. Keohane, Michelle Z. Rosaldo, and Barbara G. Gelpi (eds.), *Feminist Theory: A Critique of Ideology* (Chicago: University of Chicago Press, 1981), pp. 1-30 (23).

Malbon, Elizabeth Struthers, and Janice Capel Anderson, 'Literary-Critical Methods', in Schüssler Fiorenza (ed.), *Searching the Scriptures*, I, pp. 241-54.

Marcus, David, *Jephthah and his Vow* (Lubbock: Texas Tech Press, 1986).

Marmesh, Ann, 'Anti-Covenant', in Mieke Bal (ed.), *Anti-Covenant: Counter-Reading Women's Lives in the Hebrew Bible* (Sheffield: Sheffield Academic Press, 1989), pp. 43-58.

McCarter, P. Kyle, *I and II Samuel* (AB; New York: Doubleday, 1980).

McHale, Brian, 'Free Indirect Discourse: A Survey of Recent Accounts', *Poetics and Theory of Literature* 3 (1978), pp. 249-87.

McKay, Heather A., 'On the Future of Feminist Biblical Criticism', in Brenner and Fontaine (eds.), *Reading the Bible*, pp. 61-83.

Meyers, Carol, *Discovering Eve: Ancient Israelite Women in Context* (New York: Oxford University Press, 1988).

—'Hannah and her Sacrifice: Reclaiming Female Agency', in Brenner (ed.), *A Feminist Companion to Samuel and Kings*, pp. 93-105.

—'Miriam the Musician', in Brenner (ed.), *A Feminist Companion to Exodus to Deuteronomy*, pp. 207-30.

Miller, Nancy K., 'Emphasis Added: Plots and Plausibilities in Women's Fiction', *PMLA* 96 (1981), pp. 36-47.

Millet, Kate, *Sexual Politics* (New York: Ballantine Books, 1969).

Milne, Pamela J., 'Toward Feminist Companionship: The Future of Feminist Biblical Studies and Feminism', in Brenner and Fontaine (eds.), *Reading the Bible*, pp. 39-60.

Moi, Toril, *Sexual/Textual Politics: Feminist Literary Theory* (New York: Methuen, 1985).

Mollenkott, Virginia Ramney, *Women, Men and the Bible* (Nashville: Abingdon Press, 1977).

Munich, Adrienne, 'Notorious Signs, Feminist Criticism and Literary Tradition', in Gayle Greene and Coppelia Kahn (eds.), *Making a Difference: Feminist Literary Criticism* (London: Methuen, 1985), pp. 244-56.

Newsom, Carol A., and Sharon H. Ringe, (eds.), *The Women's Bible Commentary* (Louisville, KY: Westminster/John Knox Press, 1992).

Niditch, Susan, 'Women in the Old Testament', in Judith Baskin (ed.), *Jewish Women in Historical Perspective* (Detroit, MI, 1991), pp. 41-88.

Nissim, Haviva, 'On Analyzing a Biblical Story', *Hasifrut* 24 (1977), pp. 136-43 (Hebrew).

Nunnally-Cox, Janice, *Foremothers: Women of the Bible* (New York: Seabury, 1981).

Ochshorn, Judith, *The Female Experience and the Nature of the Divine* (Bloomington: Indiana University Press, 1981).

Ostriker, *Beyond God the Father* (Boston: Beacon Press, 1973).

—*Religion and Sexism* (New York: Simon & Schuster, 1974).

Otwell, John H., *And Sarah Laughed: The Status of Woman in the Old Testament* (Philadelphia: Westminster Press, 1977).

Pardes, Ilana, *Countertraditions in the Bible: A Feminist Approach* (Cambridge, MA: Harvard University Press, 1992).

Pedersen, J., *Israel: Its Life and Culture* (London: Oxford University Press, 1926).

Perry, Menakhem, and Meir Sternberg, 'The King Through Ironic Eyes', *Hasifrut* 1 (1968), pp. 263-92 (Hebrew).

—'Caution: A Literary Text! Problems in the Poetics and Interpretation of Biblical Narrative', *Hasifrut* 2 (1970), pp. 608-63 (Hebrew).

Polzin, Robert, 'The Ancestress of Israel in Danger', *Semeia* 3 (1975), pp. 81-98.

—*Moses and the Deuteronomist: A Literary Study of the Deuteronomic History* (New York: Seabury, 1980).

Pratt, Mary Louise, *Toward a Speech Act Theory of Literary Discourse* (Bloomington: Indiana University Press, 1977).

Pressler, Carolyn, 'Sexual Violence and Deuteronomic Law', in Brenner (ed.), *A Feminist Companion to Exodus to Deuteronomy*, pp. 102-12.

Rashkow, Ilona, 'Daughters and Fathers in Genesis... Or, What is Wrong With This Picture?', in Brenner (ed.), *A Feminist Companion to Exodus to Deuteronomy*, pp. 22-36.

Rauber, D.F., *Literary Interpretation of Biblical Narratives* (Nashville: Abingdon Press, 1974).

Reinhartz, Adele, 'Samson's Mother: An Unnamed Protagonist', in Brenner (ed.), *A Feminist Companion to Judges*, pp. 157-71.

Rich, Adrienne, *Of Women Born: Motherhood as Experience and Institution* (New York: Bantam Books, 1976).

Ricoeur, Paul, *Interpretation Theory: Discourse and the Surplus of Meaning* (Fort Worth: Texas Christian University Press, 1976).

Ridout, George, 'The Rape of Tamar', in Jared J. Jackson and Martin Kessler (eds.), *Rhetorical Criticism* (Pittsburg: Pickwick Press, 1974), pp. 75-84.

Robinson, Lillian S., *Sex, Class and Culture* (New York; Methuen, 1978).

Rush, Florence, *The Best Kept Secret* (New York: McGraw-Hill, 1987).

Russel, Diana E.H., *Rape in Marriage* (New York: Macmillan, 1982).

Russell, Letty M. (ed.), *Feminist Interpretation of the Bible* (Philadelphia: Westminster Press, 1985).

Sakenfeld, Katharine Doob, 'Old Testament Perspectives: Methodological Issues', *JSOT* 22 (1982), 13-20.

Sarna, Nahum M., *Understanding Genesis: The Heritage of Biblical Israel* (New York: Schocken Books, 1966).

Sasson, Jack M., 'The Issue of *Ge'ullah* in Ruth', *JSOT* 5 (1978), pp. 52-64.

—*Ruth: A New Translation with a Philological Commentary and a Formalist-Folklorist Interpretation* (Baltimore: The Johns Hopkins University Press, 1979).

Schneidau, Herbert N., *Sacred Discontent: The Bible and Western Tradition* (Berkeley: University of California Press, 1976).

Scholes, Robert, 'Reading Like a Man', in Alice Jardine and Paul Smith (eds.), *Men in Feminism* (New York: Methuen, 1987), pp. 204-18.

Schor, Naomi, 'Fiction as Interpretation, Interpretation as Fiction', in Susan Suleiman and Inge Crosman (eds.), *The Reader in the Text: Essays on Audience and Interpretation* (Princeton, NJ: Princeton University Press, 1980).

Schüssler Fiorenza, Elisabeth, *In Memory of Her: A Feminist Theological Reconstruction of Christian Origins* (New York: Crossroad, 1983).

—*Bread Not Stone: The Challenge of Feminist Biblical Interpretation* (Boston: Beacon Press, 1984).

—*But She Said: Feminist Practices of Biblical Interpretation* (Boston: Beacon Press, 1992).

Schüssler Fiorenza, Elisabeth (ed.), *Searching the Scriptures: A Feminist Introduction* (New York: Crossroad, 1993).

Schwartz, Regina M., 'Adultery in the House of David: The Metanarrative of Biblical Scholarship and the Narratives of the Bible', *Semeia* 54 (1991), pp. 35-55.

—*The Curse of Cain: The Violent Legacy of Monotheism* (Chicago: University of Chicago Press, 1997).

Schweickart, Patrocinio P., 'Reading Ourselves: Toward a Feminist Theory of Reading', in Elizabeth A. Flynn and Patrocinio P. Schweickart (eds)., *Gender and Reading: Essays on Readers, Texts and Contexts* (Baltimore: The Johns Hopkins University Press, 1986), pp. 31-62.

Scott, Joan Wallach, *Gender and the Politics of History* (New York: Columbia University Press, 1988).

Searle, John R., *Speech Acts: An Essay in the Philosophy of Language* (London: Cambridge University Press, 1969).

Shargent, Karla G., 'Living on the Edge: The Liminality of Daughters in Genesis to 2 Samuel', in Athalya Brenner (ed.), *A Feminist Companion to Samuel and Kings*, pp. 26-42.

Sheintuch, Gloria, and Uziel Mali, 'Towards an Illocutionary Analysis of Dialogue in the Bible', *Hasifrut* 30-31 (1981), pp. 70-75 (Hebrew).

Sherwood, Yvonne, 'Boxing Gomer: Controlling the Deviant Woman in Hosea 1–3', in Brenner (ed.), *A Feminist Companion to the Latter Prophets*, pp. 101-25.

Showalter, Elaine, 'Feminism and Literature', in Peter Collier and Helga Geyer-Ryan (eds.), *Literary Theory Today* (Ithaca, NY: Cornell University Press, 1990), pp. 179-202.

Simon, Uriel, 'An Ironic Approach to a Bible Story: On the Interpretation of the Story of David and Bathsheba', *Hasifrut* 2 (1970), pp. 598-607 (Hebrew).

Speiser, E.A., 'The Wife-Sister Motif in the Patriarchal Narratives', in Alexander Altmann (ed.), *Biblical and Other Studies* (Cambridge, MA: Harvard University Press, 1963), pp. 15-28.

—*Genesis: A New Translation with Introduction and Commentary* (AB; New York: Doubleday, 3rd edn, 1983).

Spivak, Gayatri Chakravorty, *In Other Worlds: Essays in Cultural Politics* (New York: Methuen, 1987).

Steinsaltz, Adin, *Women in the Bible* (Tel Aviv: The Ministry of Defence, 1983) (Hebrew).

Sternberg, Meir, 'A Delicate Balance in the Rape of Dinah', *Hasifrut* 4 (1973), pp. 195-231 (Hebrew).

—'The Structure of Repetition in Biblical Narrative', *Hasifrut* 25 (1977), pp. 109-50 (Hebrew).

—'The Truth vs. All the Truth: The Rendering of Inner Life in Biblical Narrative', *Hasifrut* 29 (1979), pp. 110-46 (Hebrew).

—*The Poetics of Biblical Narrative: Ideological Literature and the Drama of Reading* (Bloomington: Indiana University Press, 1985).

Sterring, Ankie, 'The Will of the Daughters', in Brenner (ed.), *A Feminist Companion to Exodus to Deuteronomy*, pp. 88-101.

Swidler, Leonard, *Biblical Affirmations of Women* (Philadelphia: Westminster Press, 1979).

Teubal, Savina J., *Sarah the Priestess: The First Matriarch of Genesis* (Athens, GA: Swallow Press, 1984).

Todorov, Tzvetan, *The Poetics of Prose* (trans. Richard Howard; Ithaca, NY: Cornell University Press, 1977).

Tolbert, Mary Ann, 'Defining the Problem: The Bible and Feminist Hermeneutics', *Semeia* 28 (1983), pp. 113-26.

Tompkins, Jane P., *Reader-Response Criticism: From Formalism to Poststructuralism* (Baltimore: The Johns Hopkins University Press, 1980).

Trible, Phyllis, 'Bringing Miriam Out of the Shadows', in Brenner (ed.), *A Feminist Companion to Exodus to Deuteronomy*, pp. 166-86.

—'A Daughter's Death: Feminine Literary Criticism and the Bible', *MQR* 22 (1983), pp. 176-89.

—'Depatriarchalizing in Biblical Interpretation', *JAAR* 41 (1973), p. 31.

—*God and the Rhetoric of Sexuality* (Philadelphia: Fortress Press, 1978).

—*Texts of Terror: Literary-Feminist Readings of Biblical Narratives* (Philadelphia: Fortress Press, 1984).

Valler, Shulamit, 'King David and "his" Women: Biblical Stories and Talmudic Discussions', in Brenner (ed.), *A Feminist Companion to Samuel and Kings*, pp. 129-42.

Vaux, Roland de, *Ancient Israel*, I (New York: McGraw–Hill, 1965).

Wander, Nathaniel, 'Structure, Contradiction, and "Resolution" in Mythology: Father's Brother's Daughter's Marriage and the Treatment of Women in Genesis 11–50', *JANES* 5 (1973), pp. 75-99.

Webster, Paula, 'Politics of Rape in Primitive Society', *Heresies* 6 (1978), pp. 16-22.

Williams, James G., *Women Recounted: Narrative Thinking and the God of Israel* (Sheffield: Almond Press, 1982).

INDEXES

INDEX OF REFERENCES

OLD TESTAMENT

INDEX OF AUTHORS